The National Center for Improving Science Education

The National Center for Improving Science Education (NCISE) is a division of The NET-WORK, Inc., a nonprofit organization dedicated to educational reform. The center's mission is to promote change in state and local policies and practices in science and technology curriculum, teaching, and assessment. We carry out our mission by providing a range of products and services to educational policy makers and practitioners who work to strengthen science and technology teaching and learning all across the country.

Our products and services are oriented toward practical guidance for those who are responsible for the day-to-day decisions that shape diverse learning environments, preschool to postsecondary. We help all stakeholders in science and technology education reform to promote better science and technology education for all students.

Advisory Board Members

William Baker, retired chairman of the board, AT&T Bell Laboratories, Murray Hill, New Jersey

Audrey Champagne, professor, State University of New York, Albany

David P. Crandall, president, The NETWORK, Inc., Andover, Massachusetts

David Imig, executive director, American Association of Colleges for Teacher Education, Washington, D.C.

David Kennedy, director of curriculum, Office of the Superintendent of Public Instruction, Olympia, Washington

Douglas Lapp, executive director, National Science Resources Center, National Academy of Sciences, Smithsonian Institution, Washington, D.C.

Susan Lewis, teacher, Middlebury ID #4, Mary Hogan Elementary School, Middlebury, Vermont

Manuel Perry, consultant, futures and long-range planning; retired, Lawrence Livermore National Laboratory, University of California, Livermore

Jerome Pine, professor of biophysics, California Institute of Technology, Pasadena

Andrew Porter, director, Wisconsin Center for Education Research, University of Wisconsin, Madison

Harold Pratt, retired executive director, Science and Technology, Jefferson County Public Schools, Golden, Colorado

Mary Budd Rowe, professor, School of Education, Stanford University, Stanford, California

F. James Rutherford, chief education officer, American Association for the Advancement of Science, Washington, D.C.

Thomas Sachse, manager, Mathematics and Science Education, California Department of Education, Sacramento

Mare Taagepera, director, Science Education Program, School of Physical Science, University of California, Irvine

Arthur Wise, president, National Council for Accreditation of Teacher Education, Washington, D.C.

TECHNOLOGY EDUCATION
IN THE CLASSROOM

TECHNOLOGY EDUCATION IN THE CLASSROOM

Understanding the Designed World

Senta A. Raizen
Peter Sellwood
Ronald D. Todd
Margaret Vickers

Jossey-Bass Publishers
San Francisco

Substantial discounts on bulk quantities of Jossey-Bass books are available to corporations, professional associations, and other organizations. For details and discount information, contact the special sales department at Jossey-Bass Inc., Publishers (415) 433–1740; Fax (800) 605–2665.

For sales outside the United States, please contact your local Simon & Schuster International Office.

Manufactured in the United States of America. Nearly all Jossey-Bass books and jackets are printed on recycled paper that contains at least 50 percent recycled waste, including 10 percent postconsumer waste. Many of our materials are printed with either soy- or vegetable-based ink; during the printing process these inks emit fewer volatile organic compounds (VOCs) than petroleum-based inks. VOCs contribute to the formation of smog.

Photos on pp. x and 146 by Patricia Hutchinson.
Photo on p. xxviii by Peter Sellwood.
Photo on p. xxx by Ronald Todd.
Photo on p. 231 by John Wells.
All photos reprinted by permission of *TIES Magazine*.

Library of Congress Cataloging-in-Publication Data

Technology education in the classroom : understanding the designed
  world / Senta A. Raizen . . . [et al.].
    p.   cm. — (The Jossey-Bass education series)
    Includes bibliographical references and index.
    ISBN 0-7879-0178-4
    1. Educational technology.   2. Education—Curricula.   I. Raizen,
Senta A. II. Series.
LB1028.3.T3968   1995
371.3'078—dc20

95-33950
CIP

FIRST EDITION
HB Printing 10 9 8 7 6 5 4 3 2 1

THE JOSSEY-BASS
EDUCATION SERIES

Technology teachers interact with youngsters in many different ways and contexts. Here eighth-graders consult with their teacher at an aviation workshop held at an airport near their school.

CONTENTS

LIST OF CLASSROOM VIGNETTES

PREFACE

Too frequently, when people hear the word "technology" in connection with school they think of computers in the classroom. Technology education is more than that. It is a new subject area that can help students learn about the world around them and help them integrate what they learn in the other subjects they pursue, thus adding relevance to all of their studies. While computers in the classroom can play a role in teaching technology, they are no more specifically linked to technology education than they are to any other subject. Rather, technology education is a combination of mastering the content knowledge concerning a variety of technologies and gaining a deep understanding of the process of designing and evaluating technologies that comes only through experience. Inherent in the definition of technology education is a model of how it should be taught. Students should not only *study* technology; they should *do* technology. Technology education includes the identification of problems and the development and evaluation of solutions.

Although technology is a major field of endeavor in its own right, it makes use of other disciplines, including science, mathematics, and communications. It can therefore be a helpful tool for linking subjects. In addition, technology education builds on the momentum toward experiential learning that exists in other subject areas, particularly mathematics and science.

Technology education can be a vital part of existing reform movements, facilitating and expanding them. Although not yet widespread in the United States, technology education has become an integral part of the school curriculum in several industrialized countries in Europe and around the Pacific rim. Within the United States, the American Association for the Advancement of Science's Reform Project 2061, the Social Studies Standards, and the national science education standards being developed by the National Research Council, all include strong technology education components. In addition, the National Science Teachers Association (NSTA) has endorsed a science-technology-and-society approach, while the International Technology Education Association (ITEA) advocates its own approach to technology education, drawn largely from the organization's industrial arts background. The National Association for Science, Technology and Society (NASTS) focuses on technological literacy as an end in itself. These organizations have each developed visions of technology education that reflect their particular perspective. This book, a report from the National Center for Improving Science Education, develops a vision that unites these disparate strands. Our vision describes a field of study that is not an add-on to another discipline but rather an independent program drawing from the strengths of technology's rich sources. As a field of study, technology education is intellectually rigorous, requires students to engage in challenging problem solving and analysis, and has students work with real materials and objects, learning about their properties by using them. Technology education has the potential for engaging *all* students, those headed for productive jobs in industry after high school as well as those headed for higher education.

The Purpose of This Report

Economic competitiveness is one of the prime movers of educational reform. To match competitors economically, the United States must match them educationally. One cannot ignore, therefore, the fact that many of this country's economic competitors place a great deal of emphasis on technology education and see it as an important tool in reforming their own educational systems. Although there are a growing number of voices calling for technology education in the United States, each group associates it with its own reform agenda. There is a dire need for a vision to unite these separate elements. The National Center for Improving Science Education has undertaken to develop such a vision, one that does not alienate any of these groups and can be supported by all of them.

Further, through analysis of existing models and through glimpses of the classroom, we here offer guidance on what technology education might look like and how it should be implemented. Those responsible for developing a policy on technology education need specific help, which this report provides. With science and mathematics receiving high priority in educational reform, as evidenced by the National Education Goals, technology education can serve as a vital element in that reform and can help meet the goals. This book gives examples of how technology can be taught, using detailed illustrations from lessons and curricula used in real schools. The examples show the expectations placed on students and teachers in good technology education activities and describe what actually takes place in the classroom. The book also provides specific recommendations on how to achieve high-quality technology education. In addition, by describing the state of technology education internationally, the book begins the discussion of what world class standards in technology education truly mean.

Audience

We intend this report for a variety of audiences. It is not meant to replace other efforts to improve education, but to complement them. We hope it will be used in schools and districts by those responsible for planning and implementing technology education curricula. At the university level, it is intended as a key text for those teaching science and related general pedagogy courses, technology pedagogy courses, and science and mathematics pedagogy courses, and as a useful resource for faculty interested in the reform of precollege education. Policy makers at the state and federal level who need guidance as to the focus of potential reforms such as those being called for by the Goals 2000 Act also will find our report useful. In fact, anyone interested in reforming science and mathematics education and precollege education in general should read and use this book.

Organization and Content

The book has five chapters that establish the need for technology education, describe its status, develop a vision of what it could and should look like, and make suggestions and recommendations about how to achieve that vision. Vignettes, mostly from real programs, are used throughout the book to give specific examples of the ideas being discussed and to make the materials approachable to a wide audience, from classroom teachers to federal policy makers. The report concludes with five appendixes that place technology in an international context, describe a slice of a K–8 technology program, and provide a list of resources for interested readers.

Chapter One establishes the need for technology education by analyzing current educational practice in the United States. It goes on to introduce a comprehensive vision for technology education in this country.

Chapter Two provides an overview of the major difficulties that lie in the way of creating a place in the K–12 curriculum for the kind of technology education discussed in Chapter One. The first obstacle facing technology education is that, as a component of general education for all students, it has no core of commonly accepted beliefs, values, standards, or practices (although the ITEA, with funding from the National Science Foundation and the National Aeronautics and Space Administration, is currently developing standards for technology education). The second challenge facing technology education is its relationship to traditional curricular subjects and curriculum sequences, particularly science and vocational education.

Educators will need a range of strategies for creating technology education programs that extend across the full sequence of schooling, from kindergarten through twelfth grade, and that are diverse enough to meet the requirements and needs of school districts across the nation. The five sections of Chapter Three respond to this need. The first section of this chapter provides a statement of guiding principles for technology education. The second section outlines explicit goals for technology education, against which all curricular components touching on technology education can be appraised. The third section describes how technology should be taught, arguing that no matter what the content, a technology curriculum must encompass processes of problem identification and solution designs and aim for an understanding of systems. The remaining sections of the chapter discuss some general guidelines for curriculum planning and for teaching and learning strategies.

Chapter Four illustrates in detail a range of specific curricular alternatives, since there are various ways of providing students with a program of technology education that meets the goals listed in Chapter Three. Because the approaches are likely to differ by schooling level, the chapter first discusses the early elementary grades, then the middle and junior high school grades, and finally the possibilities for secondary schools. These categories clearly are overlapping, as are the different typologies suggested for organizing the curriculum.

Chapter Five deals with implementation issues. Since no single option is likely to take account of the interests of all parties in technology education, how will choices be made? How will classrooms and schools be organized and equipped to accommodate students' active project work? What are teachers' concerns likely to be, and how can these be overcome? What do teachers need to know and be able to do? Who will teach the new curricula? How will teachers be trained? How will equal access to rigorous technology curricula be ensured for all students? How can girls as well boys be attracted to fields they generally avoid? Finally, how will students' work and progress be assessed? The chapter reviews these issues and makes recommendations for action designed to deal with them.

The book has five appendixes. The first appendix provides descriptions of technology education in various countries, including England and Wales, Germany, Japan, and the Netherlands. The second appendix is a slice of a K–8 technology program, describing how one technology-based topic—houses and homes—would serve as a coherent, integrated curriculum sequence. The third appendix offers fictitious excerpts from a high school handbook and student transcripts that illustrate a linked set of science/technology programs for grades nine through twelve. The fourth appendix gives an annotated list of additional readings useful in planning and implementing a technology education program, including relevant magazines, as well as a list of professional associations that can be consulted. The final appendix provides a list of school sites and teacher education collaboratives active in technology education.

Senta Raizen   *Washington, D.C.*
                                                               July 1995

ACKNOWLEDGMENTS

This report is the product of hard work by many people. Senta Raizen conceptualized the work and was the chief editor. Margaret Vickers, Rod Todd, and Peter Sellwood were the primary authors, writing the majority of the text. Sally Crissman wrote several of the vignettes. Susan Mundry and Bruce Rigby contributed specific sections. Patricia Hutchinson contributed much of the information in Appendixes D and E. Many people read advance drafts of the report and provided useful advice, including George Bugliarello, Michael Hacker, Rob Larson, David Layton, Gerhard Salinger, Kendall Starkweather, John Truxal, and John Wirt. The center's advisory board also reviewed the draft report, and several members provided comments that strengthened the text. In addition, Simon Hawkins provided assistance in editing and reviewing the existing literature. Thanks also are due to Susan Callan for her patient work in word processing the many drafts of this book. Our colleagues at The NETWORK, particularly Susan Martin and Denise Blumenthal, provided assistance in preparing the final manuscript. We wish to express special thanks to the Andrew W. Mellon Foundation, the John D. and Catherine T. MacArthur Foundation, and the Pew Charitable Trusts, which funded the book. The content of the book does not necessarily reflect the views of the sponsoring foundations.

THE AUTHORS

Senta A. Raizen is director of the National Center for Improving Science Education. She is responsible for the overall direction of the center and for its work in evaluation and assessment. She is the major author of several of the center's reports on science education in elementary, middle, and high school. Her most recent book is *The Future of Science in Elementary Schools: Educating Prospective Teachers* (with A. M. Michelsohn, 1994). Since the center's inception, she has provided leadership in policy development in science and technology education and in assessment at the state, national, and international levels.

Raizen holds undergraduate and advanced degrees in chemistry and began her career as an industrial chemist. She is also certified as a high school chemistry teacher. She is a fellow of the American Association for the Advancement of Science and a member of the American Educational Research Association.

From 1980 to 1988, she staffed several education activities for the National Academy of Sciences/National Research Council (NRC). She was study director for NRC's Committee on Research in Mathematics, Science, and Technology Education, as well as for the Committee on Indicators of Precollege Science and Mathematics Education, and she was responsible for the reports produced by these committees, including *Improving Indicators of the Quality of Science and Mathematics Education in Grades K–12* (1988).

From 1974 to 1978, Raizen was associate director of the National Institute of Education and in charge of its programs to disseminate and apply research results to education. Before that, she was a senior researcher at the Rand Corporation and, for ten years, a program official in science education at the National Science Foundation. She has authored numerous papers and monographs on educational assessment, education policy, and science and technology education. Her monograph *Reforming Education for Work: A Cognitive Science Perspective* (1989) is based on an extensive review of relevant research and policy commissioned by the National Center for Research in Vocational Education. She led the development of the science framework and curriculum analysis for the 1995 Third International Mathematics and Science Study, which involved some fifty countries and for which she serves on the International Steering Committee. She is also working on the national science assessment to be conducted in 1996 by the National Assessment of Educational Progress. In addition, she serves in an advisory capacity to several national and international education and research organizations, including the National Center for Education Statistics, the National Goals Panel, the Council of Chief State School Officers, and the Organization for Economic Cooperation and Development.

Peter Sellwood is president of Peter Sellwood Associates, an educational consultancy to schools, colleges, and industry. In this capacity, he is employed as a senior consultant to Westminster College, Oxford, and is involved in planning and lecturing on a range of postgraduate courses on their behalf. He is also involved in a wide variety of management training initiatives, and in liaison with the Professional Development Foundation, London, and the Tresco Trust, he has been commissioned to provide a series of executive training courses for companies within the European Commission. He is a prolific and respected author, having written a number of educational books for elementary and middle schools on science, design, and technology. He has also acted as a consultant to the British Broadcasting Corporation on a number of school education programs.

Sellwood was initially trained as an industrial designer and worked on automobile and other durable goods design. He was a member of the product design team that received the Duke of Edinburgh Award for Industry for a new refrigerator design in 1958. He also worked on automobile design and manufacturing processes for a range of models prior to returning to full-time studying. After rounding out his practical design experience, he completed an art and art history degree and, in 1964, began teaching in secondary schools and colleges in England.

In 1970, Sellwood undertook educational research at the University of Wales, Cardiff, into the development of integrated programs of study in secondary schools involving art, design, and technology. On completion of these studies, he was appointed County Inspector for Art, Design and Technology in Dorset. In 1978, he was appointed general adviser to North East Wiltshire and was responsible for the management and curriculum development of twenty secondary schools.

In 1986, Sellwood engaged in a research project at Bristol University on the development of technological literacy in five- to thirteen-year-olds. During the same year, he was invited to prepare a paper, "Practical Problem Solving in Schools," for the national conference of the British Educational Research Association (BERA). His studies at Bristol University led to his appointment as director of the National Project: Practical Problem Solving 5–13. The project, which lasted three years, involved ten counties in England and Wales and researched the value of investigative learning processes in the practical curriculum of elementary and middle schools.

Sellwood has been a member of the Schools Examination and Assessment Council (SEAC), a member of the Primary Education Committee of the Design Council, and co-chair of the Engineering Council's Primary Education conferences. His keynote presentations have included the ITEA conference, "Technology: An Educational Must," at Roanoke, Virginia, in 1986; the Netherlands National Conference for Technology Education in 1992; and, as a representative of the Design Council, the World Design Education Conference in Yugoslavia in 1988.

Ronald D. Todd is a director of the Center for Excellence in Design and Technology Education at Trenton State College, where he is also a research professor in the Department of Technological Education Studies. He earned his B.S. degree (1956) in industrial arts and mathematics, his M.A. (1963) in industrial education and administration at Kent State University, and his Ph.D. (1970) in education and the history of technology at Case Western Reserve University.

Todd has been active for more than three decades in developing technology education as an area in the public school curriculum. He has taught and implemented new programs of study at the elementary, middle school, high school, and university levels. He has collaborated with his wife, Karen, on technology-related efforts, including several books on technology education, the most recent of which is a high school set, *Introduction to Design and Technology* (1995). He currently works closely with several states and the Urban Systemic Initiative in Philadelphia, preparing teachers to use design and problem solving as a vehicle for integrating science, mathematics, and technology education.

Todd has been a member of the International Technology Education Association (ITEA) for over thirty years. He served as chair of the Curriculum Committee for two years, the Futures Committee for four years, and the Committee on International Relations for six years. Most recently, he helped found and chair the new section of design and technology.

In the mid 1980s, Todd cofounded *TIES* magazine, a national periodical that supports forty-six thousand teachers in technology as a school subject. At Trenton State College, he serves as director of Project UPDATE (Upgrading Practice through Design and Technology/Engineering Education), a funded initiative of the National Science Foundation for the development of design- and technology-related curriculum materials for grades K–8. Todd also coordinates the program for advanced research and doctoral study offered in collaboration with Goldsmiths College, University of London. His current interest is to support the establishment of design and technology education as a new and potentially powerful component of schooling for all students, K–12.

Margaret Vickers is director of the Center for Learning, Technology and Work, a division of The NETWORK. She holds undergraduate and advanced degrees in science from the University of Melbourne and a Ph.D. from the Harvard Graduate School of Education. Prior to joining The NETWORK, she served for a period as co-director of the Science Center at TERC Inc. and assisted in the development of science and technology curriculum frameworks for the state of Massachusetts. She is also director of the Working to Learn project, funded by the Pew Charitable Trusts.

Vickers is the author of several articles and monographs on education, technology, and training policy, and on school-to-work transition policy in the United States and other countries. She is currently a member of the Expert Group on Integrated Learning for the Organization for Economic Cooperation and Development (OECD).

Before leaving Australia, Vickers held executive positions in the technology policy and youth policy divisions of the Australian Department of Employment, Education and Training (from 1980 to 1986). In 1986, she became a research administrator of the OECD in Paris. In 1988, she was awarded a Larsen Fellowship for doctoral study at Harvard University. From 1992 to 1994, she served as an instructor at the Graduate School of Education, teaching courses on comparative education and on school-to-work transition policy.

THE CONTRIBUTORS

Contributors

Sally Crissman, Shady Hill School
Simon Hawkins, National Center for Improving Science Education
Patricia Hutchinson, *TIES* Magazine
Susan Mundry, The NETWORK, Inc.
Bruce Rigby, TERC Inc.

Reviewers

George Bugliarello, Polytechnic University
Michael Hacker, New York State Education Department
Rob Larson, Northwest Regional Educational Laboratory
David Layton, University of Leeds
Gerhard Salinger, National Science Foundation
Kendall Starkweather, International Technology Education Association
Karen Todd, Montclair State University
John Truxal, State University of New York, Stonybrook
John Wirt, Office of Technology Assessment

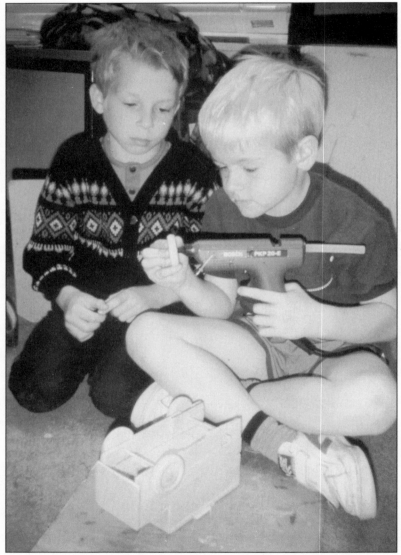

Good design and technology learning depends on classrooms with appropriate resources, materials, and tools, such as this low-temperature hot-glue gun. Such tools can help children translate their ideas into real objects and gain a sense of empowerment.

TECHNOLOGY EDUCATION IN THE CLASSROOM

Well-designed learning activities not only enhance technology skills and content understanding but enrich key concepts in other subjects—in this instance, concepts of electricity related to science.

CHAPTER ONE

A CALL FOR TECHNOLOGICAL LITERACY

Technology involves the application of knowledge, resources, materials, tools, and information in designing, producing, and using products, structures (physical and social), and systems to extend human capability to control and modify natural and human-made environments. In this book, technology education refers to K–12 school programs designed to teach understanding and competence in technology and to assess the appropriateness of technological actions. As a school subject, technology education leads to technologically literate citizens and enables young people to consider a wide range of careers in the high-performance workplace, as scientists, mathematicians, engineers, engineering technologists, and technicians (National Science Foundation, 1994).

The idea that technology should be part of everyone's basic education was first advocated in national projects in the United States and in England and Wales well over twenty years ago. Among the most prominent were, in the United States, the Engineering Concepts Curriculum Project, which developed the textbook *The Man-Made World,* and in England and Wales, Project Technology, both of which were developed in the 1960s. Despite the quality of the work done at the time, these projects had little impact on what was taught in the vast majority of schools (Layton, 1994b), in part because there was no legitimate place for these curricula, and in part because most teachers were not prepared to teach them. Today, however, there are renewed calls from politicians, educators, and employers, arguing that technology education should be a key component of the general education of all young Americans.

The publication of *A Nation at Risk* by the National Commission on Excellence in Education in 1983 can be seen as the starting point for the current generation of K–12 education reforms in the United States. This document and several subsequent influential reports have consistently advocated including technology in the context of wider plans for the reform of science and mathematics education. For example, the 1983 report of the National Science Board, *Educating America for the 21st Century*, is defined as "a plan of action for improving mathematics, science and technology education for all American elementary and secondary students." *Science for All Americans*, published by the American Association for the Advancement of Science (AAAS) in 1989, devotes a chapter to the nature of technology, in it discussing many of the process skills associated with designing, implementing, and evaluating technology, and another to the designed world, which investigates broad technological topics: agriculture, materials and manufacturing, energy sources and use, communication, information processing, and health technology. Both of these chapters are amplified in the AAAS's 1993 publication *Benchmarks for Science Literacy*. In addition, one of the six centers (San Antonio) charged with developing curriculum models to support these goals is building its model around technology themes: information processing, materials and manufacturing, human presence, health technology, energy sources and use, and agriculture. The draft of the *National Science Education Standards* (National Research Council, 1994) includes science and technology as one of its seven content areas. Recent publications by the National Center for Improving Science Education (Bybee and others, 1989, 1990; National Center for Improving Science Education, 1991) dealing with K–12 science discuss both science and technology education. The Federal Coordinating Council for Science, Engineering, and Technology (FCCSET) and its successor, the National Science and Technology Council, the agency charged with coordinating scientific activities across all federal agencies, considers its purview in education to include mathematics, science, engineering and technology (see the FCCSET 1992 report). The recommendations in these and similar reports reflect a growing desire among the nation's leading scientists, engineers, industrialists, and educators to ensure that the citizens and workers of tomorrow not only know *about* science, but are able to *use* science effectively in their everyday lives. President Clinton put the issue succinctly in a conference in the fall of 1993: "There can no longer be a division between what is practical and what is academic" (*Washington Post*, March 13, 1994, p. H1).

The movement toward technological literacy is not confined to the United States (see Appendix A). There is a burgeoning international literature on the emergence of technology education as a subject in the school curriculum, as exemplified by the United Nations Educational, Scientific, and Cultural Organization's (UNESCO) recent *Innovations in Science and Technology Education*, Volume 5

(Layton, 1994b). But what is technology education, and what is its role in the school curriculum? Ask any K–12 educator in the United States and you will be told that technology is already a part of the curriculum taught in his or her school, classroom, and district. When pressed to elaborate, he or she may refer to the use of technology in delivering instruction: the use of computer laboratories in elementary schools, the provision of vocational courses that use sophisticated equipment and aim to prepare students for skilled technician jobs, and the use of graphing calculators in mathematics or microcomputer-based laboratories in science, and so on. They may also describe such courses as Chemistry in the Community (referred to as ChemCom) that embed the teaching of scientific concepts in a technological context; design-oriented projects that culminate in products meeting certain specifications; science classes that follow up presentations of theory with discussions of technological applications; or science-technology-society courses that deal with societal issues that have some scientific and technological components.

If all of this and more is occurring already, why is there a need for a book that urges all schools to make technology education a key component of the K–12 curriculum? The answer lies precisely in the level of confusion about what technology education is, and in the lack of coherence of the activities that most schools offer under this label. Notions such as the ones given above demonstrate this confusion, because they fail to distinguish between the use of educational technologies (devices for facilitating learning) and technology education (which aims to help students understand, use, and evaluate the effects of current and emerging technologies). If coherent, carefully planned sequences of technology education from kindergarten through twelfth grade were to be found with any frequency in the schools of America, we could simply report on them, presenting a synopsis of the alternative ways in which schools are meeting the challenge of linking science with technology and technology with other subjects. This is not the case. In most instances where schools do offer technology education, it comes in bits and pieces—an isolated project here, a replacement unit there, or at best, a single yearlong course that provides in-depth treatment of a few topics, but offers no continuity or sequence from one year to the next.

It is now time to go beyond this fragmented approach. The goal of this book is to provide a vision of what a coherent K–12 technology education program for America's schools might look like and what it might achieve. The technology education program we envision would be based on a clear educational rationale. It would comprise a series of carefully constructed multiyear courses or course sequences; each of these would give students direct experience in designing products, structures, and systems to meet individual and social needs. Each course would demand that students actually make, use, and evaluate a range of such technologies. The courses would aim to develop an understanding of the two-way interactions between society and technology that have influenced the course of our civilization from earliest times, but especially over the last two or three centuries, and would seek to make students familiar with the technologies they encounter at home and at work. A few examples of courses that meet at least some of the criteria listed above will be referred to throughout the book. However, technology education courses that meet the majority of these criteria, although on the increase, are still relatively uncommon in the United States.

Current Practice

When technology is present in the K–12 curriculum in the United States, it is generally in one of two ways. First, many science teachers use technological devices to demonstrate how scientific principles work in action. A common practice in science education is to finish off a theoretical presentation of a topic by teaching students about relevant technological applications. Second, technology is a core element of vocational education. A major rationale for the vocational courses taught in high schools is to develop the skills associated with particular occupational technologies.

These two approaches to integrating technology into the curriculum—technology as a context for science, and technology as a basis for occupational training—correspond to the dominant roles that technology currently plays in the K–12 curriculum. The problem is that neither approach provides an adequate context for the kind of technology education envisioned in this book. There is a risk of oversimplification in attempting to characterize these two existing approaches, but the risk is worth taking if it helps us to conceptualize the general topic more clearly.

Technology in Science Courses

The first approach might be called "technology for science." Proponents of this approach favor technology-enhanced methods because they seem to provide more effective ways of acquiring scientific knowledge. They see the introduction of technology into science courses as a way of making science more accessible to the ever-broadening populations now studying their discipline. The technology-for-science approach attempts to augment science learning with teacher-generated "design challenges"—activities in which students are encouraged to use concrete materials and to solve problems usually selected by the teacher for their potential to stimulate discussion of key scientific concepts. As students make sense of what is happening in these design challenges, they learn—guided by the teacher—to construct their own understandings of the relevant scientific principles. Following is an example of an activity in which students use concrete materials to begin an investigation of a scientific concept.

Mousetrap Power

Mr. Frey has taught ninth-grade physical science for some years now. Over the summer he attended a workshop titled "Enhancing Science Learning Through Technology." The main message of the seminar was that students understand physical science concepts better if their learning is based on designing, building, and using real devices.

The fall semester has begun, and Mr. Frey has decided to use this approach to introduce key concepts such as motion, force, and kinetic energy. For their first assignment, he asks his students to design a system in which a vehicle is powered by a mousetrap spring; the goal is to have the vehicle cover the greatest possible distance. He asks each student to bring in a vehicle of some kind for this challenge. After showing his students how the mousetrap operates, he asks them to think of how they can connect the mousetrap to move the vehicle and how to show the design on paper.

As he moves among the students, he notices that some of them seem to have very few ideas or solutions. Others think of something right away. Methods are quite different from one student to another. He assigns students to pairs in which to test their designs.

Perry brings in his younger brother's plastic toy stagecoach. He and his partner, Sal, who has only vague sketches, begin with Perry's plan. Perry looks at his drawing, sets the mousetrap against the wall, pulls back the metal bar, hooks it in cocked position, slides the stagecoach next to it. With a stick he knocks out the prop, the spring flies forward and hits the stagecoach, which moves forward a few feet. He is pleased, but Sal is not.

"I thought we had to have the mousetrap *attached* to the car," she says. "I never thought of using it as a pusher. What if it was in the middle of a street and there wasn't a wall to push against?"

Perry moves the mousetrap away from the wall, cocks the spring, slides the stagecoach in place. This time when the spring hits the coach, the mousetrap slides back and the vehicle travels a shorter distance.

"If we're going to have it in the middle of the floor, we'll have to tape the mousetrap down so all the energy goes to moving the stagecoach. Mark how far it went this time so we can see if it goes farther."

They tape the trap firmly to the floor, release the spring, and the stagecoach moves a bit beyond the thirty-centimeter mark.

Sal wants to try moving the stagecoach with the mousetrap attached to the vehicle. They have no design on paper, but they have ideas in their heads that they begin to put to work. The mousetrap will pull a string that will be wound around the rear axle. But which way should they wind it? They move the wheels on the floor and finally come up with a rule: whichever way we want the wheels to go, we turn the axle in the opposite direction to wind the string. The string is tied to the axle and secured with tape. Next, they tape the mousetrap firmly to the top of the stagecoach and tie the free end of the string to the spring wire. They pull the spring back, prop it in place, and straighten the front wheels. When the spring is released, the axle turns rapidly, the plastic wheels spin on the hard floor and the stagecoach moves forward only about five centimeters.

"We need more friction so the wheels don't slip and spin so fast. This time friction is on our side. Let's run it on the carpet. Let's add a little weight to increase the friction."

This time the spring arches slowly over the top of the stagecoach, pulling on the string that turns the axle, and the stagecoach moves slowly and elegantly thirty-five centimeters along the carpet. They cheer! Now they want to make a good thing better. They think that if they can extend the length of the mousetrap spring wire, the arc will be longer and the string will unwind around the axle for a longer period of time. They attach a ball point pen to the spring, move the string out to the end, let the spring go, and this time the stagecoach travels forty-five centimeters.

"Maybe it's heavy enough now to stay on the floor and with less friction it will go farther."

With an extended arm, increased weight, and a hard surface, the stagecoach travels sixty-four centimeters on the uncarpeted floor.

Mr. Frey asks the pair how long the spring arm could be and still work. He asks them to measure and to show graphically the relationship between the weight of the vehicle and the distance covered, or the length of the spring arm and the distance covered. He then asks them to compare the push-off method versus the attached-to-the-vehicle method to determine which is the better way to move the stagecoach forward.

Mr. Frey asks Perry and Sal what helped them be successful. Perry says that thinking it through and planning ahead, then testing and redesigning, worked for him. Sal says that she needed to tinker with the materials before she could begin to design a solution to the problem. Both students say they would not have been successful working alone, that they needed each other's ideas and hands.

This first assignment seems to have gone well overall; however, Mr. Frey is not exactly sure about the next steps he should take. He wants to feel clearer as to which scientific concepts are important, to know how to introduce the notion of kinetic energy to build the students' science knowledge, and to know how to assess what they have learned. He noticed that the students were very caught up in the process of making the stagecoach move, but he is not sure whether they really understand why increasing its weight or extending the length of the arm made it go farther. Mr. Frey wishes there were other teachers in his school he could talk with about using technology to enhance science learning.

In following up this experiment, Mr. Frey asked his students to think about concepts like friction, force, and motion, but he ignored design-related issues. For example, he did not ask what other methods could be used to power a buggy, or when and where a spring might be the most useful source of power. His focus was more on changing *how* students learned rather than on changing what they learned. Nevertheless, the use of design challenges, as illustrated in this vignette, is a fine activity if the goal is to deploy technology to improve science learning. Because Mr. Frey did not attempt to add specific technology education subject matter to the curriculum, his approach does not represent technology education as we would define it.

The technology-for-science approach reflects the more conservative views of high school science teachers and their university colleagues. It can be traced back to one of the classic rationales for schooling: that the pursuit of the academic disciplines is the highest aim of education, and that therefore the major purpose of the school curriculum is to equip students to undertake higher levels of study of these disciplines in colleges and universities. It is consistent with this view to see science education as an end in itself, and those who hold this view support technology-enhanced approaches to teaching and learning science as means of achieving that end.

Technology in Vocational Education

The second approach defines the function of education primarily in terms of equipping people to do jobs. Historically, the subject matter of technology has mainly been taught in high schools by vocational and technical teachers. This approach could be called "technology for employment," because its main goal has been to teach students the knowledge and technical skills needed to qualify for employment in particular occupations. To describe it as one single approach is a gross oversimplification, because there are many different approaches and rationales for teaching the various occupational technologies. While the practice of some vocational teachers remains firmly fixed in the craft-based tradition, others go beyond this approach by focusing on current or high-tech industrial practices. Yet another approach, popular among instructors drawing on the engineering disciplines, focuses on systems theory and on the flow of matter, energy, and information, emphasizing cognitive competencies rather than manual skills. These approaches are discussed in more detail in Chapter Two.

The technology-for-employment approach is illustrated in the following vignette.

A Solar Hot Water Heater: Using Science in the Technology Classroom

Students in a twelfth-grade technology studies class have been invited to design and construct a solar water heater. Their teacher, a veteran both of the classroom and the metal working trade, has ensured that students are proficient in the skills required to form and join tinplate and copper into an effective solar collector. After a discussion of general principles, students work in groups to design a system that aims to heat a liter of water at least five degrees in ten minutes. The type and quantity of materials are agreed upon at the beginning of the activity.

Students must decide on the detailed design of the solar collector (shape, surface color, and so on), as well as on the configuration of the system components (for example, collector, plumbing, insulation, and storage tank). In doing this they harness knowledge about energy transfer (absorption, conduction, and convection), the electromagnetic spectrum, and the relationship between temperature and density of fluids, which they first learned in science classes.

During the design phase, each group must describe and defend its design in appropriate language, either to the class or to the teacher. When the models have been completed, they are tested in sunlight for performance against the design criteria. Standard scientific procedures are used in evaluating the solar collectors. The results are recorded and notes are made about possible improvements to the design. Each group presents its findings, as well as any plans for design improvements, in the form of a poster, report, or class presentation. The presentations also include comments on the possible practical applications for solar water heating.

The solar water heater project is an example of technology education set in the context of a vocational education or industrial arts course. Many such courses now adopt titles like "technology studies" or "technology education." This example shows how science knowledge is needed to help students produce good designs in response to a challenge, and how a scientific approach to evaluation can help isolate features of the design that need improvement. The example also illustrates the essential difference between technology education and vocational education. In a traditional vocational program, students would be given a blueprint for making the solar water heater; the blueprint would have been designed for them by a teacher or a curriculum developer. In the program described in the vignette, responsibility for designing the device lay with the students.

The technology-for-employment approach has its origins in the economic rationalist's view of education. Its popularity has grown in the last two decades, as politicians and industrialists have placed great stress on the role education might play in improving the industrial strength of the nation and increasing its international economic competitiveness. Since 1990, several federally funded programs have been launched in an attempt to secure the levels of technological competence needed for high-skill employment in today's economy. These programs include the 1990 Tech-Prep Act, which aims to upgrade secondary vocational education; the 1993 School-to-Work Opportunities Act; and the Advanced Technological Education program which, under the auspices of the National Science Foundation, is providing grants and technical assistance to upgrade the quality of technological education in community colleges and other postsecondary institutions.

This brief overview is far from complete, but it does illustrate what have historically been the two main approaches to the inclusion of technology in the K–12 curriculum. Alternative approaches to the role of technology in the curriculum are discussed in greater detail in Chapter Two.

A Comprehensive Vision for Technology Education

The two approaches to technology education presented above—that of the academic scientist and that of the economic rationalist—can lead to effective teaching in science and in vocational courses, as the two vignettes illustrate. Yet these approaches are rather limited compared to the comprehensive vision of technology education we are endeavoring to put forward in this book. As we define it, technology education entails much more than an intensive training in the technical skills needed to earn a living. Also, because it involves students in designing, building, and evaluating artifacts, it unites cognitive activity with practical action in a way few other subjects can.

Technology education also goes beyond the academic orientation of the "pure sciences," which tend to ignore the made world in which students live. The popular image of the scientist as someone who is divorced from the real world is, of course, a media myth, but the orientation of much of school science is so abstract that it often fails to counter this myth. The recent experience of New England educators at a summer science camp illustrates the extent to which the students there saw "science" as separate from life and "scientists" as people who did not have practical jobs.

What Is a Scientist and What Is a Technologist?

In 1994, a group of students ages ten to thirteen attended a summer science camp for girls in New England. One part of the program evaluation asked the girls what two or three careers they would like for themselves when they become adults, and if any of these choices was to be a scientist. Because these girls had chosen to spend part of their summer vacation at a science camp, it was not surprising that many of them said they hoped for careers such as marine biologists, physicians, or veterinarians, but with startling consistency they also said that these were not the careers of scientists.

Further probing revealed that these girls viewed the scientist as the person who finds information. Conversely, the girls said, the marine biologist or pediatrician or vet *uses* the information ferreted out by scientists to do helpful, useful, and interesting work. The girls were drawn to the using rather than to the finding out.

Later in the program these girls were introduced to six women who use science or technology in their work: a nuclear safety officer, an electrician, a sheep farmer, a horticulturist, a pediatrician, and a water quality tester. Based on the questionnaire responses, the program director changed the name of this event from "Career Fair" to "Visiting Scientists Day." Each of the professional women was asked to bring something from her work that lent itself to a "hands-on" experience for the campers—for example, a Geiger counter and a variety of objects to test for emitted radiation, or a light socket to wire. After spending time with these women and conversing as they did activities together, the girls said they liked Visiting Scientists Day, learned a lot, and had a new view of some ways science can be used in the workplace.

A classroom teacher participating in the science camp remarked, "I integrate all subjects in my classroom so completely that I am now wondering if my students know what is science and what is not. Perhaps I need to name or label the science more explicitly and talk about some ways science is part of daily life and work."

This vignette illustrates the separation, confusion, blur, or lack of distinction between science and technology from the student's point of view. The girls attending the summer camp did not describe science as the domain of the brilliant white male. (On the questionnaire, almost all of them said they liked their science classes.) However, they were naive in their understanding of how science enters into the career of the marine biologist, the physician, and so forth. It is quite possible that these students' teachers are also unclear regarding the distinctions between science and technology. Generally, both students and teachers believe that the subject matter in school is science and that technology means computers. The differences between the sciences and technology as disciplines must be clarified, not only for students but for their teachers. The girls attending the summer camp showed keen interest in solving problems leading to better health for people, animals, and the environment. Such interests in real-world problems can be tapped in a technology education program in which learning science and preparing for careers are integrated and which incorporates a number of disciplines.

From the objects and systems that surround them—microwave ovens, calculators, computers, sports equipment, VCRs and stereo sound equipment, subways and automobiles—to the more exotic technologies discussed in the daily news—

genetic engineering, organ transplants, magnetic resonance imaging, rocket launches and space stations, and the information superhighway—the products and systems of technology continue to shape and reshape our daily environment. The world that surrounds today's students is a world designed by humans, a world in which the impact of technology cannot be ignored. Technology is an important part of human culture. As such, it should be studied and experienced by all as part of general education.

The model presented in Figure 1.1, drawn from models by Roger Bybee and others (1989) and David Layton and his colleagues (Layton, Jenkins, Macgill, and Davey, 1993), reflects our view of the relationship between technology and science and our approach to technology education.

Drawing implications for education from this model, we conceive of technology education as involving much more than "using" science to explain how devices work or tacking a few "applications" of science onto the end of a theoretical presentation. In a typical technology education project, students might be asked to think about an everyday problem from several perspectives and to design, build, and evaluate an artifact that represents one possible solution to that problem. Even a deceptively simple problem, such as the one presented in the " 'Best' Jar Opener" vignette, may have many solutions, depending on who the jar opener is for, whether the cost matters, whether it needs to be portable, and so on. A typical feature of design projects is that there is no single right answer, and for this reason technology education programs will always put the student in the driver's seat.

The "Best" Jar Opener

Ms. Charpentier's seventh-grade students are used to science and mathematics classes in which there are single right answers; the rest are wrong. These students have not needed to venture outside of the textbook to be successful in their school work. The experience of having to consider multiple criteria to find a "best" solution to a problem will be a new one for them.

As an introduction to the relative complexity and the potential fun of solving a problem in technology, Ms. Charpentier has brought in a widemouthed jar of pickles and has explained to the class that her sixty-four-year-old father-in-law, who lives by himself and because of his arthritis is unable to open jars, has asked her to buy him a jar opener. Their assignment is to visit their local hardware store, research available types of jar openers and recommend the best one for her to purchase. She tells her students that their task includes not only doing their own investigations but coming up with a way to share their findings and make a single report to her father-in-law from the class.

As their hardware store investigations progress, the students come to class with

FIGURE 1.1. THE RELATIONSHIP BETWEEN SCIENCE AND TECHNOLOGY AND THEIR CONNECTION TO EDUCATION GOALS.

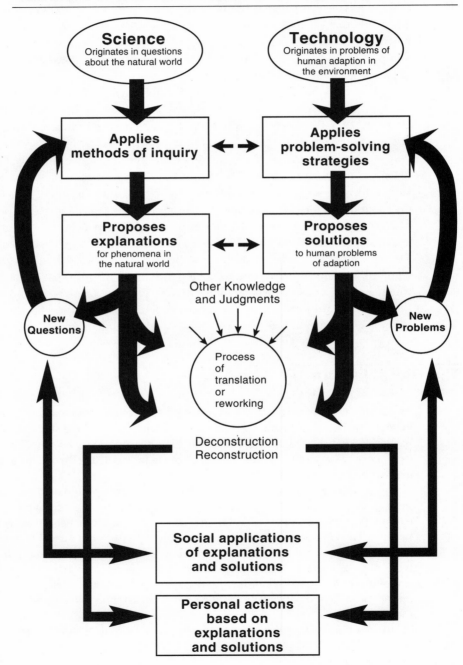

an increasing number of questions that Ms. Charpentier records on a sheet of newsprint:

- How much money have you got to spend?
- Can the opener be attached to the wall?
- What is his problem with jars? Slipping hands or lack of strength?
- Does size or weight matter?
- How can we compare one kind of jar opener with another?

To Ms. Charpentier's delight, some students begin to survey their families and neighbors, asking them what they have found to be the best way to open a tight-fitting jar lid. Two students even bring in jar-opening devices they have created themselves, complete with a cost analysis for manufacture and sales, a name, and an advertising slogan.

Each student displays the results of his or her investigation, listing price and pros and cons for each jar-opening device. The class compiles the results of their survey of effective methods for opening jars. They also design a method for comparing jar openers and test as many of the jar openers as they can gather. When the time comes for the class to make a recommendation to Ms. Charpentier's father-in-law, vigorous argument and debate takes place over the definition of "best." Finally, the class decides to define "best" in terms of cost, size and weight, strength-saving, grippability, and recommendations from experienced users.

The students have become involved in their investigations, motivated by utility (genuinely helping an elderly person to solve a practical problem), active learning, and student-selected criteria for decision making. Some students, accustomed to achieving high grades by dutifully following the steps outlined by a teacher or textbook, were initially flustered when they realized that success depended on decisions about their own investigations and learning, and that there was more than one route to success. Ms. Charpentier acknowledged that learning a new way might be difficult, but that the reward is the ability to think and decide for oneself.

It is the students' own designs, rather than the instructions in a workbook or the ideas of a teacher, that define what they will do with their projects. Technology education courses are deliberately open-ended, but they do need to be guided by some kind of a framework, so a key task for curriculum developers will be to define a common set of learning outcomes that everyone taking a technology education course will be expected to achieve. It may be that the International Technology Education Association (ITEA) will provide the needed guidance with its forthcoming standards for technology education. At the same time, teaching these courses will tax the ability of even the best teachers, because the range of things a student might do in a technology education project will be so diverse. The artifacts students build must be viewed as serious and assessable pieces of work. Design-and-build projects cannot be assessed using standard pencil-and-paper instruments, but because technology education places such a high value on these activities, it is essential that we develop valid ways of assessing them.

Because technology education projects take place in the real world, students will need to draw on knowledge from many disciplines—for example, geography, art, mathematics, business studies, and the social sciences—as they follow through on their designs. Instead of trying to absorb a collection of facts and concepts chosen and delivered by their teachers, students will be searching for the concepts that are needed to support their designs, to explain how things work, or to explore why something is not working as they expected it to. In this context, the subject matter disciplines and their boundaries cease functioning as ends in themselves. Rather than constituting separate ways of defining reality, the subject matter disciplines function as props that help students to develop their thinking and to build products that reflect what they had in their minds and their imaginations.

Intrinsic to the vision of a K–12 technology education curriculum we are putting forward in this book is the natural integration of technology with the rest of the curriculum. Model technology education curricula would bring together technological content and process, the integration of technology with other subject matter, a hands-on design and problem-solving approach, and reflections on the implications and consequences of different technologies and their impacts on society. As students work on technology education projects, they will learn to take responsibility for their own work, to apply the skills they have acquired, and to cooperate with other students. Because it uses knowledge from several disciplines in the service of practical action, the skills and qualities developed through technology education provide an essential component of the basic education required to live confidently as a citizen in today's world.

The following vignette illustrates the use of a local physical feature as a theme for linking various subjects.

Building Model Bridges: A Design and Technology Challenge

The theme for the year in Ms. Nunes's fifth-grade class is rivers, particularly the Cuyahoga River, which runs through the city where she teaches. Her students have studied some science of rivers themselves—for example, water quality, sinking and floating, and what lives in the river. They have worked with topographical maps and figured out which direction the river runs, how much higher it is at its source than at its outlet, and the slope of the river bed. The class has borrowed some stream tables from the earth science teacher at the high school and has explored the interaction of water and the land it flows over and through. Each year, Ms. Nunes has increased the number of hands-on science activities provided for her students. She is convinced that manipulating materials increases her students' motivation to learn and their depth of understanding.

Recently, Ms. Nunes has studied a framework, not just for science but for science and technology. The framework recommends technology education as well as science, and in response she has been thinking about highlighting the built environment of the Cuyahoga.

She decides to add a hands-on technology challenge to her curriculum. As part of the river theme, her students study bridges. They look at photographs of bridges and take a bus trip to look at eight bridges in the middle of their city. Ms. Nunes invites her class to make a model truss bridge that will span a thirty-centimeter river and allow boats that are five centimeters tall in the water to pass underneath this model bridge. Their materials are limited to toothpicks, wood scrap strips, and white glue. Ms. Nunes makes and displays prominently a poster outlining the steps these young engineers will follow:

Design your bridge.

Construct your model.

Test the strength of your model bridge.

Evaluate your design.

Redesign.

Students work in pairs, drawing their plans on centimeter-squared paper that they cover with wax paper and then build over. Each side of a model is lifted off the waxed paper, held vertical by securing it in plasticine, and connected top and bottom. It has taken more than a week of patient work, but now the bridges are standing over a poster-paint river that weaves its way across one side of a refrigerator carton. Today is strength-test day. Each pair of model builders weighs their bridge and estimates how many times its own weight the bridge will support.

"I think ours can hold three times it own weight. Maybe four."

Spanning a space between two desks, a container hangs from a pencil stretched along the deck of each bridge. As they begin to load in weights, the students are stunned by the strength of their constructions. A twelve-gram bridge holds 2100 grams before a piece of the roadbed gives way. An eleven-gram bridge holds 1200 grams, and as each additional gram of mass is added, the roadbed twists until one end slips out and the bridge falls over. One very sturdy looking bridge falls without much load when its relatively unsupported base gives way.

"We need to strengthen our supports. We didn't have enough triangles. The part of the bridge that crossed the water was fine. The part of the bridge that's on the land is just as important as the part that goes over the water."

"If there was a flood and the river was moving very fast it would push hard against the supports, so you'd have to build them strong enough in case there's a flood."

"What about a hurricane? Does wind ever blow down bridges? Maybe we should test ours with a strong fan."

"When we built our bridge, the two sides weren't exactly even. It looks like that's what made the bridge twist and then fall over."

"Ours felt very strong when we held it, and it was. It could have held a bigger load, but we worked hard on it and didn't want it to be destroyed. If this was life-size and made of steel it would carry a train or a lot of cars and trucks."

"You have to know the biggest number of cars and trucks that can get on the bridge at one time and how much the bridge itself weighs. You would only have to make it strong enough to hold that much."

"Yesterday on my way to my aunt's I saw a bridge exactly like this one. Instead of glue, the pieces were held together with bolts and rivets."

"Do bridges ever collapse after they are built?"

"Do they always make models before they build structures?"

"I was downtown and noticed a bridge that went over a street so people could walk between two buildings without going outside and it was made of triangles, too. I guess the buildings were like the towers of the bridges over rivers."

Ms. Nunes's technology challenge is inextricably linked to her science curriculum and to her students' community. The design challenge was circumscribed by Ms. Nunes when she designated the bridge type, the materials, the width of the river, and the height over the water. From then on, it was up to the students. Their comments reproduced in the vignette show the development of their thinking, derived from their construction attempts and relevant observations of their surroundings. In order to design, the students had to call on what they had learned about what makes strong structures and about the forces acting upon these structures, and their own experience and observations. Their knowledge of measurement and symmetry were important in the design process.

Important elements of technology became real as the students went through the design and building processes, put their models to a test, and evaluated their designs. While the students were competitive in their designs, they learned to work in groups and to value each others' contributions. Completing this project required sustained work; the students became interested not only in the product, a model bridge, but in the bigger questions, such as does the process of design, test, and redesign ever fail? How do you decide how much flooding to plan for? They began to notice and question other aspects of their built environment. Ms. Nunes, who is committed to a hands-on science program, is convinced that design engineering projects will be equally powerful in helping her students understand technology as an important field of study.

While using a social context to make schoolwork real to students is an important pedagogical technique, it has a broader instructional purpose. The social context in which new technologies emerge plays a critical role in shaping how that technology develops in different contexts. For example, the particular applications of telecommunications technology that have been taken up most eagerly in Australia, Europe, and the United States are quite distinct from each other, reflecting distinct social and geographical differences among the three continents. Society shapes how technology is used, and conversely, new technologies can have powerful impacts on society. If technology education programs are to help students understand and evaluate the two-way interactions between technology and society, a well-designed social sciences component must be built in.

The design process, crucial to technology (and discussed in greater detail in Chapter Two), should integrate well-developed communication skills with critical thinking skills. Students must learn to communicate their ideas if they are to convince others of the efficacy of their designs. Language proficiency is an obvious requirement for effective communication. Another critical communication tool is mathematics; mathematics and technology reinforce each other. Mathematics provides a method for modeling the design process, for assessing implications of changing the design, and for evaluating the outcome. It is a key tool throughout the technological problem-solving process. Often neglected, however, is the importance of the perspectives and skills of the visual arts. In many cases, a successful design is aesthetically appealing as well as an effective solution to a problem. The artful expression of a design is clearly augmented by the integration of art with technology. Further, the ability to sketch ideas and to modify a sketch as thinking develops is an integral part of the communication process of design and technology.

In fact, just as technical and science teachers are beginning to look to design as a way of enriching their instruction, so too are art teachers. The National Endowment for the Arts (NEA) began supporting a Design Arts Program in 1967, and in 1992 initiated a study to understand how design curricula assist teachers and students in meeting the national education goals (Spilka and Nutter, 1995). A number of the programs funded by the NEA focus on architecture, with activities that teach students many basic principles of structure and building and how to investigate the competing demands of form and function. Design can reconcile and combine the traditionally separate realms of science and art education. One such program has students design and build a city, requiring them to address the issues of economy, land use, building structures, energy, public policy, and many others (Nelson, 1984). Such a city must be designed to operate effectively and to be visually appealing to its inhabitants. Design activities such as those developed under NEA auspices are oriented to the real world, in which how something looks may be as important as how it functions. Some commercial software, such as

SimCity, is available which addresses similar issues, although these programs do not have a hands-on component.

The design and technology education program we advocate, as delineated in this book, is intended for all students. Democratic societies can no longer afford to have technological knowledge relegated to a handful of specialists while the population at large remains ignorant of the modes of thinking, the basic knowledge and skills, and the processes that bring about technological inventions and change. To have only a small percentage of people knowledgeable and comfortable with technology in an advanced industrial society not only decreases the ability of the majority of people to deal with and use the products of technology effectively, it also relegates them to minor status in making decisions about the development of new technologies and their likely consequences. In *A Nation at Risk,* John Slaughter, former director of the National Science Foundation, warned that "a chasm is growing between a small scientifically and technologically educated elite and ill-informed citizens" (p. 10). Everyone must be technologically literate in order to make informed decisions in today's world. Uninformed groups make uninformed decisions. Leaving the decisions to "the experts" threatens the premises on which our democratic society was founded.

In short, design technology involves practical reasoning and relevance in authentic contexts and provides for dynamic and reflective practice among both student and teachers. It creates opportunities for addressing student conceptions in mathematical reasoning and scientific understanding and in implementing *integrative* strategies in teaching, as opposed to implementing *integrated* curriculum (Rob Larson, personal communication, February 16, 1995).

CHAPTER TWO

MAKING WAY FOR
TECHNOLOGY EDUCATION

Although the idea of technology education has generated substantial interest only in recent years, its development has spanned nearly a century. John Dewey was one of the first educational thinkers in the United States to consider the role and place of technology in the school curriculum, although it was fully fifty years before technology education was given serious widespread consideration. During that long interim period, two individuals played pivotal roles in setting the stage for and nurturing the development of technology as the basis for industrial arts. Formed during the 1930s through the leadership of William E. Warner, the American Industrial Arts Association (AIAA) and its successor, the International Technology Education Association (ITEA), played key roles in the ongoing and often difficult process of considering technology as the content base for industrial arts, and later, in considering technology education as a completely new school subject. Influenced significantly by Dewey, Warner developed what he called a curriculum to reflect technology, which he presented at the first meeting of the AIAA following World War II. During the 1960s, with funding from the Department of Education, several projects located at universities in the Midwest developed curricula aimed at an organized study of industry (Phillips, 1985).

The ideas and philosophy behind the curriculum to reflect technology were considered by some, however, as focusing too strictly on industry. Of the efforts to move beyond this limited perspective, the most significant was the work of Delmar W. Olson. His research in the 1950s and his book *Industrial Arts and*

Technology (1963) served as the foundation for a new generation of initiatives to establish technology education as a subject worthy of inclusion in the curriculum for all students.

During this same period, a curriculum project emerged that held much promise for technology education. Supported by the National Science Foundation, *The Man-Made World* integrated science, mathematics, and technology into curriculum materials that introduced pre-engineering activities into secondary schools. The concepts and activities included in the *Man-Made World* materials reflected the study of technology from an engineering perspective. The materials provided an innovative approach to technology education, particularly in their introduction of such concepts as systems, modeling, and optimization. They were targeted for use by science and mathematics teachers with very able students; however, they lacked the type of hands-on activities we see as essential in technology education that is intended for all students. (The deep roots of gender bias can be seen quite clearly in the language and assumptions evidenced in these early initiatives. While there are objections on many levels to this bias, not the least of them is the limiting effect they have on the options available for solving practical problems—that is, for doing technology. For example, the terminology of "man-made world," "engineered goods," and "industrial technology" seem to preclude or discourage the consideration of textiles, food, and many other malleable materials in a comprehensive examination of the resources of technology. The issue of gender bias in the study of technology will be treated in greater detail in Chapter Five.)

Since the mid eighties, technology education has mobilized numerous powerful supporters, and the likelihood that it will find a legitimate place in America's schools is far greater than it has ever been. A range of pilot programs have emerged that demonstrate the promise of technology education (see Appendix E). Many of the frameworks that have been developed under the auspices of the Goals 2000 Act explicitly describe themselves as "science and technology frameworks," not just as science frameworks. While these events signal general support for technology education in the school curriculum, it is not at all clear at this stage exactly *what it is* that is being supported.

This chapter provides an overview of two major difficulties that lie in the way of creating a place in the K–12 curriculum for the kind of technology education that was discussed in Chapter One. As different stakeholders have entered the arena, they have attempted to influence the form technology education will take. As a result, diverse and often competing definitions of technology education are emerging. The primary challenge for those who are seeking to make technology education a school subject is that, as a discipline, it lacks both a history and a tradition, despite sporadic past efforts to introduce it into the schools. As a component of general education for all students, it has no core of commonly accepted beliefs, values, standards, or practices. The second challenge is that unlike the "classic" subjects of the school curriculum such as English, mathematics, and chemistry, technology education does not correspond to a firmly established academic discipline with a clear educational path from high school through advanced university training.

Diverse Definitions of Technology Education

The inability to settle on a single definition of technology education is due in part to the multiple definitions given to technology. The search for clarity about what technology is, and consequently about what technology education might be, is essential. There is some concern, however, that a premature crystallization of ideas resulting in a single definition might serve to limit technology rather than to reflect the rich field it actually is (Todd, 1989).

The continuing process of exploration is very important because, in a sense, technology education is still being invented. David Layton (1994b) suggests that we may be seeing a "subject in the making," but the exact shape it will take when it comes of age is far from clear at this stage. Under the heading of technology education, one can find programs and approaches with widely varying goals, depending on where, how, and under what auspices the program was created. In a review of technology education in western Europe, de Vries (1994, pp. 32–33) identified eight approaches that can be differentiated in relation to the following factors:

- The kind of activities that pupils carry out
- The way classrooms are equipped
- The way teachers are educated
- The social contexts by which the approach is stimulated
- Gender aspects
- The concept of technology that students acquire

The following categories, based on those recognized by de Vries, illustrate the diverse range of approaches found not only in Europe but also in the United States and Australia, where various attempts at reform in technology education have taken place over the last two decades. (Appendix A provides further details about the development of technology education in several countries.) The categories are not intended to represent accurately the practices in any particular classroom or region, but rather to highlight the different directions in which technology education has developed in different settings. None of these approaches is ideal, but something can be learned from each of them.

The Craft-Based Approach

This is the oldest approach to technology education and it is found in every part of the world. It places emphasis on knowledge about materials and the skills required to transform them into fabricated objects. Learning activities typically involve making things based on prescribed designs in classrooms equipped with machines and tools from the woodworking, metalworking, electrical, catering, and textile trades. Much emphasis is placed on psychomotor skills; little is placed on design.

The craft-oriented approach to technology education traditionally has provided a foundation of skills for students moving into a vocational craft or trade. It has also been used to provide a balancing "practical component" or alternative path in the curriculum of schools that focus primarily on academic achievement. Teachers typically come from a trade background or technical discipline, and the course content tends to emphasize traditional materials and techniques (wood, metal, electrical wiring) rather than incorporating contemporary manufacturing equipment and techniques. Courses also tend to emphasize traditional gender characterizations of interests and occupations (de Vries, 1994).

The absence of a craft-oriented curriculum tradition in U.S. primary education may impede the introduction of design-and-construct activities at that level. This is in contrast to a strong European tradition of crafts education in the elementary grades, which is also manifest in such transplants as the Waldorf schools, currently growing in popularity in the United States.

The Occupational or Vocational Approach

This approach is often similar to the craft-based approach. It involves a high degree of "hands-on" transformation of materials into products, but it emphasizes current industrial practice rather than traditional craft skills, though these often overlap. This is what de Vries refers to as "the industrial production oriented approach." Classrooms are similar to those used for the craft-based approach, but typically include machinery from industry, either models retired from the factory floor or scaled-down, purposely built classroom versions. The teachers usually have been trained in industry.

In some cases, there is an expectation that students will spend time in a workplace setting undertaking a "work experience" or internship program. There is certainly an expectation that by undertaking such a program, students will be well equipped to enter current technical or practical vocations after leaving school.

As with the craft-based approach, there is usually little connection between technology education and other disciplines within the school program. There frequently are, however, valuable links with local industry. This approach is the one most consistent with the conception that links education with preparation for work and an economically productive life.

The High-Tech Approach

This approach typically occurs in schools in which a substantial amount of new technology has been introduced into a traditional technology education setting over a relatively short period of time. The infusion of technology (for example, CAD-CAM systems, numerically controlled manufacturing tools, processes involving new materials, or robotics) is usually made possible by fundraising efforts in conjunction with industry partners or by grants from technology promotion initiatives. Technology education employing sophisticated equipment is generally seen as being more relevant to both boys and girls than approaches based on the older craft traditions.

The reasons for pursuing this approach vary and include a desire by industry to shape the skill base of the future workforce and a desire on the part of schools to appear progressive in an environment of technological change. In some countries—Austria, for example—specialized technical schools offer, in the context of a rigorous secondary school education, not only advanced training on sophisticated equipment but also entry (given satisfactory performance on qualifying exams) to either an academic or technical university as an alternative to entering technical positions in cooperating industries.

In his review of technology education, de Vries (1994) notes that in western Europe, teachers using this approach have usually come from a traditional technology education background but have undergone retraining. He finds, however, that the retraining typically does not empower them to use the technology in a pedagogically sophisticated way. There is a risk, therefore, that rather than developing a generalized understanding of the role of new technology in industry and society, students simply learn a new set of useful but limited skills. The approach tends to emphasize the role of technology in producing objects, rather than the processes of planning and design.

The Applied Science Approach

In contrast to the approaches previously mentioned, which have grown from the crafts and from industry, the applied science approach has been developed by science educators. Rather than teaching scientific ideas as isolated abstractions, familiar products and processes are used as both the dissection table and the test bed for scientific ideas and theories.

The applied science approach generally is used by science teachers, more often than not in a physics classroom. Although there is clearly potential for using this model to explore new applications of technology—to design and to build—practical work has generally been regarded as less important than the cognitive elements important to the given science course. Though it does not have the "workshop" association that is often thought to discourage girls, applied science tends to be more attractive to boys, because the sciences in general—and physics and engineering in particular—tend to be male dominated.

The Technology Concepts Approach

This approach focuses on learning about the processes that enable technological developments to take place. As with the applied science approach, it emphasizes theoretical understanding rather than practical action. The systems concept is frequently used, for example, to present an overview of technological processes. It focuses on the flow of matter, energy, and information rather than on understanding how to make or repair any of the components of a system (de Vries, 1994).

This approach typically is aligned with the academic engineering disciplines and taught by those with an engineering background. It is also sometimes adopted by science teachers who wish to infuse their science teaching with important ideas from technology, but who lack the classroom time or practical experience required to fully explore the design and product development process; consequently, they tend to resort to flow charts and models that represent the process in a form familiar from their own discipline. Thus, this approach all too easily can be turned into yet another set of abstractions to be learned without any experiential base that would allow students to acquire a deep understanding of the concepts involved in technology.

The Design Approach

In contrast to the several approaches already described that focus on the function and manufacture of specified products, the design approach assumes that students will be responsible for major decision making about what kind of product is needed and what the product will look like, how it will work, and how it should be made. Students typically begin with or are asked to produce a design brief that describes a need or a problem that must be solved using a certain set of resources, which may be narrowly or broadly specified. They progress through stages of concept development, construction of prototypes, and testing, and then redesign and perhaps manufacture.

The design approach has doubtless been used in isolated classrooms for many years, but it developed into a national movement in England and Wales during the 1980s (Layton, 1993). In that country, the approach was originally know as Craft, Design, and Technology, or CDT (see Appendix A). As the name suggests, it emerged from the craft tradition, but it incorporated a newer, more constructivist approach than that found in most craft-based technology courses. The current curriculum title is Design and Technology, or D&T. In addition to concentrating on design, the approach includes consideration of such issues as user response to products under development and product marketing, which have not traditionally been dealt with in school technology courses. Moreover, D&T courses have been seen in England and Wales as an appropriate place to teach or reinforce ideas from scientific disciplines such as physics and electronics. Although the approach to teaching D&T is far from uniform, the original CDT movement in England and Wales made an important contribution to the elevation of technology to the status of an essential component of general education, and much of it is now enshrined in the national curriculum (Layton, 1993).

The design approach has been incorporated into technology education curricula in other countries as well. In the United States, design technology as a curricular component was highlighted by Susan Dunn and Rob Larson in their 1990 publication *Design Technology: Children's Engineering;* since then, groups of teachers in several states, but particularly in the Northwest, have been involved in exploring design technology strategies in K–12 classrooms. In Australia, the Victorian Technology Studies Framework (Victorian Curriculum and Assessment Board, 1991) places a major emphasis on design and problem solving. (Greater detail on the Victorian curriculum guide and teaching suggestions is provided in Chapter Four.)

Classrooms in which this approach is taught are often equipped and arranged similarly to those used for craft-based teaching; at the secondary level, the teachers typically have a craft or industrial background. Where schools have had the opportunity, technology centers have been developed, giving students access to a sufficiently wide range of technologies to enable the design and construction of artifacts requiring more types of material and processing than would be found in a traditional technology classroom.

The Science/Technology/Society (STS) Approach

Courses in STS became popular during the 1970s, when concerns about the impact of science on society were at their height. Many of these courses were first introduced by universities, including major research institutions. By 1990, two thousand universities and colleges offered STS courses (Yager and Roy, 1993). They are also available as an elective in many high schools; for example, the STS approach is being used in Iowa as the basis for integrating the grades seven to twelve science curriculum. The objective of STS courses is to set science in the context of human action, particularly with respect to economic and social considerations and the consequences of these interactions between science technology and society. In contrast to traditional science education, in which the curriculum is driven by key concepts, STS curricula are organized around societal issues and use them as an avenue to uncover key concepts. Teachers of STS courses work to establish connections between their classrooms and the outside world by explicitly focusing on local issues relevant to the students, discussing the knowledge and skills needed to address these issues, and bringing in outside speakers or taking the students on field trips to places in the community where science is practiced. STS places great emphasis on the way students are taught. Activities are based on problem solving and investigation, with students asking questions and searching for solutions. Teachers in STS courses act as facilitators or guides, rather than as the more traditional purveyors of information. Students in STS courses are expected to see science as a way of dealing with problems rather than as a body of information to learn (Yager and Roy, 1993).

The hope is that through taking up some contemporary issues, such an approach will make science more relevant to young people and encourage them to apply their science knowledge to personal and societal decisions. Indeed, one of the goals of STS courses is to change students' attitudes toward science. Rather than develop students who know a body of knowledge, STS courses seek to develop responsible decision makers who ask questions about the world around them, such as, Is it a problem? How did it become a problem? What are some alternative approaches to its solution? What are the potential effects of applying the alternatives to individuals and/or society (Holbrook, 1992, p. 9). STS courses—not unlike technology courses—have been criticized, however, as lacking an integrated body of knowledge that could be made available to students.

Although the word "technology" generally is an integral part of the titles of STS courses, this approach had widely been interpreted as applied science—perhaps not surprisingly, given that these courses were developed by scientists and science educators. We have argued elsewhere that this is an entirely insufficient conception of technology. In our view, if STS courses are to make good on their promise of connecting science, technology, and society, they must move to a view of technology that appropriately mirrors its complex relationships to science and makes it an equal partner, as pictured in the model provided in Figure 1.1 in Chapter One and discussed in greater detail in the rest of this chapter.

The Integrated Subjects Approach

This approach is unique among those described here because, rather than creating or modifying a single approach, it involves the integration of several subjects or areas of study into a framework that aims to provide both an understanding of technology and its interrelatedness with other disciplines and with life outside school.

Considerable attention and support has been given to the meaningful integration of the school curriculum in the United States and in other countries. One result of this curriculum restructuring has become known as the integrated science, mathematics, and technology (SMT) approach. Technology in this context includes the role of computers and other new media and technologies as tools for learning and program delivery but is not limited to using computers in the classroom. Within the SMT approach, technology should also be considered as a subject area with its own content, goals, and contributions.

A number of statewide efforts directed toward developing standards for integrated SMT have emerged in the United States. Some states are integrating all three subjects into one set of standards, some are pairing science and technology, and some are maintaining separate subjects and standards. Notable is the New York State initiative (see Chapter Four), where a single set of standards is being developed for all three subjects. The New York standards have used the addition of technology education to help provide connections with real world applications, a connection that has been difficult to make when the focus is on separate subjects (New York State Education Department, 1994). Other states, including Pennsylvania, New Jersey, Virginia, Montana, Ohio, and Maryland, have technology education frameworks or programs.

Also included in the acceptance of integrated SMT is the growing concern that the students of tomorrow will be seriously handicapped if they are unable to apply what they know from studying the three subjects separately. The integrated SMT approach is seen as an important step in helping students to become accustomed to and proficient in solving problems that have not as yet been identified, and to gain skills in acquiring knowledge that has not yet been developed. The potential these efforts hold for educational change is matched only by the complexity they add to the already confused circumstances of curriculum change.

A different example of the integrated studies approach can be found in Scotland, where technology is grouped with science, social science, health education, and information technology under the umbrella of Environmental Studies (Scottish Office Education Department, 1993). Study of the environment provides a context for learning, which is deemed to be meaningful for all students and which provides rich opportunities for the exploration and application of technologies of many kinds (see Chapter Four). Whereas CDT courses have been identified as being less gender-specific than the traditional craft-based approach (de Vries, 1994), integrated studies based on an inclusive theme such as the environment are believed to be even more gender neutral (Hynes, 1994).

In Victoria, Australia, the curriculum frameworks reform of the mid to late 1980s laid the groundwork for extensive interconnection between technology studies, science, mathematics, and the humanities for all grade levels up to grade ten, but by still a different path than the American reform. In this case, the integration took the form of themes common to all areas of study, establishing links between the content of each study area and its impact on society and personal development, and making students aware of vocational opportunities. The Victorian Frameworks movement also encouraged collaborative activities across disciplines such as science, mathematics, and technology studies.

The Relationship of Technology Education to Existing Curricula

A second challenge facing technology education is its relationship to traditional curricular subjects and curriculum sequences. Although some of the approaches summarized in this chapter illustrate that technology can be integrated with many other subjects, it has the closest links with science and with technical/vocational education. We discuss next the problems associated with these two critical relationships.

Science and Technology

The model of the relationship between science and technology provided in Figure 1.1 presents these fields as separate but closely intertwined. There are dynamic features in both the study of science and of technology. Existing ideas in the form of laws, principles, and models are challenged and changed on a regular basis. Within both science and technology, all such "facts" are exploratory and subject to question and improvement. Sound and tested theories and principles can be very powerful, however, in helping students gain and organize knowledge. Similarly, the processes and procedures of technology can help students identify and develop knowledge and then put it to work toward the solving of practical problems.

Technology and science represent uniquely different yet mutually supportive bodies of knowledge and methods of discovery. Science is about *knowing.* Its major goal is to understand nature and its functioning. Although viewed by some as the source of "truth" and as a body of "facts," it is more appropriate to consider science as a source of models, theories, and processes that attempt to explain not "what is" but "what we know," and as a method for expanding what is currently "known." Historically, the scientific community has seen the acceptance of usable concepts and ideas that are later found to be limited, misleading, or wrong. From this perspective, science is a collection of concepts and theories that help people understand and deal with nature, and a method of inquiry that can be used to expand the body of scientific knowledge.

While science is concerned with knowing, technology is essentially concerned with *doing*. Technology starts with an idea or need (sometimes drawn from science, but usually not, as technology tends to be driven by economics); through the procedures and processes of problem solving, the idea or the solution to the need is converted to physical reality. Technology does not exist until that transformation takes place. Science, by contrast, is essentially a body of ideas that are not required or designed to relate directly to practical action. The exception comes when theories must be put into practical application in order to test their validity. (Layton, 1993, points out that a recent application of scientific knowledge has been for policy regulatory purposes. This kind of practical action also requires the transformation of scientific knowledge into a form appropriate for the intended policy or regulations.)

Science as a way of knowing and understanding (Moore, 1984) and technology as a way of adapting and solving problems (Harlen, 1985) are important themes for learning in the successful classroom. By pursuing these themes, students can grow to appreciate that, while science and engineering are separate fields of endeavor with distinctly different approaches, the two are inextricably bound (National Center for Improving Science Education, 1991, p. 61).

Within science, there is only modest interest in putting ideas into application. Technology represents the domain of application. Individual scientists may have applied interests; in such cases, they essentially shift roles from being scientists to being technologists. Similarly, when individuals working as technologists turn their attention to research and inquiry of a more theoretical nature, they take on the role of scientists. Individuals unable to make these role shifts must find others who are willing to provide the missing expertise. As students enter the real world as future workers, they will benefit from schooling that is designed to enhance movement across these artificial boundaries.

An increased understanding of the symbiotic relationship between science and technology is emerging from the work of the epistemologists and historians currently focusing on this topic. In their view, technology is more than applied science. Technologists form a distinct knowledge community. Technological knowledge entails an experiential component, or as John Staudenmaier (1985, echoing Nasmyth) wrote, "The nature and properties of materials must come in through the fingers' ends," and as a result, "no technological praxis is completely reducible to abstract theory." The knowledge communities of scientists and technologists are distinct, but interacting and interdependent.

Between these two distinct knowledge communities, influence flows in both directions. Occasionally, a scientific discovery paves the way for a technological invention. In other instances the reverse occurs, and technology functions as the driving force for scientific discovery. For example, the development of the steam engine and the problems encountered with boilers that resulted in explosions and the loss of life and property helped spur the study of the fledgling field of thermodynamics. Similarly, binary mathematics remained largely undeveloped as a field of modest importance until the development of the digital computer. The two fields now raise each other symbiotically to progressively new levels of importance.

Throughout recent history, many technological objects and processes have been developed and put into practice with the inventors and users often unaware of how and why they worked. Although science and technology have become symbiotic endeavors, there remain many instances of processes that work even though they are poorly or incompletely understood. For example, many processes in the field of biotechnology operate to produce usable end products, yet their inventors and developers often have only a hazy idea of what is actually taking place.

Technology and science in the real world may be quite different from each other, and the efforts of science and technology often remain separate, even though they are supportive of each other. Technology provides the instrumentation, both hardware and software, through which scientists can observe phenomena beyond the range of their unaided senses. Technology also provides the hardware that enhances the scientist's capacity for memory and creativity; the computer is perhaps the most evident example. Not infrequently, technology even provides critical questions for science to address. Often, technology is such an integral part of the work done by scientists that, for all practical purposes, the technology becomes invisible. Similarly, science provides a theoretical backdrop that makes the training and work of technologists more efficient and productive. Science uncovers opportunities and sets limits for what technology can create. In this sense, science, through knowing, helps technology to continue its business of doing. Similarly, part of doing for technology is to support science's major purpose of knowing.

The Second-Class Position of Technology. If the arguments in favor of considering science and technology as equal partners in a symbiotic relationship are accepted, why has technology as a field of study never attained the privileged position that science has attained in the school curriculum? According to Layton (1991), the reasons for the subservient position of technology can best be understood by looking at the struggle that took place during the nineteenth century between scientists and technologists in the academic world of the universities.

Despite the fact that the nineteenth-century practitioners of technology were mostly craftsmen and tinkerers, who were largely divorced from academe, their influence on the cultural and economic life of their societies was substantial. As Clinchy (1994, p. 746) notes:

A close examination of the process of historical change in the West from medieval times through the Renaissance and the Industrial Revolution and on into quite recent history makes it clear that technological innovation has brought about most of the great social, economic, and cultural transformations in Western society. Until the advent of World War II and the scientific/political alliance that produced nuclear weapons, as well as nuclear energy and the digital computer, the crucial inventions that have most changed our lives did not emerge from the disconnected world of university-based scholars but from the everyday life of the workaday world.

In denial of this historical reality, it is commonly thought that scholars in general and scientists in particular have provided the important knowledge and insights necessary for the inventions that have helped to shape the modern world. Technology remains an undervalued arena of knowledge and study, in part because of the misplaced credit given to scientists for the important developments of the past. Most of the major technological developments that have irrevocably shaped the world in which we live drew little from science. Clinchy's (1994, p. 747) discussion of some of the key inventions of the last 150 years makes this clear:

Of the men and women who brought about the Industrial Revolution . . . none were university scholars or even particularly well-schooled people. Just as in the late 19th and early 20th centuries, those who created some of our most transforming modern inventions—Daimler's internal combustion engine; Ford's mass-production line; the Wright brothers' airplane; Edison's incandescent bulb, movie camera, and phonograph; Telsa's alternating-current electrical power system; and the radio of DeForest and Armstrong—were all extraordinary tinkerers rather than learned university savants.

Given the very tangible contributions made by tinkerers such as these, a key question that must be asked is how and why abstract science gained its current privileged position in the academic world, while technology was more or less forced to the margins. Epistemological and historical research on the relationship between science and technology provides some useful insights on this issue. This research suggests that science has no "natural" superiority; rather, its preeminent position only arose after a century of struggle between natural philosophers (scientists) and practical men (technologists). By the mid nineteenth century, the scientists had gained the upper hand, asserting the superiority of science and theory over practice. (This analysis is based on British research, but the idea that theory—that is, science—is superior to practice—that is, technology—is common to the English-speaking nations. Intellectual traditions in Germany possibly grant a more equal place to technology. See Layton, 1991.)

The outcome of this struggle had obvious implications for how different kinds of knowledge were valued by the universities and, ultimately, by the schools. Pure science detached from practical contexts achieved high status, while practice was seen as demeaning and lacking in prestige. The work of historians of science and technology suggests that science achieved a privileged position in the British university by the late nineteenth century. The political success that scientists had achieved in the academic world by that time created a situation in which technologically oriented faculties (such as engineering) had to struggle to find a secure place.

As a consequence of the political success of science as an academic discipline, it was science rather than technology that became an established subject in the school curriculum. The contrasting fortunes of science and technology in the academic world also mean that attempts to establish technology education as a school subject today are hindered by the absence of a strong tradition of technology studies in the universities. Science education has its reference point in the university science faculties, just as mathematics education has mathematics faculties and mathematicians and history education has history faculties and historians. There is no corollary for technology education.

Because the scientists won and the technologists lost, technology came to be represented as "applied science." A series of pervasive impressions was created by this representation: that scientific discovery comes first while usable products based on scientific inventions come later; that technology is dependent on science; and that technologists merely take the implications of science and give them some physical representation. As noted earlier, careful analyses of the actual processes of invention and production suggest a very different picture: instead of hierarchical dependence, there is constant "horizontal" interaction between scientists and technologists. In the real world of research and product development, technologists make creative use of science, and scientists make creative use of technology.

Modernizing the Curriculum. Given the needs of today's students, who need to prepare for the twenty-first century, it is time to redress the school curriculum balance so as to reflect the real world outside the classroom. Technology education can add a dimension often missing in science education: by adding the more active dimension of doing, technology can put science to work in a range of applications that will require students to think more critically and creatively about the content and processes of both science and technology. Similarly, science can augment and extend technology activities by providing insights into the objects and processes that emerge from the applied activities. Collaborative science and technology can help increase students' level and complexity of thinking and doing in both subjects, setting the stage for more vigorous and robust learning activities.

The utility found in linking science and technology also helps students apply what they have learned to practical situations. Technology supported by science should help students learn that there are many ways to solve a problem, and at the same time, learn to establish criteria and processes whereby they can choose the "best for now" solution. By gaining experience in the practice of application, students can learn even more science. Thus, technology plays the role of enhancing the utility of science for students. Utility in this sense is far more than a pedestrian application of scientific concepts to simple problems. An integrated science and technology approach introduces the use of concepts at several levels of application, including operation, improvement, and design. The usefulness of what students learn is increased through concrete experiences as they (1) learn how to operate specific technological devices, (2) use that knowledge to improve those devices, and (3) integrate what they have learned as they design and develop new devices and artifacts. For example, students can be given the opportunity of using different types of water-lifting and pumping devices. After they have had a range of experiences, the students can use their knowledge to identify means of improving those devices. The students could then be challenged to use the new insights they have gained to develop new devices or to use wind power or the power of flowing water to replace muscle power.

The utility of scientific knowledge is also increased as students learn how the concepts of science relate to practical instances. The use of Newton's ideas and theories in practice, as illustrated in the vignette "Mousetrap Power" in Chapter One, would be a significantly different experience from simply seeing those ideas and theories presented in a textbook or hearing them described by a teacher. The opportunity to use science concepts in practice will help students develop concrete instances that can serve as the basis of relating these concepts to new and different circumstances. Through technological activities with vehicles and moving devices, for example, students can apply and learn important concepts of force, energy, and acceleration. Because of such active involvement, these students will view other instances of "mass in motion" with an insight unlikely for more passive learners. Learning and applying scientific concepts represent important steps in helping students transfer knowledge to new and unfamiliar instances.

Technology Education and Vocational Education

Vocational education is defined in the Carl D. Perkins Vocational and Applied Technology Act of 1990 as "organized educational programs offering a sequence of courses which are directly related to the preparation of individuals in paid or unpaid employment in current or emerging occupations requiring other than a baccalaureate or advanced degree." Technology education as an idea or as a curricular area in vocational education remains relatively invisible at the national level, yet it would appear to be an essential foundation for vocational education, which has as a goal preparing students for the contemporary workplace. Lacking the knowledge and skills provided through technology education, students tend to remain naive and negative about technology—poor attitudes for success in a work world being continually transformed by technological developments. Technology education helps provide the base that is required for most advanced technical training, whether at the workplace or through additional formal education. Because of its concern with results and impacts, technology education also helps shift student thinking more toward a future orientation. This shift makes it much easier for students to focus on the need for continued learning, which will enable them to deal with and not be as threatened by the changes that continue to evolve.

Perhaps even more important than learning to deal with change are the negative attitudes that students often have about technology. The cross-national research work of Falco de Klerk–Wolters and his colleagues (1994) on student attitudes indicates that students who have had little or no experience in technology tend to hold negative values regarding technology. With more experience, students tend to hold more positive attitudes. These research results suggest that early experiences in technology education at the elementary and middle school levels may be key factors in determining whether students go on for further vocationally oriented education, which could lead to science- and technology-related careers. Of course, since technology covers such a wide spectrum, students may very well have different preferences regarding different manifestations of technology (for instance, genetic engineering as opposed to video games).

The relationship between technology education and vocational education is not so direct and simple, however. Currently, technology educators view their subject as essential to the general education of all students, but at the same time, as suited to prevocational and vocational offerings for some students. The dual general and vocational education function of technology education has been the source of considerable ambiguity and misunderstanding. When is technology education general education for all students, and when is it vocational education for some? For example, in the technology preparation effort commonly called Tech Prep (Parnell, 1985), the term technology is used, but little has been done to clarify what it means in this context and how it relates to other forms and meanings of technology. For many in technology education, the current shift in vocational education seemingly has created curricular overlaps and introduced considerable ambiguity in the relationship between the two fields.

As the world continues to become more technological, the foundational role that technology education can play will increase in importance for all students, both those going on for advanced vocational training and those going on for baccalaureate degrees and beyond. As indicated in the SCANS (Secretary's Commission on Achieving Necessary Skills) report from the U.S. Department of Labor (1992), the workplace continues to change and to require new competencies for those who are to enjoy a productive, full, and satisfying life. The workplace know-how described in Exhibit 2.1 is not achieved through a narrow work-focused education, but through education that is considerably broader and more demanding.

Nearly all of the concepts, language, and concerns identified in the previous section are found in the new frameworks, missions, and objectives of technology education, although there is some concern that the desired competence levels may have been set too low in existing documents. Rigorous technology education represents a key school subject for delivering the kind of essential competencies identified by the SCANS report, competencies needed by all who will work and live in the coming century. Preparing graduates for that world is a job of enormous proportions, and technology education is far too important a contributor to remain invisible and underutilized in that effort.

The task ahead will be made even more difficult because vocational education lacks respectability, technology education lacks visibility, and general education lacks credibility. Senta Raizen (1989, p. 18) captures the essence of the problem in the following statement made within the context of the periodic shifting of the goals and expectations of schooling:

> Vocational education is criticized for reifying a second-class educational track that not only forecloses access to high-status professions but has little pay-off of any kind. The academic and general tracks are criticized because they do not provide young people who are not college-bound with an adequate preparation for the workplace. From time to time, this criticism of formal education—vocational and academic both—has extended beyond inadequate preparation for the workplace to include inadequate preparation for citizenship and family responsibilities as well. As a result of the criticisms there have been attempts to integrate hands-on education with academic courses and academics with vocational education. During periods when academic achievement has been de-emphasized in favor of learning to think as a goal for everyone, the schools have responded by making a few manual skills courses mandatory—home economics for girls, shop

EXHIBIT 2.1. WORKPLACE KNOW-HOW.

The know-how identified by SCANS is made up of five competencies and a three-part foundation of skills and personal qualities that are needed for solid job performance. These include:

Competencies. Effective workers can productively use

Resources: allocating time, money, materials, space and staff

Interpersonal skills: working on teams, teaching others, serving customers, leading, negotiating, and working well with people from culturally diverse backgrounds

Information: acquiring and evaluating data, organizing and maintaining files, interpreting and communicating, and using computers to process information

Systems: understanding social, organizational, and technological systems; monitoring and correcting performance; and designing or improving systems

Technology: selecting equipment and tools, applying technology to specific tasks, and maintaining and troubleshooting technologies

The Foundation. Competence requires

Basic skills: reading, writing, arithmetic and mathematics, speaking, and listening

Thinking skills: thinking creatively, making decisions, solving problems, seeing things in the mind's eye, knowing how to learn, and reasoning

Personal qualities: individual responsibility, self-esteem, sociability, self-management, and integrity

---

[*sic*] for boys—as part of a secondary school education. At present, because schools are being criticized for their lack of academic rigor, more mathematics and science courses are being introduced into vocational programs to meet increased high school graduation requirements.

Too often, technology education is still seen as "shop." Although the designation may or may not be warranted, it indicates the pervasiveness of an old paradigm and image that denigrates what technology education might contribute to the development of all students. The United States is one of a few countries that continues to see science and mathematics as separate from technology. Science and mathematics alone will be inadequate for preparing young people for the real world. As the goals and expectations of schooling shift, adding technology education to the school curriculum could further the goal of enhancing connections with the real world for students, connections so sorely missing from schooling as it currently exists.

The case has been made often that the work of the future will continue to be influenced significantly by technological developments. Students entering the adult world of the coming century without a sound grounding in concepts and skills related to technology will be placed at an unfair advantage. The response of almost all of the industrialized countries has been to expand their educational delivery to ensure that all students become technologically literate, capable, and responsible.

Unfortunately for those who are seeking to implement it as a new subject, technology education continues to be a field faced with imposing barriers. There are, however, very encouraging developments from within the United States and abroad that illustrate the part that technology education can play in revitalizing the K–12 curriculum. The next two chapters return to the approach to technology education that was developed in Chapter One and use this approach as a point of reference for a review of a selection of the technology education programs and frameworks that have been developed in the United States, Australia, and England and Wales over the past few years.

CHAPTER THREE

STRATEGIES FOR CREATING COHERENT PROGRAMS

The kind of technology education we envisage in this book is of such importance to understanding and participating in the world of the twenty-first century that we believe all school students should have access to it. Yet, as we noted
in Chapter Two, technology as a school subject is still in the making, with its roots
in several disciplines traditionally represented in the curriculum as well as in
vocational education and the craft tradition prevalent in Europe. Given the need
for technology education and its as yet fluid state, how might curriculum designers move toward a "best possible" scenario for technology education? Educators will need a range of strategies for creating technology education programs
that extend across the full sequence of schooling, from kindergarten through grade
twelve, and that are diverse enough to meet the requirements and needs of school
districts across the nation. In responding to this need, we provide in the first section of this chapter a statement of guiding principles for technology education.
The second section outlines explicit goals for technology education, against which
all curricular components touching on technology education can be appraised.
The remaining sections discuss some general guidelines for curriculum planning and for teaching and learning strategies. (Chapter Four illustrates in greater
detail a range of specific curricular alternatives designed to achieve the goals
for technology education.)

Guiding Principles for Technology Education

By reviewing several of the existing approaches to technology education, we have identified a number of "guiding principles" that we believe should underpin the development of such programs in the future. In summary, technology education should:

- Be equally accessible to all students, irrespective of their gender, their ethnicity, or their social backgrounds.
- Empower all students to use technology appropriately and effectively in their own lives, through a planned program of learning from kindergarten through grade twelve.
- Make extensive use of projects involving design, construction, and evaluation, and in general employ constructivist learning principles.
- Provide a "real world" context for learning science, mathematics, and communication arts, and create opportunities for interdisciplinary projects at school.
- Lead to an understanding of both the positive and the potentially detrimental effects of technology on human lives and the environment.
- Lead to an understanding of the properties of commonly used materials (wood, plastic, metal, semiconductors, adhesives, and so forth) and to an understanding of the use of tools and processes to transform materials into useful products.
- Lead to an understanding of how commonly used devices and processes operate (manufacturing processes, communication and information sharing systems, domestic appliances, transportation, and so on), as well as an understanding of their underlying principles (energy, control, and so forth).
- Develop students' ability to operate at the system level as well as at the detailed operational level.
- Prepare students for the world of work, including giving them an awareness of the need for flexible skills in an environment of changing technology.
- Develop the personal skills necessary for working effectively with other people.
- Promote innovation and entrepreneurship. Students should leave school appreciating the opportunities for enterprise available through the creative application of technology.

How could programs of technology education that conform to these principles be introduced into America's schools? It is unlikely that most schools will suddenly see the need to introduce technology education as an entirely new subject, pushing aside existing courses in an already crowded curriculum. What is more likely is that technology education will come in on the coattails of other reforms. For example, science teachers at the elementary and middle school levels may introduce technology education topics in order to develop in their students an appreciation of the role science can play in the development and evaluation of technologies that are commonplace in the designed world in which they live. At the high school level, as illustrated in the following vignette, creating technology education courses that are carefully articulated with science courses can play a key role in helping a school get rid of tracking.

Porter High Ends Tracking

For years, the middle schools in the Porter school district had taught different kinds of mathematics and science courses to different groups of students from grade seven onwards. This practice had the effect of creating a hierarchy among the students; as early as age twelve, some students were being programmed for the low-status vocational track, while others were being pushed toward the college track. When the students arrived at the local high school, they already knew to which track they belonged. The school committee of the Porter school district decided that in 1991 they wanted to begin to eliminate tracking.

During the 1991–92 school year, the discussion among parents, teachers, and administrators about alternatives to tracking went into full swing. After a few weeks of debate, the science teachers and the vocational teachers discovered that they shared very similar ideas on the need for reform. The science teachers wanted their students to understand that the science they were teaching was not just a lot of abstract ideas. They wanted students to see how useful the key concepts of science are in helping people to understand and use modern technologies both at home and at work. Among the vocational teachers, the motivation was different, but related. They wanted to move students beyond just knowing "what to do" when working with tools and materials, to knowing why particular techniques and practices worked. Many of the "why" questions the vocational teachers asked of their students led them back to basic principles of science and technology.

The science teachers and the vocational education teachers recognized that, in practice, their thoughts about what was needed overlapped a lot. They suggested a major reform of both science education and vocational education at Porter High. The first step would involve the creation of a carefully articulated program covering grades nine and ten. In both grades there would be a science course and a technology course that every student would be expected to take. Each course would comprise six units. Each of the six science units would be taught in parallel with a related unit in the technology course. For example, the unit on materials and technology would be synchronized with a unit on chemistry, the unit on design and movement would be synchronized with a unit on force and motion, the unit on health science would be synchronized with a unit on human physiology, and so on. The science teachers and vocational teachers recognized that this would involve a lot of work and close coordination, but they thought it was worth it. They were determined to give every student (not just a select few) a solid grounding in science. They were also convinced that it was time for technology education to become a key part of the education of all young people.

The next step at Porter High would be to develop new science and technology programs for grades eleven and twelve (see "Reshaping Educational Pathways" in Chapter Four).

Goals for a Technology Education Curriculum

A set of goals provides a lens through which classroom practice can be appraised. In addition, the use of explicit goals to evaluate technology education curricula leads to the identification of gaps, points of articulation with other areas of study, and unnecessary duplication. A statement of goals creates an expectation of ongoing review and improvement in the process of learning and teaching. This type of appraisal is important in every area of the school program, but never more so than in technology-related areas, in which the subject matter content demands frequent revision. Following are some useful goals for technology education.

As a result of undertaking K–12 technology education students should

1. Understand and have experienced the role technology plays in the process of transforming materials and creating things, and in the practice of science, mathematics, and other school disciplines
2. Understand and have experienced the role that science, mathematics and other disciplines play in the development and application of technology
3. Understand and reflect on the way technology supports and constrains personal and societal endeavors, and on how it has in turn been shaped by society and culture
4. Be confident in bringing knowledge and skills to bear on practical problems through the process of design, construction, and evaluation
5. Be able to collaborate, communicate, and work productively with others

The first goal proposes that technology should be used to provide a context for learning about science (and other school disciplines), and also for developing an appropriate attitude toward personal uses of technology both in and out of school. For students specializing in science, this means, for example, understanding how measuring instruments work and being able to describe the error and accuracy inherent in a particular measurement. For all students it means understanding enough about devices and processes to make informed decisions in selecting between alternative technologies.

The second goal acknowledges the rich opportunities technology education offers for enhancing vocational and technical education. For example, in a traditional craft-based approach to vocational education the goal is to teach students how to carry out standard operating procedures. Rarely are students asked why these procedures make sense or to identify concepts that can be transferred to other instances. Technology education asks students to make sense of technological devices and processes by focusing on the scientific ideas embedded in the technology. Equipped with a more general theoretical understanding, as well as with a knowledge of technique, students are able to work in a more flexible way to solve a greater range of technical challenges. For example, students are better able to understand and even design refrigerating devices if they understand the basic principles of thermodynamics.

Goal three focuses on how technology has always helped to shape human culture and on how it has in turn been shaped by culture. For example, the Scottish guidelines for technology outcomes include the following goal: "Recognize the impact technology has on societies, lifestyles, and the environment; recognize the part which technology can play in making effective use of natural resources . . . [and] think about the opportunities for enhancing people's lives by appropriate use of technology and design" (Scottish Office Education Department, 1993, pp. 58–59). Technology has had a profound effect on the size and arrangement of the communities in which people live; on the ways they communicate and relate with each other; on the ways they feed, clothe and entertain themselves; and on the ways in which they organize and defend their societies. In the age of "just-in-time" manufacturing and inventory control, genetic engineering, and the "information superhighway," the importance for every citizen of understanding the shaping forces of technology has never been greater. Citizens also need to understand the role society plays in deciding along what paths technology will develop—that is, the social, economic, and political factors that influence the choice and nature of specific technological processes and systems.

Goal four highlights the importance of design-based activities in integrating a broad range of content and procedural knowledge, the importance of the skills needed to use simple and complex tools, and the importance of the cognitive processes needed to develop and carry out problem solutions. When undertaken in groups, design projects also assist in developing collaborative behavior and communication skills.

Goal five acknowledges that technology education should provide a context for developing personal skills and self-confidence. The processes of designing and making something and then modifying the design in response to user feedback provide an ideal setting in which to develop teamwork, collaborative problem solving, and communication—capabilities that are as eagerly sought by industry as they are valuable in personal and civic life.

Curriculum Elements

As with any area of study, it is necessary at some point to decide exactly what will be learned and by what means. We argue that, no matter what the content, a technology curriculum must encompass problem identification and design processes, including cognitive modeling, and an understanding of systems.

Problem Solving Through Design

For the purposes of technology education, problem solving can be identified as a structured component within a general investigative approach to learning. It conforms to a defined though far from rigid methodology, the process of design, long recognized by designers, engineers, and technologists. The process of designing things is vital to both the aesthetics and the mechanics of our culture, and yet it is not comprehensively dealt with in U.S. schools. Some educators argue that the activity of designing is a fundamental capacity of mind that leads to a distinctive kind of knowledge and knowing; it not only enables people to create things but helps them to make sense of the forms and symbols in the built environment (Roberts, 1994). This is analogous to the dual roles of language in giving people a voice and in helping them make sense of the world around them. In addition to this capacity, we argue that the design process is a valuable way for students to combine knowledge and skills learned elsewhere and to apply them to the solution of new problems. The posing of open-ended questions and tasks are the tools of a problem-solving methodology. The degree of open-endedness employed is critical to the required outcome. Questions or tasks can, on the one hand, be narrowly focused and lead to the acquisition of specific knowledge; on the other hand, they can be broadly planned and lead to wider and more interrelated understanding, usually within an appropriately chosen context. By giving abstract concepts a context, the design process can motivate students to learn those concepts.

The design process model, developed by John Hutchinson and Patricia Hutchinson (1991), is representative of the problem-solving approach being implemented in education programs in countries that have established a design and technology component within their school curriculum (see, for example, Kimbell and others, 1991, p. 19). The diagram shown in Figure 3.1 is one of various models that effectively describe the many different approaches taken toward design. For example, the draft of the National Science Education Standards (National Research Council, 1994) suggests five abilities that make up the design process:

1. Identifying appropriate problems for technological design
2. Designing a solution or product
3. Implementing a proposed design
4. Evaluating technological designs or products
5. Communicating the process of technological design

The element common to all such models is that they do not prescribe a specific path that must be followed in design activities.

The design process often is depicted as a "design loop" with different tasks to be accomplished. The tasks are intended to mirror an iterative and dynamic rather than a linear process, and they should be considered as suggestive rather than prescriptive. In actual use there will be marked differences in how individuals pursue a task and implement the process. As Dunn and Larson (1990) suggest, there are many points at which students may enter and exit the design process. Moreover, while we provide a full description of the design loop here, the concepts and activities that flow from it obviously must be appropriate to the developmental levels of particular groups of students.

Analysis and investigation. Detecting a problem or opportunity and understanding its nature often requires critical examination and analysis of a real-world setting.

Framing of a design brief. To bring the problem into finer focus, a statement is generated that concisely describes what the solution must do and what constraints are being imposed. The designer refers to the brief throughout the design process to ensure that the work stays on track.

Information gathering. Before attempting to develop solutions, the designer must become familiar with the influencing factors associated with the problem. What attempts have others made to solve this problem? What are the sizes, stresses, loads, power requirements, appearance, and ergonomic factors involved? These are some of the subproblems that must be addressed if viable solutions are to be found.

Generation of alternative solutions. In a design problem, there are no exclusively right answers, but rather a range of possible solutions, some better than others. To arrive at a good solution, a designer will need to look at many alternatives, deferring criticism until a range of solutions has been proposed. Students often find this the most challenging stage of the process, calling for originality, flexibility, and self-

FIGURE 3.1. THE DESIGN PROCESS MODEL (THE DESIGN LOOP).

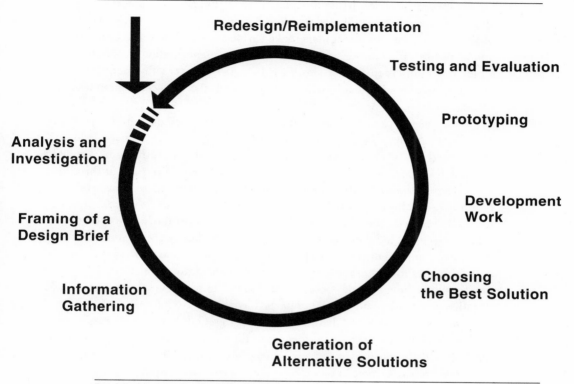

Reprinted by permission of *Ties Magazine*.

confidence. A critical component of generating alternative solutions is cognitive modeling—that is, imagining problem solutions in one's mind and exposing these ideas to others. Richard Kimbell and others (1991) note that the attempt to express an idea forces one to clarify it, as well as exposing it to suggestions and improvements made by others. This expression must be followed by the concrete manifestation of the refined idea, as mirrored in the other design stages. Kimbell and his coauthors hold "that this interrelationship between modeling ideas in the mind and modeling ideas in reality is the cornerstone of capability in design and technology. It is best described as 'thought in action'" (p. 21).

Choosing the best solution. From the alternative solutions generated, the student must narrow down to one which solution best satisfied the demands of the situation and the design brief. He or she should be able to defend the choice with reference to each requirement of the situation and the brief.

Developmental work. To develop the idea into a tangible device or system for solving the problem, the designer may use sketches and color drawings, evolutionary models in flexible materials, mathematical simulations, and technical drawings. The design brief and initial problem statement will specify the final outcome of this step. Often, the student will make various models before making an operational device. Appearance will take on importance after testing of working principles has confirmed that a chosen solution meets specified requirements. Developmental work also includes technical planning of procedures and resource management.

Prototyping. A prototype is a full-size working model, executed after functional problems are solved and size and material decisions have been made. A prototype need not be made in final production materials, but rather must simulate the material effect of the actual solution. Appearance is important at this stage.

Testing and evaluation. The solution should always be evaluated against the requirements established by both the design brief and the original problem statement. In addition, the solution should be tested against more universal design criteria to see if it handles specified loads, functions reliably, meets appearance requirements, and fits the user. Evaluation of the results should address the need for improvements and observations that might enhance future design work. Evaluation should include an analysis of unanticipated consequences, both positive and negative. For some solutions, the impacts may negate the solution.

Redesign reimplementation. If time in the design schedule permits, further modification and retesting can be performed to fine-tune the solution. This is particularly true if the product is to be produced in any quantity. Even if, as in most school design work, the product is not taken to real-world application, consideration should be given to how the solution would "change the world." Such consideration closes the loop, reinforcing the nature of design suggested by the model, and provides a forum for considering the idea of the impacts of decision making in the design process.

We reemphasize that the design process should be seen as iterative in its interplay of the active and the reflective modes (Sellwood, 1989a). An understanding of the process will help structure thinking at all levels and at each stage. During the process there will always be the problem of the moment and the overall problem or main objective. The development of creative thinking and problem-solving skills is likely to result in pupils "short-circuiting" the process by one or more stages and arriving at a sound and operable solution. Therefore, once students are familiar with the model, a slavish stage-by-stage adherence to the model may impede the learning process. For example, many designers see the evaluation stage as the most likely starting point of the industrial design process, claiming that most products are variations or improvements of existing models (Sellwood, 1991). After working through the design process, time must be allowed for reflection so that the process of design is thought about and articulated. Such reflection should also include the other disciplines brought into the solution, which will help students transfer knowledge from one sphere to another.

The Systems Approach

Although it is rarely referred to explicitly in the school setting, systems theory, or at least the idea of coming to understand complex systems through the techniques of systems analysis, has much to offer the field of technology education (Chen and Stroup, 1993; Todd, McCrory, and Todd, 1985; Todd, 1975). In particular, systems thinking helps students to understand how microlevel operations fit into macrolevel processes. The concept of "systems" has sometimes been expressed through a universal model. Such a model and associated language echo ideas that were introduced in *The Man-Made World* project, which gave primacy to the concept of systems as the major organizers of knowledge and the curriculum (Engineering Concepts Curriculum Project, 1970). The Universal Systems Model (shown in Figure 3.2) provided one of the first usable and defensible frameworks for curriculum developers and teachers of technology. While largely ignored in standard school curricula—whether in traditional science teaching or in vocational education—the model has become such a central focus for technology educators that it must be viewed as the major paradigm that has influenced the profession since the mid seventies.

In the model, *inputs* include people, knowledge, materials, energy, capital, and finance. The *process* aspect of the model is the technical means of action and practice, deemed appropriate for bringing about products, services, or conditions (results) that are valued. The *outputs* of the system represent the goals (or ends) to which all the inputs and processes are applied. The goals or ends might be products, services, or other desired conditions within the environment. The importance given to the systems model in the early 1980s is captured in a benchmark position paper (Hales and Snyder, 1982) developed within the technology education profession. The document took a definite stand on the importance and role of systems thinking for technology, stating: "The goal of the system is to place people in harmony with their culture and society. The value of the outputs must be judged ultimately on the basis of their impact on the quality of life for the total world population" (p. 13).

In addition, the document introduced four subsystems of human technical endeavor: communication, construction, manufacturing, and transportation. The Universal Systems Model, and the four subsystems that served as the major organizers of curriculum, became the conceptual paradigm that directed and shaped much of technology education throughout the 1980s and into the 1990s.

FIGURE 3.2. THE UNIVERSAL SYSTEMS MODEL.

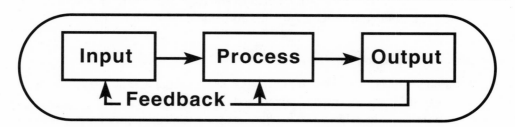

The influence of systems thinking on technology education is evident in the landmark efforts in New York State that resulted in the first mandated course in technology for all students. A description of that development follows. (A summary of the March 1994 draft version of the New York mathematics, science, and technology framework is provided in Chapter Four.)

The Development of Technology Education in New York State

A comprehensive review of the industrial arts program was initiated in 1981 by the New York State Education Department in an endeavor known as The Futuring Project. Educators, business and industrial leaders, social scientists, futurists, and engineers deliberated for two and a half years during which time experts were called upon to present papers, professional literature was reviewed, approaches were debated, missions were clarified, and a philosophical base was built. Practitioners from within the field were intimately involved in all phases of the project.

The Futuring Project occurred at a time when the social climate was right for education about technology. It was the time of excitement about space shuttles and satellites; and there was a growing interest in technology in general. It was during this time that the National Commission on Excellence in Education stated that the United States was at risk of losing its preeminence in science and technological innovation. The National Science Board, in its report *Educating America for the 21st Century* (1983), identified technology education as an entity and recommended that a full year of technology education should be required in grades seven and eight. John Naisbitt had just written *Megatrends,* and Alvin Toffler had just written *The Third Wave.* There was visible broad-based support for an educational response that addressed the need to develop a technologically literate population. In January 1983, the Futuring Committee recommended that the name "Industrial Arts" be changed to "Technology Education" in New York State and identified the development of technological literacy as the paramount mission of the new discipline.

While the Futuring Committee was drawing up its recommendations, the New York State Board of Regents began work on its "Action Plan to Improve Elementary and Secondary Education Results in New York." As a result of these parallel state-supported efforts and the timeliness of the national reports, the Board of Regents saw fit to include a one-unit technology education mandate as one of the new middle school requirements.

The Systems Analogy

In considering the elements of a technology curriculum, the Futuring Committee came to the view that understanding the common principles that apply to all systems could help students transfer knowledge from one specific occurrence to the next. Students would be able to see familiar patterns recurring, even when a particular technology might be new to them. The systems analogy could be used to model virtually any technological system; it was therefore proposed as a means through which course content could be organized in any technological context (such as manufacturing, construction, communications, transportation, or bio-related technology). Consistency was thus achieved in the way subject matter was presented. Transfer of learning was thus facilitated for students.

Problem Solving as a System

Problem solving and design-and-construct activity underpin all course work in the New York program. The problem solving process itself can be viewed in systems terms. The goal, or what the student wants to accomplish, is the input in the problem-solving system. Generating, selecting, and implementing alternatives is the process component. The actual student result is the system output. Systems thinking can help students to develop a problem-solving routine, and it can create the perception that people don't have to be satisfied with initial results. Failures are feedback that help improve future performance. Thus, the basic systems model becomes a simple conceptual tool that the student can easily picture and employ to assist in the analysis of technical (and nontechnical) systems and in the solution of problems.

The systems analogy provided the content organizers for the New York technology education program. At the middle school level, system inputs (desired results and resources), processes, outputs (impacts), and feedback and control were topics of curriculum modules in a course called Introduction to Technology. At the high school level, courses such as Communications Technology, Production Technology, and Principles of Engineering served as contexts within which many technological subsystems could be studied (M. Hacker, personal communication, 1994).

Curriculum Planning

There are a number of approaches curriculum planners may take in developing a curriculum, particularly since school systems vary in their needs. Some school systems may require a formal statement of the syllabus; others promote flexibility within broad guidelines. One approach, for example, is the prescriptive "scope and sequence" approach. An alternative approach that we will discuss here is one that can be described as the "knowledge sampling" method of curriculum design. Traditional "scope and sequence" approaches have been criticized because they tend to constrain the creativity and responsiveness of classroom teachers. Such approaches function as recipe books; teachers often follow them to the letter, creating a lockstep style of pedagogy, so that all students in the class are expected to cover the same topics at the same pace and in the same way.

In contrast, the "knowledge sampling" approach can support more flexible and open-ended curricular planning. It begins with the recognition that no curriculum can encapsulate all that is known in a particular field of science or technology. In this approach, curriculum developers agree on a core set of knowledge and skills that are to be covered by all the students in the class. In addition to learning the key concepts, skills, and knowledge entailed in the core, students are encouraged to build up their own knowledge of related fields. They are encouraged to choose topics that make sense to them for a variety of reasons—vocational, academic, or personal. This knowledge building is done through negotiated projects and individual assignments. (Negotiated student projects play a key role in the grades eleven and twelve curricula in Victoria, Australia. The centrality of negotiated projects is such that they are included in the high-stakes assessments used to determine admissions to the universities and technical postsecondary institutes. Carefully designed forms of performance-based assessment have been developed in Victoria to evaluate student performance on these projects. See Howe and Vickers, 1993.) In general, a knowledge sampling approach is consistent with the goals of technology education.

The following vignette provides an example of the knowledge sampling approach.

Working to Learn

Working to Learn is a project whose aim is to develop curricula that will integrate the scientific and technological knowledge entailed in three fields of science and three closely related occupational areas:

Anatomy and physiology ⟷ Health science

Physics ⟷ Applied engineering technologies

Ecology ⟷ Environmental maintenance and water testing

All of the students in Working to Learn are engaged in part-time internships at actual work sites—in hospitals, in manufacturing firms, and in public and private water quality and sewerage control facilities.

Working to Learn, a Technology Education Research Centers (TERC) project, has adopted the "knowledge sampling" approach described earlier. First, TERC's curriculum developers and the science teachers whose students are involved in the internship programs have formed three design teams (one for each of the fields just listed). Within each team, the science teachers and curriculum developers are seeking agreement on a core set of knowledge and skills that must be covered by all the students in their respective classes. Learning the core is one strand of student activity; the other strand comprises negotiated projects that students may carry out either individually or in pairs.

The projects are "negotiated" because (1) the students themselves have considerable choice as to which topics they will choose, provided the topic is clearly related to their field of study, and (2) students are expected to negotiate with their teachers and workplace mentors regarding exactly how their investigations should be carried out. One of the goals of Working to Learn is to help students learn how to design investigations, so the design teams decided against giving students "recipe cards" to direct their research.

The goal of the negotiated projects is to create the strongest possible links between the technological knowledge of the workplace and related fields of scientific knowledge. Each student project starts with a real problem that practitioners actually face on the job, or with a standard operational procedure technicians carry out routinely. The projects then proceed as follows: First, the teachers and curriculum developers work out what is involved in carrying out the practice or solving the problem (the "how-to" questions). They then seek to understand why the solution or strategy works. They ask: What are the scientific principles that lie behind this practice? Complementary learning activities are then created for students in the classroom and at the worksite, in the manner indicated below:

At the worksite:

1. Students gather data.
2. Students learn to carry out certain procedures.

In the classroom:

1. Students make sense of the data they have gathered.
2. Students learn why the procedures work, and reflect on their work experiences.

A student may, for example, gather EKG data on samples of normal and "septal hole" babies. At the same time, the student would be learning the standard procedures for carrying out EKG diagnoses with infants. Using student project guides developed by the Working to Learn team, the student would then develop an explanation of the differences between the abnormal and normal EKGs, and would discuss why the standard procedures used in EKG diagnoses make sense.

Teaching and Learning Strategies

Recent evidence from cognitive science research—based on investigations of both schools and workplaces—shows that people learn much more efficiently when the desire to solve real-world problems is driving them, or when the skills being developed are needed for tangible purposes. Learning is less efficient when formal knowledge is delivered in the abstract and when opportunities to situate it in realistic contexts are absent. While formal knowledge is powerful, students learn less effectively when such knowledge is divorced from its potential applications. Conversely, learning is enhanced when formal knowledge and its relationship to practical tasks and purposes is evident (Raizen 1989, 1991).

In U.S. schools, and until recently in Britain, the practical has been deemed less significant and less valuable than academic learning (see Chapter Two). Schooling places emphasis on knowledge that is out-of-context and isolated from the real world. Subjects that enhance practical knowledge tend to be at the lower end of the academic pecking order, while subjects that are customarily taught with little connection to the practical, such as mathematics, tend to be highly valued. As Resnick (1987) argues, the mismatch of learning in school and out of school is typified by four discontinuities. First, school learning focuses primarily on unaided, pure thought rather than on applied thinking supported by physical and cognitive tools. Second, it focuses on isolated, individual performance rather than on collaborative, shared performance. Third, school learning focuses on the decontextualized rather than on the context specific. Finally, it focuses on generalized skills and knowledge rather than on context-specific skills and knowledge. All of these discontinuities contribute to the mismatch of the world of schooling and the world of living.

The conflict between the lack of practicality in schooling and the demand for practicality in living is not lost on students. Many, unfortunately, deal with this conflict by dropping out of school. Gardner (1991, pp. 301–302) speaks directly to this conflict in his observation that "a pervasive antagonism often develops between the school's logical, out-of-context, knowledge system and that practical participation in daily activities fostered informally by the culture. If this antagonism is to be lessened, schools . . . must be designed and viewed as comfortable and significant environments, rather than hostile providers of useless knowledge. This means that schools must contain everyday life within their walls and must make clear the relation between the skills they teach and the problems children find significant."

The introduction of technology education into the K–12 curriculum represents a fundamental challenge to traditional instructional models of teaching and learning in the classroom. Technology education demands that teachers, teacher educators, and curriculum developers create and sustain programs in which students learn both through academic study and analysis and through the practice of working in and on the physical environment. By introducing real-world experiences and by engaging students in solving problems of interest to them, technology education creates a different relationship between the process of learning and the content to be learned. Students engaged in technology-oriented design and problem solving begin to think differently about all their school subjects as they put knowledge from several fields to work in an attempt to solve practical problems. Faced with real-world problems, students are required to apply what they have learned—and often to go back and relearn concepts they need to solve a particular problem. Contextualizing knowledge in real-world settings not only increases the relevance of what students learn, it also increases the engagement of students in higher-order critical and creative thinking.

Strategies for curriculum delivery, in technology as well as science, should reflect the best contemporary practices. The teaching model reproduced in Table 3.1 has been developed by the National Center for Improving Science Education as appropriate for both science and technology education and would serve well any school, such as Porter High School, in rethinking its curricular practices and developing a coordinated curriculum. Though the model portrays teaching in sequential fashion, it is intended to be dynamic and cyclical, like the processes of science and technology themselves. The model implies a shift toward student-directed learning, which requires teachers to act more as directors and facilitators of learning rather than as instructors. Teachers will need opportunities for professional development to support this change. Guidelines for assessment and reporting, appropriate to new styles of learning, should also be provided. (These matters are taken up in Chapter Five.)

Hands-On, Minds-On Learning

As the vignette on Working to Learn demonstrates, knowing and doing science and technology involves both hands-on and minds-on engagement in learning by students. "Hands-on," a phrase that has been used regularly within education over the past decade, suggests a down-to-earth, direct way of learning, but its use appears to differ in each of the many subject areas and contexts in which it is used. From the perspective of science, educators see hands-on activities as learning that takes place when critical observation is acted upon. From the perspective of technology, educators define hands-on activities as learning through practical engagement in investigating, designing, making, testing, or improving a variety of objects, systems, or environments. Both uses of hands-on activities recognize "experiential" learning as a powerful tool in making learning meaningful. For the purposes of this book, we define hands-on as experiential learning that provides a degree of independence for the learners when they interact with their environment. It is direct learning that results from exploration, manipulation, or observation of the physical world.

To accomplish significant learning, hands-on engagement must also become minds-on learning. Hands-on experiences can be trivialized, resulting in time spent in entertaining activities that keep students busy but not engaged in learning. Well-designed activities can provide the active concrete experiences through which students gain new insights into the nature of things and how they work. Such activities must elicit levels of critical and creative thinking that help students question, rethink, and reconstruct their understandings. The lack of such engagement will significantly reduce the potential power of students' learning experiences.

Since much of science and technology happens in places not readily accessible to children, schooling must help provide students with direct involvement that provides essential, foundational experiences in science and technology. Clearly, students can learn more about physical constructs through critical observation, recording from direct observation, and handling and manipulating materials than they will ever learn from being told. The thinking and doing of technology include designing, making, estimating, measuring, and testing, all drawing upon the skills of mathematics, science, and technology, and all learned best through "hands-on, minds-on" learning tasks.

Although all tasks should be stimulating and engaging, the type of task should vary to match the different learning objectives encompassed in a coherent technology education curriculum. Educators in Scotland, England, and Wales have developed useful typologies for describing the range of tasks that should be part of a well-rounded technology program (David Layton, personal communication, January 21, 1995). In selecting activities to include in their course sequences, teachers have found it helpful to consider the following typology and to draw on the full range of these tasks:

1. Tasks leading to the development of fundamental skills and knowledge that students will need throughout their design and technology education, and beyond.
2. Activities through which students learn the traditions and standard procedures that have been developed by technologists for dealing with recurring situations (such as translating linear motion into rotating motion), including tasks in which students investigate, disassemble, and evaluate familiar products.
3. Problem-solving tasks, in which students define and formulate a problem

TABLE 3.1. TEACHING MODEL.

STAGES	EXAMPLES FOR SCIENCE	EXAMPLES FOR TECHNOLOGY
Invitation	Observe the natural world. Ask questions about the natural world. State possible hypothesis.	Observe the world made by humans. Recognize a human problem. Identify possible solutions.
Exploration, Discovery, Creativity	Engage in focused play. Look for information. Observe specific phenomena. Collect and organize data. Select appropriate resources. Design and conduct experiments. Engage in debate. Define parameters of an investigation.	Brainstorm possible alternatives. Experiment with materials. Design a model. Employ problem-solving strategies. Discuss solutions with others. Evaluate choices. Identify risks and consequences. Analyze data.
Proposing Explanations and Solutions	Communicate information and ideas. Construct a new explanation. Undergo evaluation by peers. Determine appropriate closure.	Construct and explain a model. Constructively review a solution. Express multiple answers/ solutions. Integrate a solution with existing knowledge and experiences.
Taking Action	Apply knowledge and skills. Share information and ideas. Ask new questions.	Make decisions. Transfer knowledge and skills. Develop products and promote ideas.

and then develop and carry out solutions, ranging from the making of a product to procedures for remedying an inadequately functioning system.

4. Case study activities, in which students analyze and evaluate an artifact in its particular context. The context might be historical, another culture, or a contemporary development; the analysis should deal with the influences that have brought about and shaped the artifact's existence; the evaluation should deal with its effects on individuals and society, both positive and negative.

These tasks represent a progression in intended student learning. At the same time, students' developmental levels must be considered in selecting a task in any of the four categories. The proposed national technology curriculum for five- to sixteen-year-year-olds in England and Wales (Department for Education and the Welsh Office, 1992, p. 49) lists a series of criteria against which the difficulty of a task may be assessed:

Generally, it was felt that progression could be achieved by requiring pupils to move from:

- making few decisions about the nature of their work to giving them greater freedom;
- working on a closely defined problem to working on a problem which is more open-ended;
- undertaking work within a familiar, personal context to working in a context which is less familiar and more abstract in nature;
- using a limited range of materials to using a wider range or a combination of materials which require a wide variety of manufacturing techniques;
- working on a small scale to planning and implementing larger-scale operations;
- working from a simple drawing or description to working from a detailed specification;
- working independently to working interactively in small and large groups;
- taking account of their own values to considering conflicting and inter-related values which impinge on designing and making;
- working to a standard which satisfies them to working to standards defined by others;
- evaluating their work by trial and error to focused objective testing to identify the cause of failure;
- explaining their work to justifying their decisions and outcomes.

The knowledge gained from experiences that demand active thinking and doing is, in most cases, more readily assimilated and used by students to reconstruct what they have learned from those experiences. At the secondary levels, this will entail elaborate reconstructions of the curriculum as illustrated throughout this book. At the elementary level, such experiences might be gained through direct observation and involvement during a visit to a science and technology exploratorium or through exploration of the children's neighborhood, or they might involve the designing and making of something. That this kind of instruction is effective with all children is demonstrated by the progress of a class of first graders in a Harlem school, as recorded by their teacher who had participated in a City Science Workshop program. (For further information on City Science Workshop, contact Gary Benenson, City College, 138th Street and Convent Avenue, New York, NY 10031.)

Teacher's Log: City Science Workshop

This log was kept by Angel Gonzalez, first-grade teacher at Family Academy, a public school located in the Harlem neighborhood of New York City.

Community and Buildings/Science
(with Herbert, City College student assistant)

April 5, 1994

We began our community study by going up Adam Clayton Powell Boulevard as a class. Kids were encouraged to look at the types of buildings, their designs, patterns, and shapes. They were encouraged to look for shapes and to count them.

We observed immediately the buildings across the street and saw squares, rectangles, circles, and arches by the windows. Color patterns were noticed. Some facades had columns holding up balconies.

Kids were encouraged to feel the texture of the buildings and they noticed brick patterns that protruded like steps at the base of the corner building. As we turned the corner on 121st Street we noticed ramps going into a beauty salon and a grocery store. One child pointed to the basement metal doors on the grocery store's sidewalk. I asked if all buildings had basements. They didn't know. (Maybe we can go to see a basement.)

Other buildings we passed were restaurants, apartment buildings, churches, and office buildings. We walked to 125th Street and eventually stopped by the A. Clayton Powell Office Building. We stood under the building by the huge columns outside, and looked up and observed. I asked, "What holds this up?" Guillermo said its the wooden pillars. (Clearly we need to look into different materials used for building to explain and teach them differences.) Guillermo believes that wood is so strong that it will not bend. (This can be challenged.) Which material is the strongest can also become a test.

Upon returning, we stopped by a Gothic-style church on 123rd Street and observed the pointed arches. They counted them nonstop. We also looked at a rehabilitated building being water-blasted clean. They asked about the water pump.

Reflections. The trip was a good introduction to teach them to observe and look for patterns. It also provided ideas (mentioned in parentheses) which can become class activities.

In class, we wrote a brief experience chart and the kids began to draw neighborhood sketches.

Building Science
(with Jose, City College student assistant)

April 6, 1994

I had to catch up on math with the class so I focused on geometry/mathematics groups, while Jose worked with half of the class. This occurred both in the A.M. and the P.M. I oriented kids with a beginning reading of a couple of pages from *What It Feels Like to Be a Building* by Forrest Wilson.

Jose guided his groups into buildings with LEGOS, Zaks, Construx, and blocks. Some of these materials were new, so this was a beginning exploration for them. With blocks, kids are being urged to build as high as possible.

In the afternoon, I demonstrated how junk boxes (which I keep in storage for class) can be used to build by using tape and glue. They were excited about this.

At sharing time, we saw Haranisha build using rhythmic patterns on her walls, alternating long blocks and short blocks:

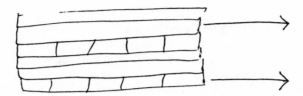

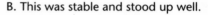

She also learned to stabilize the arch of her church by simply changing the direction of her base columns.

A. This toppled.

B. This was stable and stood up well.

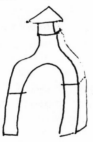

(I believe Jose taught her this technique. I will ask her.)

Can we use this crisscross technique to build even higher? (My new question?)

This reminds me of the "Jenga" game. Will bring in and challenge kids to play. This may inspire some to build high up in "Jenga" crisscross patterns.

Kids enjoyed and shared Zaks and Construx.

When Guillermo built with junk, he had trouble keeping a glued cap on the side of the structure from sliding off. He accused the glue of making the cap fall off. This led to a discussion of gravity.

The next day I used a magnet to explain how gravity works and that without it, bricks and things would float away and not be stable on the ground.

Reflections. Kids are building and are beginning to take off on their ideas. Mario says that if we sketch our ideas for a construction first, we might change what we actually build. I said this is OK and that in real life it happens. We can just change our plans or "blueprints."

I think this is a very important idea that should be strongly encouraged. Sketching and planning save time, because they allow you to experiment with ideas before actually building anything. They involve a host of important skills: visualizing, drawing, comparing, imagining, and (when groups do it) negotiating.

Architecture Classroom Science
(with Jose, City College student assistant)

April 13, 1994

I have been reading *What It Feels Like to Be a Building* to teach concepts of columns, beams, gravity, walls, buttresses, and tension-compression. Kids are able to demonstrate or dramatize concepts by acting like the aforementioned structures. I am reading this book daily before each science workshop.

I have provided the class with different challenges:

1. In block area, I am asking them to build the highest stable structures possible that will sway (or topple) the least.
2. With straws and clay or toothpicks and marshmallows, again they must build the sturdiest and tallest structures.
3. With paper and tape only, make paper stand so as to withstand blowing and to take greatest load (of notebooks) possible.
4. Build structures with junk.

Some kids are building nicely, while others get frustrated quickly, given their less experience with construction or less inclination toward creative arts. Kids are building on each others' explorations with materials. Jose has played an excellent role in guiding these activities.

Architecture Science
(with Jose, City College student assistant)

April 20, 1994

Our class hiked past Morningside Park and down to the Cathedral of Saint John the Divine for our study of the community and architecture. Jose was good in asking relevant questions and in eliciting thoughts about structures and patterns in the built environment.

In an empty lot, two construction workers were at an initial building site where the foundation had just been built with concrete. We discussed the importance of this structure. Kids initially called it a "perimeter"—rightfully so as they learned in mathematics class. Later during our hike, Jose was able to point out the visible foundations to other completed buildings.

We looked at masonry brick patterns on buildings:

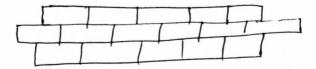

We looked at a zigzag ground brick pattern:

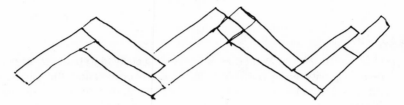

We discussed monuments, retaining walls, buttresses.

At St. Luke's Hospital, we observed the patterns on the building's "walk bridges" (two). On one bridge, we noticed the triangulation formed by X's:

On the other, the patterns observable were squares:

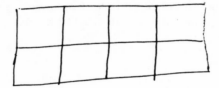

At the Cathedral's facade, we observed and elicited the shapes seen. The rose windows provided circles; other structures created triangles, squares, rectangles, crosses, and so on. Inside the children were in awe at the immensity, the darkness, and the solemnity worked by the architecture. The kids expressed a sense of nervousness. They felt the place was "spooky." We discussed how buildings can generate feelings. We saw the stained glass windows, the high columns, the statues, altars, the arches, and so on. In the cathedral, we all sat on the floor and sketched what we observed. It was very calming and "therapeutic" to have kids draw.

Upon returning to the classroom after lunch, we had science groups engage in investigating structures using:

1. Toothpicks and marshmallows
2. Clay and straws
3. Paper and tape
4. Building blocks

I wonder whether and how the children see the relationship between their neighborhood experiences and their experiments with structures. It would be important for them to establish these connections.

1.   Alexis and Amber have succeeded in using square and triangle shapes in building with toothpicks. They are finding the stability of those shapes.

2.   With straws and clay, kids have succeeded in building with square shapes, but these still lack stability. I have urged them to try including triangles in their buildings.

3.   The paper and tape challenge (to make paper stand and withstand wind and top load) has been exciting. A good number of kids have made cylinders with paper that take lots of wind and weights of notebooks on top.

4.   Three kids worked well collectively (Paul, Dymitris, and Antoinette) to build a cathedral-like structure. They included masonry brick, patterns, arches, columns, and buttresses. Their building is becoming taller, more methodical, and inclusive of concepts discussed.

On April 22, at the Queens Zoo, our class observed a geodesic dome with triangular frames.

Architecture
(with Herbert, City College student assistant)

April 26, 1994

The class was divided between Herbert and me. Herbert managed the group in the science center, where kids built using clay and straws or marshmallows and toothpicks. I managed the groups building with junk and woodworking. At the blocks, I challenged them to work together on one structure alone, a really tall one.

Reflections. Kids are getting better at building. They are generally managing to build squared cubes with sticks with triangular-type roofs.

Others are succeeding at building and tessellating a structure using triangles made from toothpicks.

At the block center, the team has been frustrated at times, but with my insistence they finally cooperate as a team. They use columns and beams to build high structures. A chair and table are utilized for "scaffolding."

The "stick" structures are frustrating for less dexterous kids, especially since structures are fragile and invasive rodents come at night to disrupt them. Junk building is going fine.

It would be useful to think about the concept they are learning via these activities.

Trip to Central Park Garden
(with Jose, City College student assistant)

May 1, 1994

Our class had a guided tour of the garden with Jose. The focus was the fountain area with statues of maidens. My students had a hard time not focusing on creeping insects (such as ants) while the guide was struggling to get their attention! The class explored flowers, their colors and shapes. The kids had adequate time to observe the garden area and sketch (adults did also). Sketching has been therapeutic in calming kids down and causing them to notice details to the greatest extent possible.

Jose was helpful in pointing out architectural structures in the garden such as arches. We also had time to tour other parts of the garden. Kids were fascinated by the twisting, adhering action of vines. (You can get this to happen in the classroom using kidney bean plants.)

By the lake, kids observed large carp, and birds such as ducks and cormorants. One girl, Haranisha, recalled when we last passed the lake, when it was frozen (that is, in January).

Tuesday
(with Herbert, City College student assistant)

May 3, 1994

Kids continue to build with straws and toothpicks, blocks (the highest wall is the challenge), junk, and paper. Herbert takes groups to use paper. They must make paper stand and then take loads using only tape. (They are continuing challenges presented by Jose. These would lead into bridge building.)

Kids are meeting the challenges, are excited and are becoming more agile and complex in their structures. They are also using the terminology: arches, beams, columns, buttresses.

Bridge-Building Day
(with Jose, his last day)

May 4, 1994

Since the students already had skills in standing paper and making paper columns that withstood loads, I asked if they were ready for bridge-building challenges. Sure enough, Jose gave the go ahead and build bridges they did. He had some children building with blocks across table spans, and some building with paper. The kids eagerly set out to create bridges and to my astonishment, they did build them quickly. When I asked Curtis, "Who gave you the idea to use columns?" he said, "Nobody, I am a scientist!" It was gratifying to hear a self-acclamation. Takeerah said, "Keep these bridges up for a show!" Jose explained some of the bridges made:

1. Suspension type
2. Post-lintel
3. Double deckers
4. Beam bridges

Jose demonstrated a rope footbridge made with twine and ice cream sticks:

Bridges made by kids:
Suspension bridge using tape and paper:

Wooden beam bridges with columns:

Wooden double decker beam bridges:

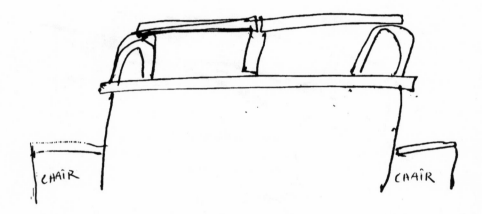

Paper towel bridge by Takeerah:

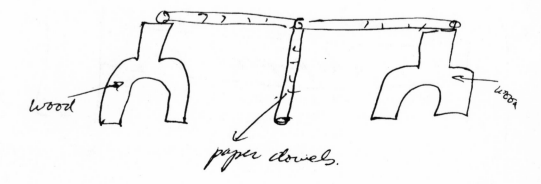

Paper sheets with tape:

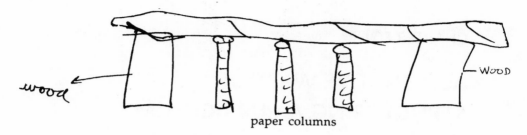

paper columns

   This is a good example of a sequence. They weren't ready for bridges until they had learned basic structure concepts. It would be useful to know precisely what they needed to be ready.

Architecture and Archeology
(with Herbert and Angel, the day of the solar eclipse)

May 10, 1994

   Herbert presented a slide show on the African burial ground found near Wall Street. The class was interested in what happens in the decay process. Where is the skin? Where is the coffin? They were very inquisitive about the skeletal remains of a woman with a child. Questions emerged also about the mechanisms of the digging process: How do sand and soil not cave on oneself, when a grave is dug so deep? These are great questions that reflect their knowledge of structures.
   My slides on housing construction in Vieques, Puerto Rico, for homeless after the Hugo Hurricane in 1990 focused on the structures, materials, and tools used in building simple homes.
   Both slide presentations were helpful in stimulating interest in scientific pursuits (that is, archaeology and architecture).

   Children can learn a great deal from studying the communities in which they live. There are a number of teaching materials and programs that focus on just this type of learning. Organizations supporting such programs include the Foundation for Architecture, publisher of *Architecture in Education*; the American Planning Association, publisher of planning-related activities and resources; the Learning Through Design Network, publisher of a resource guide for design activities and *Process*, a newsletter promoting design education; and the National Building Museum, publisher of *The Design Wise Workbook*.

CHAPTER FOUR

ALTERNATIVE WAYS OF STRUCTURING A CURRICULUM

The introduction of technology education programs would change the context for science education in American schools. We envisage a close articulation between science education and technology education. At the elementary and middle school levels, it may be appropriate for science and technology to be taught as a single, integrated course. In fact, one could argue that a technology approach at these levels could serve to integrate the whole curriculum, that it holds the potential for students to learn science, mathematics, language arts, social studies, and the fine arts in the context of designing and making artifacts that fill a human need.

At the high school level, the problems are more complex. In an already overcrowded curriculum, where should technology education fit in? What will be the relationship between science and technology courses? What effect will technology education have on vocational education programs? Is it intended to upgrade the current vocational education curriculum so that students can obtain good jobs after high school or continue with technical education beyond high school? Would technology education continue to serve as replacement for industrial arts courses? Could a well-designed technology education program help schools find a way of avoiding tracking and provide a balanced program of studies that is suitable for all students?

It is not appropriate to elevate a single approach above all others. Different school districts will need to find solutions that are acceptable to local needs and requirements. There are various ways of providing students with a program of technology education that meets the goals listed in Chapter Three. Because the approaches are likely to differ by schooling level, we first discuss the early elementary grades, then the middle and junior high school grades, and finally the possibilities for secondary school. These categories clearly are overlapping, as are the different typologies we suggest for organizing the curriculum.

Elementary Education

The best elementary classrooms have always featured practical activity as one of the most important elements of early learning. Whenever children use materials to build or make things that serve a purpose, whether in an imaginative or real-world context, they are involved in technology. Although elementary teachers rarely identify these activities as technology, they are practical design experiences that lay a foundation for future technology education studies.

Language, mathematics, and humanities tend to dominate during the elementary years. Practical learning is either very prescriptive or seen as "play." The important foundations of the early years, including sensory learning and investigation, are neglected in favor of more academic learning strategies. Early concepts of structures, movement, control, and simple mechanisms can be built upon and extended to reinforce science and mathematics learning. Technology education can provide an opportunity for students to study and discuss environmental issues, their problems and possible solutions. Content and process must include study of

- Materials and their properties and how they can be used
- Energy in a variety of forms
- Control, in the form of switches, catches, valves, and mechanisms
- Information used for communication

Although the problem of softening the boundaries between subject areas is less acute in elementary than in secondary schools, even at this level the curriculum is often planned under distinct headings. Hence, special efforts are still needed to integrate subject matter. By adopting a carefully planned "topic" approach at the elementary level, technology can be integrated into the present curriculum. A broad and comprehensive view of the concepts of structures, movement, control, and communication/information needs to be built into existing programs. This would provide a practical means of extending and reinforcing science, mathematics, and language learning. Technology education should provide an opportunity for students to study and discuss environmental issues, their problems and possible solutions. A description of an elementary school that is incorporating technology education into the classroom follows.

Experiencing Technology Education for the First Time: The Early Elementary Years

A group of six- and seven-year-olds had completed some grouping and sorting of materials (fabrics, plastics, glass, wood, paper products, and so on) and an exploration of "connectors" (glues, brass fasteners, string, clips, nails, and so forth). They had learned how to use saws, drills, and hammers. They were given a twelve- by eighteen-inch sheet of paper and asked to design something they would like and be able to build that moved in some way. They were told they could use materials from their classroom recycling center such as cartons, containers of all sorts, fabric, dowels, cardboard, wheels, and centimeter wood strips. They could also use materials brought from home. The connectors they had explored were available.

Drawing was not new to these children. They had drawn from nature in their science studies, they had illustrated stories, and drawing materials were always an option for art or classroom choice times. They had built three-dimensional constructions in the block corner and in the classroom recycling center. However, they had never been asked to draw something to be constructed in the future and then to build from their drawings. The process of moving from two to three dimensions and of committing themselves to a plan (as opposed to planning and creating as they went along) were new experiences for these children.

Ben, a six-year-old, drew a rather conventional house with a chimney on the roof and smoke coming out of the chimney. Looking over the materials, he passed by the rectangular boxes and selected a one-liter soda bottle as the basic structure for his house. He cut out freehand a door and some windows from construction paper and taped them to the bottle. Then he chose a dowel, taped a curvy piece of black construction paper to the end and showed his teacher where he wanted the two holes for the dowel to pass through the bottle. He inserted the dowel and proceeded to push and pull it up and down, making the "smoke" extend and retreat from the chimney. He was not bothered at all by the fact that the house looked nothing at all like his drawing. What counted was that the smoke moved in and out of the chimney. With construction successfully completed, his teacher asked him to evaluate his product. Did it come out the way he had planned it? Was there something that moved? A huge smile of satisfaction spread over his face. Yes, this was exactly what he had in mind, he said; the smoke moved out of the chimney (and back in), and he wondered if he could take it home and show his parents what he had made.

Across the room, two eight-year-olds were constructing boats they wanted to move by rubber-band-powered paddle wheels. They had completed their planning and construction and were now ready to test the boats. A small plastic wading pool was filled with water, the paddle wheels were wound up, and the boats were launched. As the boats moved forward, their structures began to come apart; the children realized to their dismay that the glue must be dissolving in the water.

"We should have used a glue gun."

Their teacher watched as they reassembled the boats, connecting the wooden frames with a glue gun, a time-consuming process; they tried them again in the water, and once again watched as they fell apart. The teacher debated whether or not to suggest that they test connecting materials in the water on just a few pieces of wood rather than take the time to reassemble the entire boat. She decided to let them do it their way, and hoped they would come to this realization themselves. If not, she would bring the subject up.

"We'll have to nail them together. Can we have some small nails?"

On the third try, the boat held together and paddled across the classroom pond. Delighted and relieved that their hard work and tenacity had paid off, the boat builders were not at all ready to think about short cuts to finding the right materials to connect wood for use in water. For these students, this lesson would have to wait for another time. For their teacher, there still remained the issue of how much to tell students ahead of time and how much to let them discover, or not discover, for themselves.

The boys' classmate Kylie eyed the recycling center, spotted a shoe box, and decided to build a car that would carry her stuffed bear. She remembered her brother once built a rubber-band-powered car. Her drawing was a rectangle with small wheels. She selected four plastic wheels and found two dowels that fit through their centers. Using a ruler, she carefully planned where to punch holes in the shoe box so the axles would be parallel to the ends of the box. She attached the wheels to the outside of the box, front and back. She then began to puzzle out how to wind up a rubber band. Once she had an idea of how it might work, she asked her teacher if there was another box she could use to try out her ideas because she "didn't want to mess up my car." Unlike the boat builders, Kylie had discovered on her own the concept of building a prototype or model. Once she worked out a rubber band system, making her mistakes somewhere other than on her car, she was ready to complete her project.

Although the entire project was ultimately successful, asking the children to draw their desired object on paper as part of the design for the project may have been too ambitious. Children this age frequently find it difficult to conceptualize three-dimensional construction through two-dimensional drawing, and they become confused by the task. They may worry about their inability to transform their drawing into the object they imagined, and shy away from the task. For example, it is unclear how Ben's drawing helped him in the design of his project, which bore no relation to the picture he drew.

What did this teacher want her students to learn? Her main objective was to have them understand something about design, namely:

- The design process begins with a problem and a plan.
- There will usually be design specifications and limitations (in this case, particular materials and the requirement for some sort of motion).
- Testing will tell whether one has been successful or needs to redesign.

Perhaps the learning would have been more successful if the students had been more involved in selecting the design challenge; perhaps, given the students' young age, the teacher was unwilling to take the chance that they would come up with feasible tasks. This vignette points out the choices teachers have to make when there is so much to be learned, especially when students do something for the first time. An important point is that there *has* to be a next time, and another after that. Students cannot assimilate learning all at once. The classroom observations that follow illustrate how teachers in one school developed a curriculum building on each other's instruction.

Technology in One School

The following classroom activities were seen in progress during a visit to a Virginia school by Ronald Todd. Twenty of the school's K–5 teachers had participated in an intense one-week summer workshop. The teachers had been introduced to a design-and-technology approach that engaged them in hands-on/minds-on teaching and learning activities. Through direct engagement in problem-solving—in a manner similar to how students would learn—the teachers gained new knowledge, skills, and confidence in designing, making, and improving a variety of technological devices and systems. Time was also provided for the teachers to apply, question, discuss, and re-organize their knowledge of science and mathematics.

During the school visit, children in fifteen classrooms were observed in different stages of designing, making, testing, and discussing the things they had developed. The activities ranged from kindergarten children making cookies to second graders designing and building models of escape routes and devices for their homes to fifth graders going to the primary wing to work with first graders in making a model of a new town. In one room, first graders were designing and making things that would help Santa Mouse do his job on Christmas Eve. In another, four second graders were showing a classroom visitor the house for Stuart Little, the eponymous mouse hero in the novel by E. B. White, that the class was putting together after small groups of students had designed and built individual rooms. Meanwhile, their classmates were preparing to test and improve the vehicles the class had made earlier. Students from two third-grade classes and two fifth-grade classes were working in small groups designing and making things in response to a range of problems that had emerged from their reading activities. Fourth graders were discovering the problems of designing and building structures such as bridges and towers similar to those being constructed nearby in their community. One fifth-grade class was busy building models that showed how they would improve the school store, while students in another fifth-grade class were working in small groups to build science apparatuses. In the corner of that room, one team of two girls and a boy worked on a problem based on a story about Paul Bunyan.

In the kindergarten, the children were working on the difficult problem of designing ways of packaging the cookies they had mass-produced the previous week so that the cookies could be mailed to some of the U.S. troops in the Middle East. They were trying to solve the problem of how to protect the cookies from getting broken or stale in transit.

The second graders who had built a house for Stuart Little were well along in additional activities that grew out of their reading about Stuart. The children were putting finishing touches on the rooms they had made for Stuart; one group of two girls and a boy were deeply involved in getting water to slosh around in Stuart's Jacuzzi (made from a plastic bottle and a panty hose container).

The second-grade class that had made vehicles was engaged in testing them to determine how far each would go. Their problem was to see how the vehicles could be improved to make them go farther. The students were measuring the distance of each test run on a test track made from a long strip of butcher paper. By recording the measured distances as well as plotting the actual distance on the strip of butcher paper, the children were quietly introduced to measuring, graphing, and statistics.

The team of fifth-grade students responding to a problem from a Paul Bunyan story (the reader may remember the story of the crowded bunkhouse in which the bunks had been built so high that the people on the top bunks had to parachute down to the ground) had built multilayered bunks that could be reached by an elevator that was raised and lowered by a hand crank. The children had encountered a number of problems and were now installing a motor from a LEGO set to replace the crank. In all of these instances, children were engaged in putting what they had learned to work, and by doing so, learning more.

In Appendix B we provide an example drawn from Project UPDATE (Upgrading Practice through Design and Technology/Engineering Education—an effort funded by the National Science Foundation) of a thematic approach to technology education carried through coherently in the elementary and middle grades.

Secondary Education

At both the lower secondary and the upper secondary school levels, educators have a number of choices for organizing the curriculum. Schools may, for example, provide a sequence of stand-alone courses or strands within courses, develop a sequence of combined science and technology courses, improve and link existing technology and science courses, or build a curriculum around design-based projects. These are but a few examples; the full range of choices is much wider.

Providing a Sequence of Stand-Alone Courses or Strands Within Courses

Technology education can conceivably, though perhaps not ideally, be offered as a series of separate courses or as a distinct strand within an existing program. Courses such as "Science, Technology and Society" (see Chapter Two), described in a recent catalog of evaluated courses compiled by the National Diffusion Network (U.S. Department Of Education, 1994), provide an example. In this option, technology education coexists with the traditional science and craft-based technology curricula. Separate courses can place a strong emphasis on design and problem solving, on the integration of theoretical and practical strands of science and technology, and on the social context of the science and technology relationship. Stand-alone courses can provide students with opportunities to deploy knowledge and skills from many different learnings in the search for solutions to challenging design problems (see the vignette called "Little Whizzers" that appears later in this chapter, drawn from a stand-alone course given in Australia). A separate course or strand can also provide a testing ground for new approaches to teaching and learning that would ultimately flow back into other disciplines and courses.

Courses of this kind can be stimulating for both teachers and students, because they are likely to be very different from regular classes. Devising such a course, or series of courses, is not easy, however. At present, few suitable resources are available "off the shelf," so a lot of the good work being done in this field depends on the ingenuity of teachers who use educational tools and devices designed for other purposes to carry out technology education activities. The two vignettes that follow provide examples of such teacher ingenuity.

Ms. Simpson's Gadget

Jenny Simpson is a fifth-grade teacher with a special interest in mathematics and a concern that her students were not learning enough about technology. While attending a summer course on computers in mathematics, she learned about LEGO TC Logo, a kit that enables students to build devices out of LEGO bricks and control them using a computer. Jenny immediately saw the possibility of linking some simple programming exercises with hands-on science and technology activities. She managed to borrow two sets of LEGO TC Logo for six weeks from a neighboring school.

During that time, with gentle guidance but little direct instruction, her students worked out how to build an automatic fairground carousel, a trolley that draws shapes on the floor, and a device for trapping bugs that only come out at night.

Some of the other teachers wanted to join in, but the shortage of equipment meant that they had to build their gadgets out of materials that were already on hand. Together, the teachers produced a set of activity guides for grades four to six. These activities were based on their own ideas, as well as on activities and "starter suggestions" from books and from an electronic bulletin board run by the mathematics teachers association. The parent-teacher organization raised money to buy some Lego TC Logo kits, and collected useful pieces of "junk" from local businesses.

What's Ticking? A Middle School Technology Unit

"They said we were crazy, but we did it anyway." That was the headline when two local teachers, Burt Friedler and Samantha Ashley, were interviewed after their students won seven out of ten major prizes at the regional science fair. "We knew we had to do more with technology. We have a good trade shop in our school and the kids have some good technology skills, but they never got to design and make things they wanted. So, we started up a new six-week unit in which kids get to design and build gadgets. They start with a design specification and then sketch out some rough plans. After they get those checked by a science teacher and a shop teacher they finish their plans and start building in our 'Invention Room,' which doubles as a science lab.

"We also do a big group project, and everybody gives a short talk called 'Technology of the Week,' in which they describe how a gadget or something like that works. We've had talks on cars, cosmetics, life in space, sports shoes, and yes, why a water meter ticks. The water-meter talk led to great rave about ratchets and clocks.

"It's hard work, and we've had to change the way we work with kids and the way we assess work, but the kids mostly love it. They really got a blast out of doing well in the science fair."

A significant disadvantage of stand-alone courses is the difficulty of guaranteeing access to all students. New stand-alone courses can only be added when the time allocated to other subjects is reduced. Alternatively, they can be offered as electives, in which case they are only studied by a subgroup of the students. Decisions about what kind of technology courses to offer often cause tensions in school communities and highlight the need for ongoing review of the total curriculum. Questions like those asked about the relationship of technology education to science could equally well be asked in relation to mathematics, social studies, and most other areas of study.

The next vignette provides a good example of a course that merges elements of science and technology.

Materials Science and Technology

In Materials Science and Technology (MST) classrooms, the boundaries between science and technology are blurred, and it is not easy to see where one begins and the other ends. MST integrates chemistry, engineering, physics, mathematics, writing, design, and technology education in an environment that mirrors the working worlds of science and technology.

To understand materials, students must experiment with them, working with their hands to discover the nature and properties of the materials. This tactile knowledge comes straight in through the fingertips. At the same time, they must also learn about the science of material, and use the scientific concepts they have learned to design and create products of their own choosing. The opportunity to design and create a product is often what draws students to enroll in the MST course. Student project work builds on concepts and skills learned in MST lab sessions, through experiments that provide carefully structured experiences with the four materials groups around which the course is organized: metals, glass/ceramics, polymers, and composites. Sample student projects include developing better airfoils, designing a night light, creating jewelry, and making stained glass windows or raku pots.

An observer in one class described students working to help each other in the former industrial arts room that is their laboratory. When one student had problems cutting a curved piece of glass, he asked another student who had mastered the skill how she did it. She demonstrated the process, and then watched while he did it correctly.

As part of the course, students kept journals describing their work. One described the final steps of making a medallion: "(11/19) Today I finally cast my medallion. I had it cooked at 900°. Then I put it in the rotating machine. In this I melted my [silver and copper] and cast my medallion. From there I broke it out. Next I have to sand and polish. . . . (11/23) Today I helped three people invest their rings. I feel like a Materials Science genius!" (Whittaker, 1994).

This unique approach to teaching materials science and technology began in 1986 when a Richland High School teacher worked at the Pacific Northwest Laboratory under the mentorship of a dozen or more scientists, engineers, and technologists in metallurgy, glass/ceramics, polymers, applied chemistry, and advanced composites. Since then, the MST program has been supported by the U.S. Departments of Energy and Education, the State Departments of Education in Washington and Oregon, and the Northwest Regional Education Laboratory. The program is now in its seventh successful year in Richland High School and is in place in more than a dozen schools in Washington, Oregon, Pennsylvania, and Alaska (Hayes, 1993; Pacific Northwest Laboratory, 1994).

Developing Combined Science and Technology Course Sequences

Course sequences that combine existing technology and science courses have the effect of amalgamating key elements of each and replacing both "science" and "technology" as separate subjects. A combined science-technology course sequence, therefore, introduces all the science that is needed to complement key technology topics. Ideally, such course sequences are project intensive, with a strong emphasis on design-and-build activities. Ideally they also cover both the theoretical and the practical aspects of technology education.

At present, few individual teachers would be able to teach course sequences such as these. Most teachers have been trained *either* to teach science *or* to teach technology. In addition, the facilities in most existing classrooms would not be adequate to support hands-on work in both science and technology. The desired result could be achieved, however, by having teachers from technology and science backgrounds coming together to form teams. The teams would design the curriculum together and would deliver it either by team teaching or by coaching each other on the components with which they are most familiar. To deal with the need to use both "shop" tools and science equipment simultaneously, the teams would need to rearrange facilities, for example, by making up a cart of science equipment to wheel into a technical workshop, or by making up a cart of "shop" tools to take into a science lab.

The efforts of individual teachers and researchers who are already doing pioneering work in teaching technology and science together should here be acknowledged (see Appendixes D and E). There is a need to harness their innovative work in a way that makes the early exemplars available to the mainstream. Special attention needs to be paid to elementary schools, where teachers often lack confidence in science and technology.

While writing this book, we attempted to locate descriptions of actual science and technology curricula. Unfortunately, outside of those already mentioned, we found very few published curricula in the United States that meet the goals for technology education outlined in this book. The recent U.S. Department of Education (1994) publication reviewing exemplary mathematics, science, and technology programs notes relevant courses. This document highlights the breadth and high quality of the work being done, but also demonstrates the lack of an overarching vision of technology education and its relationship to other disciplines. Another review document, *The Consumer Guide to Science Curriculum* (Boyce, 1993), also describes curriculum packages and support materials in this field. Although both of these documents claim to address aspects of technology education, the emphasis in the great majority of programs listed is on enhancing science education themes through the use of educational technology, that is, the provision of science education through technology, not technology education as we or others in the field envisage it. Thus, most of the programs described reflect the common misconception that technology equals computers.

Improving and Linking Existing Technology and Science Courses

This approach retains separate subjects called science and technology, but guarantees that the separate curricula will be developed under a plan that ensures attainment of the new goals for technology education. This may require some adjustment to the content and classroom practices in both areas of study to ensure that the studies are truly complementary and that collaborative activities are possible.

Under this linked-studies approach, students in technology classes would solve problems by conceptualizing, designing, constructing, and evaluating a device or procedure. In the process, they would employ scientific principles and the language and organizational methods from systems theory to achieve their goals. In science classes, students would learn how everyday things such as refrigerators, CD players, or automatic security gates work. They would use industrial processes as a vehicle for learning about mechanics and chemistry, as illustrated by the course "ChemCom: Chemistry in the Community" developed by the American Chemical Society (1988). Students would also undertake design and construction activities that require knowledge of materials and production as well as scientific knowledge and principles.

This approach has been used in a number of states as well as in other countries to guide the development of new and sometimes complementary curricula (as discussed later in this chapter in the section called "Systemic Reform: The Frameworks Approach"). There are now many examples of programs or curricular sequences that emphasize the use of technology in the study of science or the use of science in technology studies. For example, the Global Laboratory project discussed in the next vignette engages students with environmental monitoring and research tasks using simple and advanced technologies; it is an example of using technology in the science classroom.

The Global Laboratory Project

The Global Laboratory project has developed a community of student scientists based in classrooms in twenty countries. Students take part in hands-on investigations of both the natural and the indoor environments, making use of advanced technologies such as digital temperature and light measuring probes, ultraviolet spectrophotometers and gas-sampling tubes, as well as simple technologies for measuring soil percolation and airborne particulates. Classrooms are linked via electronic mail and an automatic data-sharing system that allows students to aggregate their data and take part in collaborative investigations. Students and teachers are assisted by curriculum materials that emphasize a project-based, collaborative approach to learning. Classes are encouraged to progress from a semesterlong introductory unit, a kind of research apprenticeship, to more open-ended "advanced research projects." Students learn to think and work like scientists by working *as* scientists, using technology appropriately for measurement, analysis, communication, and publication. (For information about the Global Laboratory, contact TERC, 2067 Massachusetts Avenue, Cambridge, MA 02140, or use a World Wide Web browser, such as Mosaic, to access http:\\hub.terc.edu.)

The Global Laboratory curriculum example illustrates the use of technology as an integral part of collecting and sharing information in science. Students gain not only the ability to use instruments in a programmed manner but also learn about the need to understand associated measurement errors and the need for standardized procedures. In addition, students are encouraged to devise and adapt technology to help them answer new questions that arise during the investigation.

Conversely, a design project in a technology studies class can be greatly assisted by the application of scientific knowledge and principles. The solar hot water heater vignette given in Chapter One illustrates the motivation and need for science learning in a vocationally oriented course. To develop a successful design, students had to draw on knowledge from both science and technology classes; to build their models, they had to use their skills with tools and equipment; to evaluate the efficiency of their solar collectors, they had to use standard scientific procedures. Student reports discussed scientific and technical aspects of their models, potential design improvements, and possible practical applications.

The challenge involved in bridging the gaps between subject areas is a substantial one in most secondary schools. Successful curriculum reform often relies on reforms in "supporting" areas such as school organization, teacher professional development, assessment, and the reporting of student results (which are discussed in Chapter Five).

Creating Integrative Design Projects

This approach envisages the retention of existing subjects but would engage students and teachers on a regular basis in multidisciplinary collaborative projects involving design and construction. The key feature of these projects is that they would be jointly developed by teachers from at least two subject areas. In addition, they might involve collaboration among students from different classes or even different grades. These would be integrated projects rather than stand-alone courses. Such projects could create a sense of team play and collective ownership in much the same way that a school drama production or community project brings everyone together. For example, a project on water treatment could involve the science class in studying the chemical and biological processes involved, while the technology class might construct a water treatment plant. The students might also use mathematics classes to calculate the dimensions of components or to suggest designs that would allow for different input and output flow rates.

In design activities, students use knowledge from science to reduce the amount of trial and error involved in making prototypes. If the device they are designing does not work at first, experimentation combined with scientific knowledge may help to identify the problem, leading to a better design. In a similar way, mathematical skills may assist in designing to specification, or in evaluating performance and redesigning the product.

Collaborative projects can become exciting foci for school life with opportunities for establishing links with the community and industry. Some examples of design projects that integrate perspectives across different subjects are

- Developing a water treatment project
- Entering a solar car competition
- Putting on a school science fair
- Developing environmental protection projects
- Doing consulting work for local businesses (for example, traffic surveys)
- Conducting opinion polls on community issues
- Setting up and maintaining mailing lists and membership databases for local clubs and societies
- Manufacturing products for charities

The following vignette outlines a cross-curricular project involving mathematics, science, and technology that has been developed for students in grades seven to nine. The project has been very motivating for students, teachers, and other participants.

Flight Project: Curriculum Planning

The main task the students face in this project is to design a model glider as a marketable product. The students begin with the following series of problem-solving exercises in preparation for the main task.

Science

- What creatures and natural objects use floating as a means of controlling descent?
- Investigate and record through observation, drawing, reference books, and photographs how some seeds use air to float to the ground.
- Why do seeds need to float through the air? Study some selected specimens and make notes and drawings on how they function.
- Dissect seeds and accurately record the seed composition through drawing and notes.
- Investigate the strength of materials in comparison to weight.

Technology

- Investigate flying machines made by humans.
- Make structures that will fly. Activities in designing, making, and testing: explore the principles of gliding using cardboard. Whose design will glide the greatest distance? Which design can glide and hit a target accurately?
- Make something that will gently float to the ground. Choose materials that you think will work best.
- Design and make a product (toy glider).
- Packaging (examining the properties of packaging materials): design, make, and test packaging structures; design graphic images for the surface of packaging.

Mathematics

- Calculate cost of materials, cost of production, and cost of advertising.
- Construct cones, pyramids, cubes, and cylinders.
- Examine areas in relation to flight performance: wingspan, length of fuselage, parachute circumference, distance of flight, and flight trajectory.
- Investigation: time the descent over a set number of drops and work out the average time it takes to reach the ground from a height of eight feet. Plot the points; compare these with seed dispersal.

These activities are particularly suited to developing teamwork and cooperation among the students. In most of the activities, students must work in teams to complete problems specifically designed to be too involved for one student. By collaborating as teams, the students will be helped to realize the importance of

- Being organized
- Making sure that everyone in the group understands their role
- Making sure that all ideas are listened to, respected, and recorded
- Understanding the design process
- Meeting regularly to discuss progress

These tasks and responsibilities fit easily within the following kinds of design and technology activities:

1. *Design a glider that will be a suitable toy for a ten-year-old. It must be in kit form.* Some considerations:

- It must be well designed and a good glider—that is, it must work.
- It must be easy to assemble.
- It must have a pleasing shape.

2. *Formulate a means of manufacturing and assembling your product; the process must be organized through at least four operational stages.* Some considerations:

- How are you going to organize the manufacturing process?
- How many operators are necessary within the system?
- What tools will be necessary?

3. *Design a presentation package.* Some considerations:

- How will the package protect the glider from damage?
- Will it be fitted with separate sections to accommodate the different parts?
- What material would be best?
- How will the package be manufactured?
- How "visible" will it be as a packaged product (color, package graphics)?

4. *Devise a marketing strategy.* Some considerations:

- How will it be sold and distributed?
- What will it cost?
- What is the profit margin?
- What form(s) of advertising will you use?
- Will you use a logo?

This junior high school project was programmed over a whole semester. Pupils worked in groups and organized themselves in tasks according to their strengths. They thought of themselves as a real team of designers. A team of four teachers acted as advisors and facilitators, only intervening when their support was essential.

The students' products were well constructed and met the requirements of the design brief. This would not have been possible if the they had not researched flight in their preliminary investigative exercises, in which they experimented with parachutes, hot air balloons, and gliders. They developed their ideas explicitly using the process of the design loop and made decisions through discussion and motivation. The packaging was made to be strong, yet inexpensive to produce; the graphics were equally well considered and complementary to the product. The instructions for use took into account the age group for which the product was designed. The typography and graphics used a selection of fonts and a design layout suitable for the product. A computer-aided design (CAD) program was used for some of the design layout. The final outcome was a marketable package that extended the students in their learning and fully employed existing skills. They developed an understanding of the vital role of mathematics, science, and technology in product design, manufacture, and marketing. A class portfolio was kept to show evidence of the project. Individual students kept a project portfolio of their own group's work; their own personal responsibilities were identified and documented.

It needs to be remembered that, even though different teachers are involved in this type of integrated project approach, mostly the same body of students will be undertaking the work. It seems that this rather obvious fact is often forgotten in individual disciplines' curriculum-planning efforts. The fact that students may recognize links between different subjects before the teachers do should not lead teachers to be complacent. Teachers should not leave to their students alone the task of discovering complementarity among the ideas and skills acquired in different areas. Teamwork among teachers from different subject departments is needed to forge explicit links, and teachers must be rewarded for this extra effort.

The critics of integrated approaches to learning believe that subjects are not taught thoroughly through cross-curricular programs of work. They argue that single subjects are not taught in sufficient depth or with adequate rigor when integrated with other subjects. Supporters of integrated approaches to teaching and learning, however, claim that young students do not distinguish one subject from another; therefore, broad relevance is more important than subject purity and depth. Indeed, when taught with rigor and expertise, integrated learning programs appear to provide greater relevance for many students than single-subject teaching alone. Obviously, there are times when subjects should be taught separately. It would be foolish to integrate subjects at all times. However, when broad projects are undertaken that involve students in practical investigation, subject integration is a far more effective learning approach than subject separation. When leading integrated lessons, teachers must bear in mind that, although they may recognize the various subjects included, their students frequently do not. Teachers need to explicitly point out the activity's connections to various disciplines (Sellwood, 1990).

The either/or argument over a thematic approach versus a subject-centered approach suggests that a teacher must accept one over the other rather than a balance of the two approaches. The melding of the two appears to happen as teachers gain experience in using a design-and-technology approach. For example, Project UPDATE teachers use the design-and-technology approach to support thematic units when appropriate, but they also are quite comfortable with using design and technology to motivate the learning of a specific subject. Project UPDATE teachers report that they are able to shift the attention of students so that the design and technology activities become the focus of content and skills in specific subjects. For example, teachers are able to shift the attention of students who may not attend well to a subject such as mathematics by focusing on activities or aspects of activities that require mathematical thinking and doing. The same can be said for science, reading, writing, and other school subjects, if teachers have been helped to see the cross-curricular connections and to apply the knowledge of the different subjects to practical purposes. Because they have so much power for holding student attention, design and technology activities can serve as a foundation upon which to build bridges to these and other subjects. Again, Project UPDATE teachers report that the power of design and technology activities requires them to learn new "disengagement strategies." Given free rein, students tend to pursue these activities for long periods of time, dispelling the myth of the short attention span of young people. In some cases, the strategy may be as straightforward as a "countdown" over a period of ten or more minutes to the end of an activity; otherwise, students tend to miss shifts in topics of study, changes of classes, and even breaks for recess and lunch. Appropriately managed, design and technology activities often help to create a level of engagement in learning that is more powerful than occurs using separate subject approaches and that facilitates guiding students into related work calling for in-depth critical and creative thinking. (Project UPDATE has shown that appropriately trained teachers are quite able to use the design-and-problem-solving approach in cross-curricular efforts with students from kindergarten through eighth grade. See Chapter Five for further details.)

Systemic Reform: The Frameworks Approach

In any attempt at systemic reform, different schools and school systems inevitably will choose different pathways, based on their readiness to change, the profiles of their teaching staffs, the nature of the student populations they serve, and the availability of resources. Systemic reform strategies therefore need to be flexible; they need to allow each school or school district to sustain its distinctive character and to proceed at a pace it can manage. At the same time, if the reforms are to mean anything, the reformers need to set some broad guidelines that define the limits of what they see as acceptable goals and standards for the schools.

This is the essential rationale behind the curriculum frameworks that are now being adopted by most states in the United States and in several other countries. Frameworks identify the desirable elements of a curriculum and advocate certain reforms in pedagogical strategy, but they do not prescribe exactly what must be taught. Frameworks provide a scaffolding for course development, but they do not constitute a syllabus. Nevertheless, the frameworks approach sets clear guidelines for curriculum appraisal and an agenda for change. The documents sometimes also include scope and sequence charts, a guide to supporting research literature, and advice about alternative strategies for assessment and reporting. Frameworks documents are typically produced by state education authorities based on advice from educators, researchers, and the community in order to advise schools under their jurisdiction. A similar approach could easily be adopted by individual schools or school districts.

Curriculum framework documents that emphasize close links between science and technology have been produced in a number of states, including California (1990), Massachusetts (1994), and New York (1994). Outside of the United States, England and Wales have mandated technology education as part of the national curriculum. As described later in this chapter, Scotland also has an environmental studies curriculum with a strong technology component. In Victoria, Australia, a centrally mandated, statewide curriculum framework has been created for technology education for kindergarten through tenth grade; for grades eleven and twelve, three broadly defined technology education subjects have been introduced to replace the old industrial arts classes that provided preparation for specific trades. In each case, the framework documents identify a set of underpinning educational principles and a set of goals for student achievement. (Further details are provided in the vignette "Curriculum Frameworks, Victoria, Australia" that appears later in this chapter.) The frameworks from New York and Scotland are especially noteworthy in that they embrace a whole range of subject areas in a single document and provide explicit links between learning objectives and assessment targets and procedures.

Curriculum, Instruction, and Assessment: New York State Education Department

Central to the New Compact for Learning released by the New York State Education Department in 1991 is the vision of "local development of curriculum, instruction, and assessment that results in student achievement of specific standards." This vision has been supported by the release of several framework documents.

The Mathematics, Science, and Technology Framework includes a set of broad educational goals and a set of nine standards. Standards 4, 5, and 6 each refer to a single area of study (science, mathematics, and technology). All the other standards are generic—none of them focus on a specific area of content. The nine standards are:

1. Analysis, Inquiry, and Design
2. Systems
3. Information Resources
4. Science
5. Technology
6. Mathematics
7. Connecting Themes
8. Interdisciplinary Problem Solving
9. Preparation for the Future

The text of Standard 1 clearly indicates the intention for an integrated approach to teaching mathematics, science, and technology: "Students will have knowledge, skills and attitudes that empower them to use mathematical analysis, scientific inquiry and engineering design, as appropriate, to pose questions, seek answers and design solutions."

Under the discussion of Standard 2 (Systems), the same set of key concepts and competencies are listed for both engineered and natural systems:

• Identifying boundaries
• Working with inputs and outputs
• Identifying interactions among elements of the system
• Working with feedback and control

Other standards refer explicitly to connecting themes (Standard 7) and interdisciplinary problem solving (Standard 8). The document includes a discussion of the links between curriculum, instruction, and assessment; consideration for students with disabilities; and exemplar materials aimed at different grade levels.

School districts, schools, and teachers are free to develop their own curriculum units within this framework. Such was the case for Alan Horowitz, chairman of technology, Clarkstown Central School District. The following article, written by Horowitz, will be published, along with some photographs of the activity, in the *Technology Educator*, the New York State technology education professional journal. It provides sufficient detail for other schools to undertake a similar project. (Further information may be obtained from Alan Horowitz, Chairman of Technology, Clarkstown Central School District, 30 Parrott Road, West Nyack, NY 10994; (914) 634–6235 or (914) 639–6410; fax (914) 634–5073; E-mail: ahorowitz@aol.com.)

Innovation

It happened one morning about two years ago. It didn't slowly materialize, with lots of planning and forethought, but suddenly, like a case of temporary insanity or the flu. I'm going to do it full speed ahead . . . and damn the torpedoes!

Yep. That's how it all began . . . the Felix V. Festa Junior High School's very own solar car project. When I announced the project to my seventh- and eighth-grade students, the looks I received went from "Yeah, right!" to "This guy is crazy." But since I was a lot bigger then most of them and was also responsible for their report card grade, I received an overwhelmingly polite silence with a lot of skepticism thrown in to boot. Well, who can blame them? No one in his right mind would tackle an ambitious project like this with twelve- to fourteen-year-olds. But I knew that the enthusiasm of my junior high youngsters would see this thing through. With the right motivation, these students are curious, energetic, imaginative, and a lot sharper than people think. Even so, it wasn't until a school district truck, loaded with aluminum and other donated materials, backed up to my room that the students took me seriously.

From that time on, not one school day went by where students didn't come to work on the car, even during some of the worst snow storms of last year. Students drew sketches of the car's design and built a wire frame model. Surprisingly, the vehicle came out very close to the model we built. Almost one hundred students planned, researched, cut, bent, soldered, welded, sanded, threaded, wired, drilled, riveted, formed, filed, sawed, body-filled, greased, and performed just about every other operation you could think of in the manufacture and production of our solar vehicle. I photographed and videotaped the students working on the car from the very beginning in order to document the vehicle's progress. Along the way, students proposed a long list of names for the car and, after a ballot, selected SPARC (for Solar Powered Advanced Research Car) as the favorite.

Description of the Car

The car is approximately fifteen feet long, five feet wide, four feet tall, and weighs around six hundred pounds. Most of the body parts and frame are made from aluminum pipe and sheet metal. The flooring is made from quarter-inch aluminum diamond plate. It has rack-and-pinion steering, hydraulic disc brakes, and a mechanical emergency/park brake. Four six-volt, deep discharge batteries drive a four-horsepower, twenty-four-volt DC motor. A Sevcon microprocessor controller and a large relay controls the speed and forward/reverse directions. The front end is a four-bar suspension system with coil-over shocks and the rear has a leaf-spring suspension. There are eight twelve-volt flexible solar panels wired in a series/parallel configuration to get the desired twenty-four volts. A charge regulator is used to keep the battery pack from overcharging. The dashboard has a digital speedometer, digital voltmeters, and a series of switches, including the ignition, forward/reverse, max speed, and headlights. The turn-signal switch is on the steering wheel, and the rear spoiler brake lights are controlled by a switch mounted near the brake pedal. The drive system is a simple chain and sprocket connected to a limited-slip-differential rear end. With the sprockets geared way down, the maximum speed is ten to fifteen miles per hour—just right for the young drivers.

Funding for the Car

The funding and donated supplies for the project came from a variety of sources. Without these supporters, this project would not have been possible. [The article then provides the names of public and private sources of funds, including fourteen national corporations and local businesses.]

Some people have asked me why has it taken so long to build the solar car. When you have between forty-five minutes and one hour a day to work on the car and you have to teach students how to perform many operations and safely use many tools and machines along the way, it takes a lot of time. It took over two months just to make the mold that was used to form SPARC's windshield. (Bondo body filler sure does stink, doesn't it?) But since time was never a factor in this activity, we were never in a rush. We didn't have any deadlines such as would be the case if we were to enter the car into a race. Our goal was not to build SPARC fast, but to build it as best as we could with the equipment and funding we had. And, most important, to give the youngsters a hands-on engineering, design, and problem-solving experience usually obtained only at the college level.

When all is said and done, the real goal of the car activity was to give students an educational experience they would never forget. And, hopefully, that goal was met. In addition, the school newspaper, the *Rockland Journal-News* (a Gannet paper), and the local cable channel did stories on the project. The publicity obtained from the activity helped give the technology department in my school a boost. And as we all know, a little positive publicity can go a long way.

At the time of this writing we are fiberglassing the front end, making some improvements on the vehicle in order to obtain a special DOT license. But regardless of whether we are finished or not, I'm planning to bring the car to the NYSTEA spring conference on May 10 to 13, 1995, at the Nevele. Write those dates down and be sure to stop by, say hello, and see SPARC "in person."

Horowitz reports that, although most of the work for the car took place before or after school hours, many areas of science and mathematics were included in the activity. Topics such as plastics, leverage, friction, measurement, electronics, electricity, wiring, soldering, welding, surface area, and metallurgy were an integral part of the project. Topics were covered on a need-to-know basis and lessons/demonstrations were given accordingly. Both boys and girls worked on the car.

Fitting the solar car activity into the New York State technology education curriculum was no problem. The curriculum basically provides an outline of the topics needed to be covered by the time students complete eighth grade. The topics include "Getting to Know Technology," "Resources of Technology," "Problem Solving," "Systems and Subsystems," "How Technology Affects Society," "Choosing Resources," "How Resources Are Processed," "Controlling Systems," and "The Impacts of Technology"—all of which the solar car activity can deal with if appropriate lessons and demonstrations are used.

Some frameworks have combined technology with other socially oriented curriculum sequences. The Scottish Office Education Department (1993), for example, has divided the traditional curriculum into five subject areas: mathematics, expressive arts, English language, religious and moral education, and environmental studies. Each curriculum area is described in a framework document that lays down a common set of goals, topics for study, strands (targeted skills and processes) and attainment targets for students in the five-to-fourteen age group (equivalent to grades kindergarten through ten). Technology and science are both included in the environmental studies framework, together with health education, social studies, and information technology (computer studies/computer literacy). The common goal of these studies is to "engender informed attitudes to the environment" (p. 2). The studies have a common language for describing strands and attainment targets and are designed to complement each other in various ways. Throughout this curriculum framework, there are "pointers" that indicate links with attainment targets in other areas of learning. Special consideration is given to students with learning difficulties and those exceeding the attainment targets set in the assessment guidelines. The framework has been reviewed, generally endorsed, and extended by the Scottish Consultative Council on the Curriculum (1994). This review group advises that implementation of the proposed curriculum will take time: "The further development of technology education in Scotland in the directions indicated by its proposals will need sustained encouragement and support in the years ahead, in order that such changes as may be necessary and desirable will be manageable by teachers and schools over an appropriate timescale" (p. 10).

A number of frameworks contain exemplary projects with suggestions for classroom management and assessment. These are particularly useful in schools where teachers may be unfamiliar with subject-matter content as well as new approaches to practice. The sample activities provided in the Australian frameworks (illustrated in the two vignettes that follow, which were adapted from examples in the Victorian Technology Studies Curriculum Framework) were widely adopted and rapidly provided a basis for dialogue between teachers in different schools.

Green Gunge

Green Gunge is a middle school science unit aimed primarily at developing knowledge and skills associated with the creation and separation of mixtures. The class works through a scenario in which the town water supply is shut off and the school community must survive using water from a nearby pond. The pond water is cloudy and has rafts of green algae (green gunge) floating on the surface for much of the year; it is thought to be undrinkable. The students will be responsible for treating the water in order to make it suitable for use. The activity does not follow a strict procedure. What follows is a description of how the unit unfolded in one classroom.

A class brainstorm yielded a list of essential uses for water, as well as the things that might need to be removed from the pond water to make sure the water was suitable for each purpose. The teacher then led the students through a series of exercises involving the separation of solids from liquids. She also prepared a sheet outlining additional techniques. The methods considered were

- Sedimentation and decanting
- Filtration (filter paper, cotton, wool, gravel, and sand bed)
- Flocculation
- Absorption (charcoal filter)
- Evaporation and distillation

During the exercises the teacher helped students develop a list of key words linking the procedures with commercial and industrial process used in water treatment.

Next, the students worked in groups to design and build a piece of water treatment equipment that could be used to produce water suitable for one of the identified needs. Each group had the task of treating a one hundred–milliliter sample of green gunge. At the end, groups described their device and compared their results. Students were encouraged to consult with their technology teachers during the design and construction phases. The unit finished with a role play concerning the location of a new factory in the town, a survey of domestic water uses, and proposals for water conservation.

The Green Gunge unit came about because a teacher was unhappy with the abstract way in which her seventh-grade students learned about "mixtures." The unit was developed by brainstorming with colleagues and finding a "real world" context for developing the identified skills. By the time they had finished, the unit not only met the original educational goals but embraced several other science topics, and it involved design and construction activities, a drama activity, and involvement in a local community environmental program.

Little Whizzers

The Little Whizzer is a toy suspended on a loop of cord that spins when the cord is alternately pulled tight between the hands and then released. Everybody has played with one of these toys, but have you considered what goes into designing and building one? That is the challenge set for a grade six or seven technology class. The activity is intended to develop the skills for cutting and shaping acrylic sheet (Plexiglas). It also provides an opportunity to learn about the concepts of momentum, center of gravity, and "centrifugal force" and to see the spinner as a manifestation of Newton's first law of motion.

Students are given a design brief that specifies the purpose, materials, and maximum dimensions of the desired final product. The design criteria also state that the product must be attractive, interesting, and safe. Determination of the center of gravity is an essential step in making a toy that will spin smoothly.

Students are then guided through a design and construction process that involves

- Selecting a shape
- Cutting the shape from the Plexiglas
- Determining the center of gravity of the cutout shape
- Drilling holes and fitting the string
- Testing for balance and safety

This activity addresses the development of knowledge and skills related to materials and tools and also provides an opportunity for hands-on exploration of some important scientific concepts. Important links can be made between the language of science (for example, center of gravity) and the language of technology (for example, dynamic balance). Concern with functionality, safety, and the aesthetic appearance of the finished product softens the hard, "boys only" image of the technology classroom.

Although different school systems decide on curriculum policy in different ways, most systems face problems when attempting curriculum reform. The frameworks approach can offer guidance in this regard. In the Australian example, for instance, detailed in the next vignette, documents describing nine areas of learning are complemented by an overarching document dealing with curriculum planning, school organization, and decision making, and by a separate document dealing with methods of assessment appropriate for the range of learning methods advocated. These have proved invaluable to school communities and faculty who have worked to revise local educational programs.

Curriculum Frameworks, Victoria, Australia

In Victoria, Australia, the Victorian Technology Studies Curriculum Framework was released in the form of nine documents that described the guiding principles and the scope and approaches to teaching and learning for nine subject areas (including science and technology studies). The frameworks also include the School Curriculum and Organization Framework and the Assessment Framework.

The frameworks were developed by panels of educators, academics, and administrators, with several rounds of consultation and pilot testing in schools between 1985 and 1988 (Johnson and Fuhrman, 1994).

Adoption of the frameworks was not compulsory; nevertheless, its use was widespread across the state. The process created a shared vocabulary of language and ideas among teachers, and exemplary activities and methods of classroom organization were quickly disseminated at the local level. One feature that facilitated effective adoption of the frameworks was the fact that they contained a timely compilation of contemporary but well-tried approaches to teaching and learning in each subject-matter area, as illustrated by the two preceding vignettes.

With respect to the new technology education courses, they carry titles that suggest a very different way of slicing up this domain of knowledge. In the place of the "old" courses such as construction, dressmaking, electrical, and metalworking, the Victorian Certificate of Education (VCE) introduced three new courses: "Materials and Technology," "Technological Design and Development," and "Systems and Technology." (The reforms leading to the introduction of these courses and their special concern with gender equity are described in Chapter Five; see the vignette "Beyond Occupational Specificity and Gender Bias.")

Related Reforms

During the same period, new guidelines for technology education in grades eleven and twelve were also developed, as part of a systemwide reform of postcompulsory education. These reforms led to the accreditation of forty-four new study designs that carried credit towards the VCE. The new VCE program aims to deliver a comprehensive postcompulsory education and to provide access to higher education and employment for all students. Assessment policies also changed from a norm-referenced competitive system based on a limited range of assessment techniques to a criterion-referenced system based on achievement of "work requirements" and participation in "common assessment tasks." The new system is performance-based; it takes pressure off the end-of-year examinations and encourages students to work more steadily throughout the year.

The VCE is a high-stakes program: successful completion of the project-based and formal assessments developed for the VCE constitutes the principal means of admission to postsecondary education in Victoria (Howe and Vickers, 1993).

Reshaping Educational Pathways: A New Approach to the K–12 Curriculum

As we explained in Chapter One, the goal of this book is to provide a vision of what a technology education program for America's schools might look like, and what it might achieve. The program we envision could take a number of forms, but a common element would be a sequence of carefully constructed technology education courses, from kindergarten through twelfth grade. Each course would

- Give students direct experience in designing products, structures, and systems to meet individual and social needs
- Develop an understanding of criteria for evaluating the two-way interactions between society and technology that have influenced the course of civilization over the last two or three centuries
- Demand that students actually make, use, and evaluate a range of technologies
- Seek to make students familiar with technologies commonly encountered at home and at work

In Chapter Three, we discussed Porter High School's decision to abolish tracking. The school decided that, after students had successfully completed common, challenging, parallel science and technology programs in grades nine and ten, they would be able to choose from among eight programs offered by the school for grades eleven and twelve. All eight programs had particular core requirements, but students would still be able to take a limited number of courses from the other programs. Six of these programs grew out of the six pairs of units around which the grade ten science and technology program had been structured. The other two programs would focus on natural science and the humanities.

Such a secondary school program would have several advantages:

- There would be no more need for tracking in the middle school.
- All students would gain a general introduction to both science and technology.
- Students could choose between an academic pathway and a technical pathway at the end of grade ten, but in any case, all the pathways would provide a sound preparation for college entrance.

The Porter High School paradigm advocates a common science curriculum to the end of grade ten, paralleled by and linked with a common technology education curriculum. The technology education curriculum would be generic, not occupationally specific, as are most of today's vocational technological courses. In grades eleven and twelve, students would follow diverging pathways. The nature of the pathways is likely to be different in different school districts and states. (See, for example, the student handbook excerpts and transcript stories given in "Technology at Merlyn High" in Appendix C.) Some potential alternatives are as follows:

- Students aiming to secure employment immediately after graduating from high school would take courses in which they would be expected to design artifacts, to select the materials and processes needed for production, and to carry out their designs. Unlike today's vocational and technical courses, these courses would demand that students go well beyond carrying out manual production tasks under instruction.

- College-track students aiming for careers as technologists or architects or engineers might take courses like the English and Welsh D&T (described in Chapter Two) or the Australian VCE Design Studies. Students interested in post-secondary education in the allied health field would take courses that focused on health technologies and professional practice, as well as providing a sound basis in the life sciences. Students might, for example, conduct experiments to test the insulating capacities of different materials. This experimental activity would lead to solving a larger design problem, for example, building an alpine shelter in an isolated area not connected to any electricity supply.

- College-track humanities students might take a general technology education course, or a technology education course specifically slanted towards the history of technology and its impact on society; for example, students would investigate a question such as "How does milk get on my table?" both currently and within a particular historical context, such as Illinois in 1800.

- College-track science students would study chemistry, physics, and the life sciences, but these courses too would be changed. The changes would mean that instead of relying on learning sheer abstractions (as many of today's science courses emphasize), science students would be challenged to explain how artifacts work, or to work with fellow students in the vocational and technical programs to jointly solve problems in areas such as designing, fabrication, materials selection, and so on. For example, by working alongside vocational/technical students on specific technological tasks, such as building the alpine shelter, the science students would acquire insights into how their theoretical understandings could be translated to become effective in the realms of practical action.

CHAPTER FIVE

ESTABLISHING TECHNOLOGY EDUCATION IN THE SCHOOLS

Technology education as we advocate it would radically change the way in which both science and mathematics, as well as other subjects, are taught and learned in the elementary schools, middle schools, and high schools. It would mean that all students, beginning in the earliest grades and continuing to grade twelve, would complete coherent programs of study that have as their aim not only to help them understand the key principles of these subjects, but also to develop their facility in making, using, and evaluating a wide range of technologies. The public acceptance of technology education as something that should be part of the general education of all young people, however, will be heavily influenced by the difficulty of implementing the necessary curriculum and organizational changes.

What is involved in a full-scale implementation of technology education in American schools? What will take technology education beyond the status of a transient innovation that exists at only a few grade levels in a few schools? As with the introduction of any new curriculum, schools interested in technology education will have to address a number of critical issues. In fact, several of these issues are particularly salient to this subject, both because it is new to the school curriculum and because the subject wrongly but all too frequently has been considered appropriate only for part of the student population—for boys rather than for girls, or for vocationally rather than academically oriented students.

Implementation Issues

The two preceding chapters have dealt with alternative curriculum models and suitable instructional strategies. This chapter takes up four other critical implementation issues. Until a satisfactory and coherent range of solutions to these implementation issues has been identified and well tested in schools, technology education will continue to follow a faltering path.

Issue One: Planning for Change

Who should be responsible for initiating the needed changes and how can the new curricula be introduced effectively? How will classrooms and schools be organized and equipped to accommodate students' active project work? How can scheduling be rearranged to provide planning time and to allow team teaching? Reorganization of the relationships between different departments in schools will be needed, and new arrangements will have to be made to ensure availability of appropriate equipment and facilities for technology education programs. No single option is likely to take account of the interests of all parties in technology education. Science teachers, technology teachers, vocational teachers, administrators, parents, and students have different interests and will continue to advocate different options. It is imperative, therefore, to identify a range of options and to gain an understanding as to which of these options are more effective in particular circumstances.

Issue Two: Teacher Development

Who is going to teach the kind of curriculum suggested in this book? What does a teacher (or team of teachers) need to know and be able to do in order to implement a technology education curriculum at given grade levels? And who will help teachers acquire the necessary knowledge and skills? Teachers need to be prepared for teaching technology education by constructing curricula out of local design opportunities and by working from frameworks rather than from packaged curricula. The new teaching demands combined with the new subject matter and the integration of various traditional subjects put heavy cognitive demands on elementary teachers. There is danger, as in some hands-on science curricula, that the curriculum will descend into "fun activities" (see the vignettes "Experiencing Technology Education for the First Time: The Early Elementary Years" in Chapter Four and "Kites" later in this chapter). Another problem for elementary school teachers is fear of technology and feeling incompetent to teach it, particularly since it is viewed as involving mainly physical science and construction.

There are considerable hurdles at the secondary level as well, including ownership of specific disciplines by science and technology teachers; the low status of technology teachers, most of whom are former industrial arts teachers; and the confusion of technology education with technical/vocational education, resulting in the relegation of the field to the vocational education teachers. In truth, however, as for the elementary school teacher, an effective technology curriculum is cognitively very demanding of the teacher educated either in any of the traditional disciplines relevant to the current high school curriculum or as a vocational education teacher. Given the integrative nature of the type of curriculum we propose, team teaching would seem an appropriate approach. While such an approach is not uncommon at the middle school level, it requires major adjustments in traditional high school teaching.

Issue Three: Technology Education for All

How will equal access to rigorous technology curricula be ensured for all students—girls as well boys, minority students in inner-city schools, rural students? How can a strong foundation be laid in the early grades to overcome the traditional failure of schools with these student populations—a foundation that will nurture their interest and achievement in subjects that lead to good technical careers or to further education in science- and technology-related fields—engineering, architecture, industrial design, mathematics, and the science disciplines?

Issue Four: Assessment of Student Achievement

How will students' work and progress be assessed? Assessment of what students learn in technology education must match its essential characteristics, that is, it must be performance based. Because projects and group work as well as paper-and-pencil tests will have to be assessed, common assessment criteria will need to be developed for such student work, similar to the developmental assessment work in Great Britain and in Australia. Good curriculum development must include development of assessment tasks and strategies; but the effectiveness of new curricula must be demonstrated in terms of student learning through assessment tasks that fit such curricula—and that preferably are embedded in them. Most important, district- and state-mandated tests must reflect the goals of technology education and must be consistent with the classroom-based assessments controlled by the teacher.

Planning for Technology Education

Implementing change within a school or across a school system is far more difficult than implementing change in a few classrooms. This is true for any educational reform, not just for technology education. Although some large-scale changes have started from individual teachers working alone, this is the exception, not the rule. For the interested administrator, it is important to find a teacher or teachers who want to implement change and then to provide support to help in the change process. The best circumstance is when teachers and administrators come together in common concern for improving what and how students learn. As an example of such collaboration, a description of the collaborative effort of the Boyertown, Pennsylvania, school system follows.

Boyertown

A school-based project of districtwide scope was implemented in the Boyertown Area School System in Boyertown, Pennsylvania. As part of an overall desire to make significant changes in the nature of schooling for Boyertown students, a new educational mission and building program was initiated. The board of education adopted a mission for delivering quality education for all students. Within that context an initiative for technology education was established to prepare individuals to comprehend and contribute to a technology-based society. As a part of their total education experience, students are expected to become technologically literate and capable in (1) the technological method, (2) identifying problems and opportunities, (3) technological processes, (4) dealing with resource questions, (5) technological knowledge, (6) evaluations, and (7) management. These capabilities are to be acquired through a curriculum based on technological systems, the interaction of efficient actions, and the application of these systems and actions to societal purposes. The systems and actions will encompass the bio-related, communication, and physical technologies.

Much of the initial planning work in technology education focused on bringing the programs in the school in line with the existing industrial arts/technology education guidelines for Pennsylvania. In order to set a larger context for the emerging directions of technology education, the district administrators were invited by the Boyertown technology education faculty to attend a presentation called "New Directions in Technology Education." The presentation was part of the program of a grassroots professional development effort in Southeastern Pennsylvania offered by supervisors and teachers of technology education for their colleagues. The superintendent accepted the invitation and participated in a planned program for administrators that considered the ongoing changes in technology education and its potential for all students from kindergarten through twelfth grade. The initial presentation was followed by a discussion of design and technology and its potential for integrating science, mathematics, and technology education.

The timing was perfect. On returning home, the schoolwide leadership team supported the idea that plans for industrial arts education should be shifted significantly and more attention turned to the implementation of technology education. This was no small task, with technology education itself in transition from programs that focused on construction, manufacturing, communication and transportation to those organized around the physical, biological, and information/communication technologies. The planned program would be student centered and focused on learning, rather than on teaching—a paradigm shift. The technology education faculty was ready to accept the challenge of remaking itself and inventing a new program of study. Hundreds of hours of work followed as the faculty launched into uncertain and uncharted territory. The potential power of linking science and technology soon became evident, and the working team was expanded to include members of the science faculty. Within a few months, members of the mathematics faculty also joined the collaborative effort. By the second year of the project, faculty representatives from other subjects became involved in the planning of an integrated school offering.

The work of that team continues. The new facilities are completed, and the first of the cross-curricular courses have been implemented and assessed. The participating faculty found the work both demanding and exciting. The general response has been positive, with a great deal of optimism concerning the effect that the new courses and the new approaches to learning are having on students.

Particularly exciting has been the tapping of the potential of the technology education program. The school faculty now realizes that technology education brings to the table a different orientation on curricular change—one that focuses on the realism and excitement provided by technology as a means of enhancing what students learn as they prepare for the coming century. Through the receptivity and work of colleagues across the school, technology education has provided an "engine of change" that links together other school subjects in new and exciting ways.

In a sense the effort has only begun. The work on curriculum redesign and staff development is now under way, but everyone involved realizes that the journey will be long and demanding. Much of what is being done has been self-funded, but the efforts now demand outside support. Observers and participants hope that such resources will support a serious program of research. Certainly the interest of other schools and colleagues suggests the importance of this effort that, since its initiation, has drawn hundreds of people for professional visits to Boyertown. The resulting load on faculty has increased to the extent that a formal visitation day is now provided once a month on a "reservation only" basis for those interested in an orientation and a chance to see the program in operation.

As impressive as the Boyertown effort is, the involved faculty members are quick to indicate that future efforts should be able to go further by building on what they have learned. The general sentiment of the leadership team that triggered the initiative is that they are convinced that technology education as a means of involving students, as a vehicle of professional collaboration, and as an agent of curricular change has even more potential. They find it exciting to consider what other schools could accomplish as they build on this base of experience.

What are the lessons of Boyertown? The following section discusses key issues that need to be addressed for the effective introduction of technology education into a school system:

- A clear mission and vision for the curriculum, subscribed to by parents and administrators as well as teachers
- Policies and leadership that support the mission
- School culture and the orientation of educators
- Management of the change process
- Teachers' concerns, including new roles and responsibilities
- Choosing curriculum materials based on effectiveness
- School organization, especially scheduling
- Space, equipment, and supplies

Mission and Vision

Teachers and administrators must have clear goals for their students and a vision of what is possible with technology education. This can come from visiting industrial sites and classrooms that use the design and technology approach, from watching videotapes of classrooms, from reading case studies of classrooms, and from attending presentations and demonstrations by teachers who use design and technology in their classrooms.

Next, teachers need to make the vision their own. Working collaboratively with colleagues, they need to ask themselves: How would this work in my classroom? What additional expertise do I need? Is it available in the school or community? How can I access it? Whom do I wish to work with? What safety policies need to be reviewed? Where does this fit into my curriculum? How will I measure performance of students? How will I report to parents and colleagues? Teachers also need to gain clarity about what they are doing, why they are doing it, what it will involve, and how it will benefit their students (Fullan and Hargreaves, 1991). This can be accomplished by individual reflection; meetings with staff developers, coaches, or other problem solvers; and collaboration with other teachers from the school or district.

Recommendation

Leading educational associations and policy makers must collaborate on the development of a vision that unites the wide range of views of technology education and what it should do and be within American education.

Recommendation

Key education associations and reformers should develop strategies for increasing public acceptance of technology education—what it is and how it will benefit children and society.

Recommendation

As schools or districts begin implementation of technology education, they should identify a design team from across grade levels and disciplines to design the courses. The design teams should seek agreement on a core set of knowledge and skills that must be developed by all the students in the technology education classes.

Policies and Leadership

Support from school leaders is critical. The school leadership must have a clear understanding of the critical role technology education can play in the general curriculum and they must communicate the value of technology education through the priority and resources they give to it. They must actively collaborate with teachers to plan and implement the teachers' vision of technology education.

Educational leaders will have to formulate policy directives to support making technology education an integral part of a district's or state's school curriculum. As noted, several states already have included technology education in state-level curriculum frameworks; other states, such as Vermont, are introducing technology through the reform of mathematics and science education. At the local level, policies that integrate design and technology into the curriculum, as in Boyertown, help to stabilize and legitimize its place in education.

High school graduation requirements should acknowledge the role of technology education and the achievements of students involved in design and technology work. District and state assessment policies must reflect the learning goals of the technology curriculum. Local employers also should play their part by establishing internships and explicit hiring policies that reward student achievements in technology courses and projects. These internships should be coordinated by the teachers and employers with instruction in the schools.

Technology education as a new school subject may face a considerable barrier in the admission criteria imposed by institutions of higher education. Recent experience with the American Chemical Society's course "Chemistry in the Community" (ChemCom) is indicative. ChemCom is a rigorous chemistry course, but it uses realistic community issues to treat not only traditional chemistry topics but also some technological and societal issues. The developers report that the course is not accepted for chemistry credit by some colleges and universities simply on the basis of its name (Sylvia Ware, personal communication, March 23, 1994). The case for technology education may be even more difficult since there is no analog in colleges and universities until students decide to obtain an engineering degree, usually at the upper division or professional school level. In fact, the *Man-Made World* project (discussed in Chapter Two; see also Engineering

Concepts Curriculum Project, 1970), although a rigorous one-year alternative to twelfth-grade physics, failed in part because there was no "slot" for it in the high school curriculum, and because colleges and universities would not award physics credit for it. Unless the more prestigious institutions of higher education are willing to recognize technology education as a legitimate field for high school study, as is now the case in Great Britain, its acceptance by schools serving privileged students will be slow. The consequence will be to reify the status of technology education as a second-class subject unworthy of rigorous treatment—just as is the case for much of vocational education.

The relative newness of technology education as a curriculum area requires school leaders to create awareness among school board members, parents, students, and teachers who are not directly involved about what technology education is and why it is necessary for students' futures. In fact, technology education programs are an obvious vehicle for involving parents and community members in school reform. One important role administrators can play in support of technology education is to broker relationships and draw resources from the community into the school. For example, architects, artists, engineers, computer scientists, medical technicians, environmental specialists, and physicists can make valuable contributions to technology education. Professionals such as these can be brought into the schools to work with students on projects, make demonstrations, support teacher development in technology education, and serve as advisors or jurors for fairs and competitions. School administrators should also arrange for teachers to share what they are doing through faculty meetings and other collegial events, at state and regional professional meetings, and through news coverage for the community.

Recommendation

State education agencies should address technology education in state curriculum frameworks.

Recommendation

School districts should support the creation of communities that collaborate to support technology education—communities of practitioners within a school who will work together across departmental boundaries—the creation of a sense of community support for technology education from the institutions of higher education, and the creation of communities of teachers who are sharing ideas about how to solve problems, across a state or across many states.

Recommendation

Universities must value and accept course credits from technology education programs.

School Culture and the Orientation of Educators

School culture must change to support ongoing learning by administrators and faculty, risk taking by teachers and students, and the pursuit of open-ended questions and problem solving in the classroom. As teachers change their perceptions of themselves from purveyors of information to facilitators of learning, they will confront many barriers—psychological as well as organizational and developmental. Getting over the psychological need to "know the answer" is hard for teachers, and even harder for students. Technology education can provide a platform leading to support of this type of teaching.

The work environment of schools can help or hinder teachers in this regard. Educators must assess the extent to which their school's culture is in alignment with the requirements of the new practice. They should review what gets rewarded in the system—for example, textbook coverage versus sustained project work. Adjustments through policy directives or more informal communiqués may be necessary. "Schools where teachers feel comfortable proposing and trying out new instructional strategies and materials and where they routinely share with each other at several levels—from talking about teaching to co-developing units of instruction—are more effective in increasing teachers' learning, as well as that of students" (National Center for Improving Science Education, 1991, p. 91).

Design and technology education requires a school culture that supports teachers as risk takers, in letting go of the need to have all the answers, and in being free to discover and explore meaning and learning with their students. Most teachers are not comfortable with the "open-endedness" of this approach to learning, in which the teacher, rather than directing every step of the way, will not even know the exact outcome of the project until it is done (Dunn and Larson, 1990; Makiya and Rogers, 1992). Add to this new approach the introduction of "teaching tools" that are unfamiliar to most teachers, such as hacksaws, vices, pliers, drills and drill bits, wire, bulbs, batteries, motors, welding rod, syringes, and so forth, and one realizes that technology education faces major implementation challenges.

Educators, students, and parents also must understand that the pursuit of open-ended questions does not equal chaos in the classroom. On the contrary, one teacher who uses design activities extensively reports that classroom management issues have disappeared because the students are so engaged in their projects. Nevertheless, even teachers who are natural leaders and "paradigm pioneers" need the organizational conditions necessary to support such innovation and risk taking.

When parents and school administrators trust teachers, invest in their ongoing learning and development, and give them the tools and resources they need to measure results, they support professional risk taking. Administrators who are willing to adjust teacher evaluation processes when they do not fit with new practices and to seek waivers and board or community support for promising innovations help to develop a culture for innovation and exploration among their faculty and in the school.

Another way of demonstrating the school's support for technology education is to organize events at which students may demonstrate their technology work to parents and community members, such as fairs, competitions, and displays in the school and community. Through such supporting activities, school leaders will be creating the school culture necessary to support teachers as they try out new strategies and approaches.

Recommendation

Incentive and evaluation structures for teachers should reward innovation, leadership, and risk taking as teachers strive to improve student learning through innovative curricula and teaching strategies.

Managing the Change Process

Several organizational supports and conditions are necessary for introducing and sustaining any educational reform, including technology education (National Center for Improving Science Education, 1991). In addition to supportive policies, leadership, and climate, these include (1) a team or individual (change facilitator) who understands and manages the change process, paying attention to both people and resource needs; (2) opportunities for high-quality staff development and ongoing support (discussed in the next section); (3) formal recognition and support for the implementation of technology education and the trying out of new educational strategies; and (4) meaningful involvement of parents and other stakeholders.

Many of the changes necessary to support technology education that we present are not unique to technology education. For example, the changes in organizational arrangements to support collaboration and teamwork, as well as changes in assessment and pedagogy, are very similar to reform efforts in other curricular areas. Some schools therefore will have already created some of the cultural and climate changes needed to support technology education. Nonetheless, introducing and sustaining this new curriculum area will be hard work. The payoff will be in the enhanced conceptual development of teachers and students, who are given the opportunity to live effectively in a contemporary world.

As an important first step in the introduction of technology education, educators need to "legitimize" and support the formation of an appropriate cross-functional team (for example, industrial arts/technology teachers, mathematics and science teachers, elementary and middle school teachers, students, curriculum directors, parents, and practicing engineers/scientists) that can manage the change process associated with the introduction of technology education. This team would be charged with investigating and introducing design and technology at the district or school level.

Recommendation

School districts and universities need to establish formal mechanisms for joint planning and implementation across departments and grade levels. At the university, engineers are particularly enthusiastic about technology education. They need to work with other educators and to communicate their enthusiasm to key decision makers in the university and local school districts.

Teacher Concerns

Change efforts that focus exclusively on the content of the change—that is, the practice or program that is changing—are less successful than those that also attend to the concerns of the individuals who are doing the changing. As schools take on technology education, they must consider what the teachers' concerns will be as they go through the change process, and they must plan to address these concerns. According to a number of researchers (Hall and Hord, 1987; Loucks-Horsley and others, 1989), teachers experience a range of concerns as they take on an innovation. One way of documenting and tracking teachers' concerns is to ask them to keep a journal of their experiences as they take on technology education (see for example the vignette "Teacher Log: City Science Workshop" in Chapter Three). A regular review of the journal will help facilitators of the change to address problems and will give teachers a chance to share their insights with their colleagues.

Teachers' concerns typically start with information and personal questions. They ask: What is technology education? What will this mean to me? Science teachers may be concerned about the erosion of their discipline, mathematics teachers about the loss of rigor in their courses, elementary teachers about the amount of setup time needed for project work, and so on. Teachers may fear that the development of a new subject area such as technology will leave them de-skilled, that what they know best to do will no longer be valued. The team of facilitators charged with implementing technology education in the schools should initiate discussions among faculty that build understanding of what the innovation is and address issues about how use of the innovation will affect teachers personally—for example, by creating more time demands, by changing schedules, or by leading them to feel uncomfortable and less competent as they learn something new. Facilitators should also share information about the change, provide examples from other schools, and give teachers opportunities to talk with others who have been successful with technology education.

As teachers begin to use the new practices, management becomes their primary concern. Professional development experiences at this stage should focus on how to implement the new program and how to help teachers anticipate problems they may encounter. Staff developers should model effective use of technology education for the teachers who will be implementing it and give them ample time to practice. After attending training programs, teachers need to have ongoing support from change facilitators who help them to solve problems they encounter, give them the extra time they need to prepare, and organize ways for them to collaborate with one another as they develop more confidence with their new strategies. At this point it is also very helpful for teachers to review materials that provide curriculum guidelines and give some examples and "how-tos."

As teachers become more competent in the use of technology education, their concerns will shift to impact. Is the program having the desired effect? How can I share and work more closely with my colleagues? Is my new instruction better than what I was doing before? How well do students achieve? How does what I am doing measure up to "best practice"? At this stage, change facilitators should help teachers evaluate what they are doing, show them what other teachers are doing with technology education, and provide them with opportunities to give and get feedback on their implementation of technology education. As teachers assess the impact of their efforts, they will need help and resources to decide which new strategies to keep and which to discard. Opportunities for teachers to document what they are doing and to reflect on what works best and why are particularly valuable as teachers experience impact concerns—for example, the rigor of courses, the loss of traditional subject matter, the need for setup time, and so on.

Recommendation

Educational researchers should identify innovative and effective practices and programs in technology education and help practitioners access information and research that may help them implement successful programs.

Choosing Curriculum Materials

Although they are limited, curriculum materials and examples of use of design are available to support technology education, as noted in Dunn and Larson (1990) and in Appendixes D and E, which provide lists of resources and sites actively implementing technology education. Instructional materials should be chosen wisely to ensure optimal learning. Materials that provide step-by-step instructions or show pictures of how something "should" look are unlikely to encourage students to be thoughtful. The goal is for students to invent and use their knowledge to design technological solutions, not to copy predesigned ones from books or instruction sheets. Instructions and examples should be true to the philosophy of open-ended problem solving and avoid spelling out procedures or processes (Boyce and others, 1993). Technology practitioners (including engineering and science faculty from cooperating universities) can help in the choice of materials.

While avoiding "cookbook" activities, curriculum materials should encourage teachers to set clear parameters for any project to be undertaken, so that the objectives are well defined and the criteria for acceptable work "knowable" to the teacher and the students. Materials that include some guidelines for assessing the products produced, as well as for assessing student understanding, are particularly helpful.

An additional criterion for selection is that instructional materials must fit state and local curriculum frameworks and educational philosophy. Also, some materials do not deal adequately with the social and ethical issues surrounding technology. Such materials may lead students to experience all technology as beneficial—for example, to see only the benefit of a new surgical procedure without considering its risks or its costs (Boyce and others, 1993).

For curriculum directors and teachers to make good curriculum choices, they must be familiar with the research base that undergirds technology education in general as well as specific curricular approaches to it. In most schools, students are expected to work in social isolation and to solve problems as mental exercises, usually with minimal access to practical aids or physical equipment. Problem solving in work and other nonschool settings is different: typically it involves interaction with the environment, with mechanical and conceptual tools, and with other people. A number of studies conducted on how young people and adults solve problems they encounter at work and in realistic settings outside the classroom suggest that they learn more efficiently and perform more competently in such situations than they do in the decontextualized environments that school usually provides (for example, Rogoff and Lave, 1984; see also the synthesis of this research by Raizen and Colvin, 1991). Formal studies of this type at school sites—for example, involving high school students in tech-prep programs, youth apprenticeships, or career academies—are rare, however.

How effective is the hands-on technology education approach? What is the role and importance of actually experiencing or using theoretical knowledge in realistic settings? Evaluations of technology education programs suggest that they may in fact fulfill the promise of the results reported so far by cognitive scientists, by extending teaching and learning methods beyond lectures, reading, and audiovisual techniques to include demonstration, group discussion, practice by doing, teaching others, and putting what is learned to immediate use. In Project UPDATE (see the "Project UPDATE" vignette later in this chapter), the indicators were once again very encouraging. There is growing evidence that the participating students scored better at the end of the school year on a range of assessment instruments than did students in comparable but more traditional classes.

Encouraging evidence on implementation comes from the response of teachers and students in pilot efforts in Delaware, Florida, Michigan, New Jersey, Oregon, Pennsylvania, and Virginia. With only modest amounts of in-service training, teachers are implementing thematic cross-curricular units that use design and technology activities as the vehicle for integration of student learning and the school curriculum. Additional research comes from England and Wales. Though the number of studies is rather modest, the emerging findings indicate the promise and potential of design and technology activities and what they can do to help students make cross-curricular connections in their studies. In addition, both the National Research Council's Science Standards and the American Association for the Advancement of Science's Science Benchmarks give prominent place to technology education and the design process.

The following vignette illustrates the advantage provided by the implementation of technology education in England and Wales.

Electricity at Age Fifteen

In a testing program conducted by science educators in England and Wales, fifteen-year-olds were found to do poorly in exercises related to electrical circuits. Although the students had studied electricity at several age and grade levels, 60 percent of those tested could not draw a circuit that showed the correct placement of an electrical switch, two lamps, and a battery in an electrical circuit. As an alternative to traditional instructional methods, a design and technology approach was developed. The design and technology activities required students to

1. Use theoretical knowledge to design and build an artifact
2. Test and improve their designs
3. Draw and document activities in their project portfolios
4. Discuss the process and results of their work

In some cases, students also were asked to help teach what they had learned to other students.

Evaluations of the learning gains for electronic circuits were conducted for electronics students using a design and technology approach based on the four elements just listed. The evaluations indicated that the acquisition of skills and knowledge by fifteen-year-olds was greatly improved by using this approach. Furthermore, by using design and technology activities, students six or seven years younger were able to build and draw circuits of similar or greater complexity than those produced by the fifteen-year-olds.

Students seem to find theoretical knowledge about electronics difficult to apply and to retain over time, but by using the design and technology activities, retention of electronics skills was greatly enhanced overall. The evaluators concluded that the power of the design and technology activities emerged from the realism and meaning that the activities brought into the classroom, and from the multiple levels of involvement that were required of students (Gott, 1984).

Despite such early documentation, a great deal of reliance currently must be placed on the judgment of teachers regarding the potential of technology education and an integrated approach to instruction. Because the adoption of a design and technology approach in the United States has been so recent, the evidence available within this country on its effectiveness in the classroom is scant. Considerable effort is needed to build a research base for making decisions regarding design and technology and its use in educational change.

Recommendation

To address the dearth of available technology education curriculum in the United States, federal and state education agencies as well as private foundations should support curriculum development efforts that establish a sequence of carefully constructed technology education courses from kindergarten through grade twelve.

Recommendation

Curriculum developers should define a common set of learning outcomes that everyone taking a technology education course will be expected to achieve. They should make early exemplars available to the mainstream of educators through active dissemination activities and planned demonstrations and scale-up efforts.

Recommendation

School districts should develop or adopt technology programs that reflect the guiding principles and goals for technology education presented in this book, choosing from several legitimate approaches to best match the educational needs of their students.

School Organization and Scheduling

As discussed in Chapter Three, there are several options for technology education courses and activities. Teams planning to introduce design and technology into their schools need to determine how the program will be provided through the different grade levels: coherently throughout K–12, or in self-contained classes at the elementary level, through team teaching that links science and technology courses at the middle school level, and through stand-alone or integrated courses or through a cross-grade project at the high school level. A number of other variations are also possible. The options the team chooses may depend on the school organization and schedule and how much these can be modified to accommodate technology education—for example, whether interdisciplinary activities or extended periods are feasible. The average fifty-minute period that characterizes secondary education may be enough to conduct some phases of a design project; however, continuity and the opportunity to explore learning in depth may be lost as students are required to pack up and move to the next class. Also, teachers in a given district or school may be bound by a time schedule that rules how many minutes are to be assigned to each subject per day or per week.

Middle schools that are designed for interdisciplinary teaching provide a good model for how schools can organize themselves to support technology education. Such middle schools provide common planning time for teams of teachers across the disciplines. During this time, teachers plan interdisciplinary units and arrange the logistics of how they will work together on technology projects. This model also empowers the team of teachers to modify the children's schedules as needed to support the learning objectives. Because all the members of a middle school teaching team serve the same students, the teachers are free to swap periods, put blocks of time together, and dedicate time—weeks or even a month—to a particular unit or project.

Elementary schools, too, have the flexibility to expand or contract the time they spend on given activities and to arrange groups of children in teams for project activities. This same flexibility is often unavailable at the traditional junior high school or high school, where organizational arrangements must be made to address two major barriers—teachers not having time to plan together or work together, and students' schedules not allowing for extended periods and time flexibility.

Recommendation

School administrators must develop structures for rewarding teamwork among teachers.

Space, Equipment, and Supplies

Once teachers have chosen design activities, they must have access to the space, materials, supplies, and equipment their students will need. Effective technology education does not require schools to have access to cutting-edge computers and software. On the contrary, most of the learning experiences for elementary students described in this book start with "low-tech" materials such as glue, toothpicks, fabric, sheet metal, rubber bands, mouse traps, and other common items. As schools introduce technology education, they must plan for having these materials on hand and for replenishing any that are consumable. Simple tools and equipment as well as common materials can be stored in a wheeled cart that can be moved from classroom to classroom. In doing research for their designs, students also need access to reference materials, including books, magazines, manuals, models, and computer software (Hill, 1994).

The use of simple equipment and common materials is particularly appropriate in the early grades. For example, all elementary school students should be able to use blocks, sand or water tables, cloth, string, paper, cardboard, wood shapes, paint, plastic, liquids, Play-Doh, tape, glue, crayons, pencils, brushes, safety scissors, plastic hand trowels, water wheels, plastic beaters, and toy cars, while upper elementary school students should also be able to use harder materials such as wood, metals, thicker plastics, wire, resins, and styrofoam (Hill, 1994).

At the secondary level, the choice of materials and resources becomes more complex. The availability of high-tech devices has made it easier to introduce technology activities into schools. Important and persistent problems emerge, however. The acquisition of technology-related resources should fit within and support the goals, objectives, and activities of the envisioned curricula. Historically, industrial arts and vocational education curricula were shaped more by the available tools and equipment than by curricular plans. In very few instances the established curricula, learning outcomes, or education standards have been used to set the specifications of equipment to be acquired by the schools. Educators have bought what they could get and often have had to make do with those acquisitions.

Implementing the design and technology approach, especially the analysis of products to meet the needs of the user, tends to create a dissatisfaction with buying only what is made available to schools. Educators must become more intimately engaged in specifying and even developing the tools and resources that are used for teaching and learning in technology education programs. Each item added must support and enhance meaningful and worthwhile student learning. Acquisitions that do not fulfill a significant support role to the curriculum should be avoided. Established standards and thoughtful planning will help educators identify materials, equipment, and computer simulation and modeling programs that allow approximations of real-world conditions, and to acquire those that are most appropriate. Similarly, these standards can help schools solicit donations of raw materials and equipment from community businesses and industry. This is a great way to inform and involve parents and community members in technology education.

Depending on the chosen activities and the equipment students are using, schools may need to provide alternative space for technology education classes. Technology education may not work in the traditional classroom. Desks are too small for many of the projects; long tables work better. Technology classes often need to make use of the auditorium or gym, hallways, or even the school grounds in milder climates to build and display large projects such as solar-powered cars, scale models of cities, or models of large animals such as dinosaurs or dragons. Some schools have created a design center within the school; some districts provide movable trailers that rotate among schools (Hill, 1994). The school community signals its support for technology and design activities by providing the necessary space and support for these activities.

Recommendation

Planning teams and participating teachers should make arrangements to procure necessary equipment and to review any district or school policies about use of equipment by students and staff.

Recommendation

As technologies in the workplace change, schools must update equipment. This is particularly important for students expecting to enter the workforce after high school. It may often be accomplished through the cooperation of local industry or scientific/technical institutions.

Preparing Teachers for Design and Technology Education

Throughout this discussion of the issues to be faced in the introduction of technology education, the question of teacher preparation and staff development has loomed prominently. We now turn to a consideration of this critical component of effective implementation of technology education. The diary presented in the next vignette records the experience of a new teacher introducing a design unit to middle school students; it illustrates well the challenges inherent in making good design and technology education happen in the classroom.

A New Teacher's Log: Wheels—a Design Unit

The following record was kept by Koyen Parikh for nine forty-minute periods devoted to teaching a technology unit to sixth graders at Shady Hill School, Cambridge, Massachusetts.

My Objectives

Process objectives:

- Inventing, tinkering, adjusting
- Meeting an open-ended challenge
- Making measurements
- Defining variables
- Creating good/fair tests
- Cooperative work
- Communication, presentation of ideas

Content objectives:

- Acceleration
- Friction
- Inertia
- Energy transfer

Personal objectives:

- To develop and implement a unit from *Problem Solving in School Science* (Johnsey, 1986), from idea to classroom activity: scope, sequence, applicability, place in year-long curriculum; homework, worksheets, discussions, assessment
- To consider the advantages and disadvantages that accompany every choice made in the process of planning a curriculum

Warmup activity: What I remember saying: We have started talking and thinking about motion. In the next few weeks we are going to continue that work by investigating wheels. You will eventually become part of a design team working on the design of a four-wheel vehicle. Today we'll start with a short independent project.

[I passed out directions and construction paper folders. Gave them time to write their names.]

I am going to ask you to start with a square of cardboard and trace this juice can lid on it. Then carefully cut the circle out. You now have the frame or base with which you will design. The task is to design something that will allow the cardboard wheel to travel straight down a slope without a push.

Discussion questions:

- Where are your ideas going to come from?
- What makes a design good?
- Are the designs likely to be the same?
- How can you tell if the design works?
- What should you do if the design doesn't work?
- How can you help someone who is designing something?

Notes: My objective for this short project was to familiarize students with the design process using a challenge that is not too difficult. I chose to have them work on this project independently, but emphasized that they could consult with anyone in the room for advice. In doing this, I wanted them to feel comfortable sharing their ideas, but I also told them that there were many solutions to the challenge and that I wanted to see the kind of creativity they, as a class, could generate. I found it important to state the parameters of the challenge very clearly. Some of my students, in the busy course of their design process, lost sight of the need to use a cardboard circle at all, and began using other materials. That left me with the question of either refocusing them so they met the challenge as I stated it, or allowing them to meet their own new challenge. It took me ten minutes to give these directions.

I did not use the worksheet described below. I have realized that sixth graders still need a tremendous amount of concentration to write. I ended class with a three-minute free write, using a large, clearly visible sand timer. This may have relieved anxiety in the room. They knew they didn't have to do any writing until the end, so perhaps they were freer to experiment and play. There will always be a few students who are so concerned about the written piece that they never even really use the materials. The timer casts a magic spell on the room. They wrote furiously, and I feel that the written information I got was just as helpful as an all-class worksheet would have been.

Day One: Introductions and One-Wheelers

Discussion (recalling warmup activity):   Talk about what it means to design something.

- How do you get an idea?
- What makes an idea good?
- Are all the designs likely to be the same?
- How can you tell if your design works?
- What can/should you do if your idea does not work?
- How can group work be helpful when you are designing something?

Challenge: Starting with a cardboard cutout, make something that will roll down a slope in a straight line without being pushed at the beginning. Additional challenges:

- Make another design that works.
- Design something that travels down the slope very slowly.
- Design something that follows a curve as it travels down the slope.

Worksheet: Requires students to

- Draw a picture of their first design
- List materials used
- Explain what happens to their design on the slope
- Describe any changes they made

Materials:

- Orange juice container lids (six-centimeter diameter circles to trace)
- Small squares of cereal box cardboard

Adhesives: white glue, glue gun, masking tape, plasticine, duct tape, string

Tools: hole punches, nails (different thicknesses), scissors, stapler, compasses

Other materials: pipe cleaners, bottle caps, lids of different sizes, spools, cylindrical objects (film containers), dowels, paper clips, thumb tacks, cardboard pieces, Styrofoam pieces, white paper (good for making patterns and finding center), craft sticks, toothpicks, straws

Ramps:

- One ramp for every two students, using wooden shelves (two and a half inches by six and a half inches) propped up about six to seven inches with test tube racks
- One longer ramp in classroom (about five inches)

Processing: Ask students to

- Talk about what makes wheels work and not work
- Explain why they think the wheels roll down the slope
- Check if it goes faster at the bottom of the slope

As I put the materials together, I asked myself several things. I wanted to ensure that I supplied enough materials to allow for several different successful solutions and to avoid leading them to any particular design. A note about respect for the materials (use everything you need, but nothing you don't need) may be helpful. Questions about what they were getting from this also entered my mind. Why can't I just stand up there and tell them that wheels travel faster at the bottom of a slope? That would take far less effort, and perhaps an equal percentage of them would "get it." I also wondered how many examples, if any, I should show them. I decided not to show them any of my successful or unsuccessful designs. (I had plenty of both.) This decision may depend on the kids' comfort level with open-ended challenges, but I feel that seeing one solution sometimes makes it hard to see things another way.

I did not set up any formal sharing session at the end. While I still feel that this would have been nice, it did happen informally, especially as children gathered around the longer slope to see if their designs met the second challenge.

Some students solved the problem quickly without any real thought or effort. To them I said, "Great, that does work. Now see if you can come up with something else." The students who knew how to do this and essentially made what I would have made, I gave them the curved line challenge. This can be done as long as the curve you give them is part of a circle. I drew it on a desk with a piece of chalk, and raised one end of the desk.

At the end of class, I wondered about sending their projects home with them. While I do not want them to become nuisances in other classrooms by being distracted by their products, I am also not sure how I feel about the idea of product. How important is that? How important should it be? I want kids to be invested enough in their designs so the end result matters to them, but I also do not want them to judge their work by that end product. What matters is the process, but the only reason you experience the process is because you are creating a product. I did not know what kind of "deal" to make of their designs. Right before they left, I let them know that they would be put into teams next time they come to class.

Day Two: Hypothesizing About Four-Wheeled Vehicles and Assembling Them

Create design teams: Students picked colors as they walked into the room, and sat at the matching-color table. Each design team thought of a name and wrote it on the wheels folders. I put these names on the board (five minutes).

Directions: I asked them to watch as I ran the vehicle across the floor three times. I told them they would fill in a chart recording seven adjustments they could make and predictions of the effects those changes would have.

Brainstorm in groups:

- What do you think is important for this vehicle to run?
- List seven things that you think will change the way it moves.
- What do you think will prevent the vehicle from running well?

Once they were finished with their charts, I gave them a bag with the materials for the original ruler racers along with directions to assemble them.

Initial check of the vehicle: Does it run in a straight line? Try it across the floor, on a carpet, and on a slope.
   Materials:

- Vehicles for each group: ruler, two bulldog clips, two dowels, eight pieces of rubber tubing that fits tightly on dowels, four small corrugated cardboard wheels. (These can be cut easily with a scalpel blade attached to a wooden block with a nail in it. The center holes can be enlarged with a fat nail.)
- Ramps: five six-inch shelves, test tube racks (mark start lines)

   Notes: I struggled with the sequence of this activity. Initially, I wanted to let them construct and play with the vehicles before making a list of predictions, but I worried that the class would become chaotic as children began unfocused experimenting. I had visions of "Hot Wheels" derbies inside my head. Although I still feel that some children would have had an easier time with the chart if they had actually held and used the vehicles, I do feel that overall the quality of work I got from them was better than it would have been if they had been writing and playing at the same time. I was pleased with their ideas on these charts; their hypotheses interested me.
   What I found to be most challenging during this activity was the group dynamics. Sixth graders consider this to be a very significant part of their work. In more than one class, I noticed that certain students were not made to feel welcome in the group they became a part of. I made announcements about how the ability to work with different people is part of becoming a successful person. I said that they might hear ideas that surprised them. I still have many questions about the best way for groups to be assembled. What should be considered when determining their size and makeup (gender, ability, enthusiasm, materials)? Although it may seem like a small matter, group formation can connect to your deepest philosophical beliefs about education by either enhancing or working against them.

Days Three and Four: Experimenting with Four-Wheeled Vehicles.

Experiments:

- Wheel size
- Axle length
- Wheel thickness
- Vehicle length
- Vehicle weight
- Three wheels versus four wheels
- Larger wheels in front, larger wheels in back
- Smooth slope versus carpeted slope versus rough slope

   Six to eight wheels were not tried.
   Materials: Initial vehicle kits, plus

- Wheel size: two additional sets of cardboard wheels of medium and large sizes
- Wheel thickness: two additional sets of cardboard wheels the same size
- Vehicle length: three sizes for body (I tried a ruler and a meter stick, but the meter stick is really too long. Wooden pieces would work better.)
- Vehicle weight: three plastic sandwich bags of rocks, small clip, spring scale
- Axle length: two additional sets of dowels of medium and long lengths

Idea for implementation: Have worksheet for each experiment (statement of purpose, materials, procedure, data table, questions to be answered). Have each group do one. Presentations to rest of class to share information learned.

Other ideas I had for this next step:

- Model the steps of one experiment from start to finish. Have them design another experiment on their own. Conference with a teacher to plan/execute experiment.
- Have each group do the same experiment.
- Have them design the fastest, farthest-traveling vehicles, then have them figure out how to tell which of their own designs is best.

What I remember saying: Last time you were here in science we looked at a vehicle I put together. I looked at all the notes you took about this vehicle and found the five most common adjustments you suggested. Here's what they were. [Wrote these on the board.]

Today we are going to be doing some testing to see what effect these adjustments actually have. I have put together kits that have three versions of what is being tested. So the wheel size kit has three sizes of wheels. The wheel thickness kit has three wheel thicknesses. What information would you collect if you were going to do a test? [Wrote their suggestions on the board.]

OK. I have a different worksheet for each test. These will help you as you go do your experimenting.

Notes: They definitely needed two forty-minute periods to do this work. They will talk about where to measure and where to time. I would rather have them talk about this than tell them exactly how to do it. I did tell them all to use the metric system and told them that the reason was because they then would find it easier to compare numbers with other groups. The topics that the group would study were determined by picking the title from a hat. I then gave them time to negotiate and trade. I don't think this is necessary. It didn't seem to matter much to them. I would love to think of a way that lets groups study what they most want to study without having huge discussions/arguments in class.

Ultimately, it's nice to have each group trade topics and study something else on the second day. Michael Horn [directing teacher] says that sixth graders tend to do more careful work on the second day of an activity because they know what they are doing and the activity feels more familiar. Also, he put together a great worksheet that helps them make bar graphs of the information they find. I finally put together a homework sheet that lets them graph an imaginary set of data and asks questions about fair tests.

If there had been a way for me to teach them how to put together a test and to make their own visual representation about their data, I would have preferred that. Some important thinking about doing tests and making conclusions was lost on them. I didn't think they were ready for such a big task, but think they may be able to do it next time a good test is called for.

Days Five and Six: Designing Your Own Vehicle

Challenge: To design a vehicle that travels either very far or very fast.

Materials: All of those listed for one-wheeler activity.

What I remember saying: Now you have completed some research on some of those things that affect the way these vehicles run. What I'd like to know from each of the researching groups is whether or not they think it makes a difference, and if it does, which helps the car travel farthest, which helps it travel fastest. [Filled in their responses on the board.]

You as a group now have a lot of decisions to make. You know what effect these had alone, but what happens when you combine them? Will the best wheel thickness arrangement enhance or ruin the effect of the best wheel size arrangement? I will give you ten minutes to discuss what you want your vehicle to look like. Write down your agreements on a white piece of paper. Each of you should sign this. Then you may begin working.

Notes: This is the portion of the activity that they showed the most enthusiasm for. The contract is essential. I was glad that they had to discuss what they wanted to do before beginning work. Otherwise, I'm afraid the most aggressive in the group would have taken charge and controlled what happened for the whole period. I found that the groups did a great deal of talking about their vehicles and the way they run.

What I found to be the most difficult about this part of the activity was the fact that the class was so nearly motivated by competition. It helps that only one vehicle can fit on a ramp at one time and that the ramps were scattered around the room. The potential for mean-spirited competition was there, and worried me.

I also wondered about the scientific piece of this activity. They needed a sufficient amount of time to work on their vehicles and to become invested in them. Until this happened they could not, nor would they want to, do any real testing. It's hard to know how much time to give them. What is enough to allow for real science to happen, but not so much that there's nothing to do but fool around?

Day Seven: Bumpers

Materials: foam, Styrofoam, rubber tubing, cotton balls, balloons, zip-closure bags, tape, egg cartons, pen caps.

Demonstration: Drop heavy object on several different materials (foam, paper construction, pillow, straight to floor, balloon, plasticine).
Discussion:

- Which crumple?
- Which are springy?
- What absorbs the impact best?
- How could we measure which is best at absorbing impact?

Assembly: Attaching passenger compartments. Introducing passengers.
Experimentation: Time to try different materials.
Challenge:

- Design something for your vehicle that will protect your passenger in an impact.
- Produce design drawing first.
- Then construct and test.

Additional challenges:

- Increase the speed upon impact by increasing slope.
- Limit materials in some way (only use white office paper).

Notes: This was the first time I didn't make everyone in the class work on the same challenge at the same time. Some groups had not finished designing their vehicle, so I told them to keep working for a while and let them know that it would be fine if they did not get to the bumper challenge.

Those who did try to make bumpers found the task very challenging. Only one group was able to make a successful bumper. I let them know that the task was difficult, and that I did not think that everyone would be able to design a successful one, when they became frustrated. Next time, I might try a passenger compartment that is deeper, or a different slope, but I do like giving students experiences with difficult tasks. As a teacher, you can learn a great deal about your students' attitudes and approaches to things that are difficult by watching them as they work. You can teach skills that enable people to deal with difficult tasks by talking to them and modeling what to do. I felt that they were experiencing enough success throughout this challenge for this piece not to be destructive.

Day Eight: Adding Elastic Power to Vehicles

Materials: rubber bands, dowels, Popsicle sticks, toothpicks, nails, saws, tape, thumb tacks.
Demonstration: Show how elastic twists and untwists.
Challenge: Attach an elastic band to your vehicle so it will travel across the floor

or up our ramps without a push (size of elastic, placement of elastic—front/back, size of wheels).

Discussion:

- Where does the energy come from?
- What are the energy changes from winding to vehicle rest?

What I remember saying: You are about to be given your last vehicle challenge. The challenge asks you to design a motor for your vehicle with a rubber band. Try to make something that will enable your vehicle to travel across the floor, or maybe even up a ramp. You will have to experiment with the size, placement, and number of rubber bands to try to design the most efficient motor. I want you to take advantage of the twisting motion of the elastic and not to design a slingshot model. Slingshots give your vehicle a push; that's not really a motor. One note about rubber bands: I was hit in the eye when I was in elementary school, and my eye was badly damaged. I don't want any of these to fly across the room. Be careful. I'll read the questions I want you to answer aloud, but will give you all some writing time at the end of class, so you do not have to answer them until then.

Notes: They loved this challenge. Many of them really had to do some experimenting before coming up with something that worked. They made important discoveries about anchoring one end, and winding the elastic backward if you want your vehicle to go forward. This was the first time I heard them talk about friction and grip. One group put rubber bands around their wheels for better traction. I did let them make small changes in their vehicles as needed to allow freer experimentation with rubber bands. It's important to have many different thicknesses and sizes.

Day Nine: Presentations and Evaluations

At Michael's suggestion I gave them questions to frame their presentations:

- What was your vehicle designed to do?
- What changes/improvements did you make and why?
- What ideas were discarded and why?

I like these suggestions because they give students a chance to tell you the story of how these vehicles came to be. It's impossible to tell by simply looking at them the kind of thinking that went on as these vehicles came together. When making these presentations, they could share what they wanted to do, what threads they were trying to pursue.

We timed the presentations with our three-minute timer, but many groups took longer, and the time limit was not strictly enforced. For this lesson we put the desks in a circle with a ramp in the middle. The evaluations were not very helpful. I'll need to work on ways of getting useful information about their experiences with the unit.

This teacher's aspirations closely match the vision of technology education described in this book; she is well prepared and teaches in a school that encourages her approach. Nevertheless, the course is not easy. Enacting the vision more broadly will require teachers, administrators, parents, and students to adopt a new view of teaching and learning. In classrooms organized around this view, children will actively encounter the problems of adapting, constructing, and manipulating materials to solve real problems in their worlds. They will develop their understanding of scientific concepts by engaging in problem solving and construction activities that challenge concepts and misconceptions they hold and reinforce learning of new concepts and beliefs. As modeled in the log, teachers will be actively engaged in the learning process alongside their students.

The next vignette demonstrates how continuous training support and assistance provided to teachers can enhance their efforts.

Project UPDATE

Gary Ball, a supervisor of technology education in Brandywine, found time to take on the development of an elementary school project, a task that fell outside his normal job duties. He was able to find two teachers interested in learning more about hands-on design and technology activities and approaches. The teachers were particularly interested in what these approaches might do for elementary classes that were almost always a full year behind grade level. The first year's development efforts were demanding, frustrating, exciting, and interesting. Limited to one day a week, the activities introduced into the classrooms had only a modest effect on student performance. The activities, scheduled for every Thursday, were exciting for students, and the classes were always well attended. On closer examination, attendance on Thursdays was found to be significantly increased, an interesting departure from the normal absenteeism found on other days.

In the second year, the teachers and supervisor joined Project UPDATE and participated in more formal training in preparing and implementing design and technology activities. Over the next two years the participating teachers gained new insights and skills in using the design and technology approach. Some interesting results emerged as the teachers used their new skills. Most notable was the success the teachers had in bringing their students back to grade level in reading and writing—a result accomplished solely by students participating in design and technology activities. These results have not gone unnoticed, and the efforts are to be expanded across the school in the coming year.

Whether teaching at the elementary or secondary level, teachers will need training and support as well as opportunities for planning and collaboration as shown by the above vignette. Several areas need to be addressed to develop and support teachers' abilities to successfully integrate technology and design into their teaching. Indeed, addressing these issues will have rewards for educational reform in general. Critical areas include:

- Teacher collaboration across grades and subject areas
- Teachers' understanding of science and technology concepts
- Effective classroom management and grouping techniques
- Use of tools and equipment in the classroom
- Providing teacher education

Teacher Collaboration

As described in earlier chapters and as demonstrated in several of the vignettes, technology education works best when teachers from different disciplines and/or specialties such as industrial arts and science work collaboratively. In the course of planning curriculum sequences and project work, teachers learn from each other and become reflective about their own practice.

Teacher teams should be formed not only across specialties but also across grade levels and the usual schooling level demarcations so that the curriculum can build on rather than ignore students' earlier experiences. Such working relationships support ongoing improvement of schools and implementation of innovation, but for the most part, they do not currently exist in schools. According to Susan Rosenholtz (1989), school organizations need to build structures for increasing collaboration and professional interaction among teachers and people outside the school. This is particularly true for technology education because it needs to draw upon several disciplines and a variety of perspectives. The following conditions in schools would support successful implementation of technology education:

1. Teachers from different disciplines and various grade levels working together to design the technology education program and curriculum
2. Teachers modeling and observing one another and providing feedback to each other
3. Open exchange of ideas, information, and materials among teachers and administrators
4. Teachers and administrators working collaboratively to introduce technology education

Teachers have busy days; they rarely have planning time. Moreover, there is little evidence that they connect even informally with their colleagues around education issues (National Center for Improving Science Education, 1991). At the secondary level, ownership by teachers of specific disciplines such as science or of advanced placement courses and the changing but still-low status of teachers of vocational education and technology presents a special challenge. New relationships are necessary between technology teachers and science teachers. They should have frequent meetings to share knowledge and plan integrated projects and activities (Todd, McCrory, and Todd, 1985; de Vries, 1991).

The burden on teachers involved in changing curriculum and teaching practice should not be underestimated. In England and Wales, teachers have become weary of what they perceive to be constant changes brought about by the introduction of the National Curriculum, including technology education. They complain of "overload" and lack of time for reflection and evaluation of practice, let alone for preparation for innovations. Where there has been success, it lies in "the depth of planning by the teachers concerned, so that they could cope with what they felt was the challenge of starting with a very keen, enthusiastic and often over-excited class, whilst being personally concerned about how to organize and control the whole initiative, and achieve worthwhile educational results" (Makiya and Rogers, 1992, p. 44). Having the authorized time to collaborate and plan is critical to teachers' success.

Recommendation

Schools must create opportunities for teachers to plan together and to pool expertise so that science teachers, general education elementary teachers, and technology or industrial arts teachers design and carry out technology education collectively.

Teachers' Understanding of Science and Technology Concepts

Getting started with technology education requires teachers to have a moderate level of comfort with the content and processes of technology education. To implement technology education effectively, teachers need technological skills and knowledge as well as scientific insight (de Vries, 1991). They must develop their understanding of the scientific concepts used in design (for example, electricity, energy, force and acceleration, measurement, and scale) and develop technology "literacy." Without these necessary prerequisites, there is a risk, particularly at the elementary level, that technology education could devolve into shallow "fun and games" activities that do not provoke deep learning.

Currently, teachers lack expertise and understanding in this area. In a study of teacher beliefs and views on science and technology topics, Uri Zoller and his colleagues (Zoller, Donn, Wild, and Beckett, 1991, p. 555) found that "the 'STS [science-technology-society] literacy' of teachers is questionable, particularly concerning the nature of science and technology, the difference between them, and their interrelationships. Special effort in the 'STS-literacy' domain should be made within both teacher training programs and student teaching."

Teachers must possess enough knowledge of the scientific concepts they are focusing on to challenge assumptions, create cognitive dissonance around misconceptions, and help students to process what they are learning so they can develop new conceptual understanding. The teacher's role is to provide physical experiences and encourage reflection.

If students are to adopt scientific ways of knowing, then intervention and negotiation with an authority, usually the teacher, is essential. The role of the authority figure has two important components. The first is to introduce new ideas or cultural tools where necessary and to provide the support and guidance for students to make sense of these for themselves. The other is to listen and diagnose the ways in which the instructional activities are being interpreted to inform further action. Teaching from this perspective is thus also a learning process for the teacher (Driver and others, 1994, p. 11).

As facilitators of learning, teachers must have the vision and knowledge to steer children, ask questions, and challenge thinking. They must learn to make good choices about what to focus on, about how many concepts their students can deal with simultaneously, and about what materials to use. The range of knowledge and skills needed by effective teachers of design and technology is well illustrated by the earlier vignette of Koyen Parikh's nine-day log of her "wheels" unit.

Eleanor Duckworth (1987, pp. 96–97) provides examples of the kinds of questions that are helpful: "What do you mean? How did you do that? Why do you say that? How does that fit in with what she just said? Could you give me an example? How did you figure that?" To develop this style of teaching and level of expertise, teachers need high quality preservice and in-service training coupled with ongoing, sustained support in the form of classroom visits, demonstrations, and coaching. They need ample opportunities to dialogue with others, in person or electronically, about what they are doing, problems they are facing, and breakthroughs they have had.

Technology education poses special challenges. Connecting, articulating, or integrating different school subjects is no mean task. In addition to this, design-based courses demand that teachers contextualize learning. There are a number of ways to do this, but all of them require skills in moving students from "tactile" craft activities to "conceptual" or knowledge-based activities, as well as skills in connecting the two. The range of content, concepts, and skills that can be built into a technology curriculum—and that teachers therefore will need to command—is illustrated in the following curriculum plan.

Topic, Grades Six to Eight: Houses and Homes in the Community

This curriculum sequence was planned by a group of middle school teachers whose school serves an inner-city population. Bob, who teaches the seventh-grade class, has worked with his colleagues in developing the program. Bob's school principal and colleagues are enthusiastic and are supported by the school district. The superintendent has worked hard to provide funds for staff in-service education and some financial backing for materials. The school board is prepared to continue backing the program as long as its progress is documented and the curriculum materials that have been developed are made available to support other local schools.

The school principal has a compatible team, but knows that success is largely dependent upon a consistency of approach; in her view, children must experience schemes of work that build on prior knowledge and experience. She insists on monitored progression and a reliable means of recording, reporting, assessment, and evaluation. For this reason the school staff meet regularly to provide each other with updated information, to discuss the pupils' progress, and to view samples of student portfolios, a recently introduced means of monitoring student progress and development.

The school has adopted an integrated approach focused on the curriculum areas of science, mathematics, and technology. The staff are committed to this type of curriculum organization, believing it to be the most reliable way in which they can deliver subject content that is rigorous and of great interest to their students and relevant to their future lives. Use of language is enhanced, particularly that based on critical observation, analysis, description, and the development of a technical vocabulary.

All topics are broadly planned by the whole team so that continuity is ensured from grades six through eight. The selected topic has been constructed to develop an understanding of built structures, mechanisms, domestic service systems, and environmental issues and concerns. The staff from the high school to which most of the students will go have been invited to key meetings to provide cross-school liaison. The hope is that similar integrated projects will be continued in the high school.

The group of teachers has identified the following learning objectives for the grade six to eight curriculum sequence:

Knowledge

Materials: Properties of materials over a wide range; appropriateness of materials—based on their properties—to match form and function; value of materials and the need to be economical in their use; need to treat some materials to protect them from corrosion, contamination, decay; need to conserve materials.

Energy: Range of energy sources; the limited resource of fossil fuels; need to conserve energy and to develop energy sources that cannot run out: wind, waves, water current, solar.

Control: Different ways in which control can be operated; comparing one method against another as to suitability.

Measurement: Linear, area, volume, weight, cubic, and fluid measurement; patterns; tolerances.

Communications

Understand and communicate: Oral, written, drawn, CAD, symbols, colors, sound, electronic; role-play a professional designer, inventor, chef, fashion designer; discuss with others the merits and shortcomings of products, systems, layouts; program simple commands.

Practical Skills

Building and assembly: Make structures using a wide range of materials; make models that can move on land, on water, and through air; design and work to scale and proportion; make working drawings to use in manufacture; design and make items using textiles; design and make jigs for assembly.

Cutting, bending, forming, joining: Use a wide range of tools safely; cut, bend, form, shape, mix, and blend to specified requirements and dimensions; select and choose the most appropriate tool to suit material and purpose; choose the most appropriate means of joining and fixing; join and fix hard, soft, sheet, and fiber materials.

Development Objectives

1. To help students acquire confidence in group discussion, become reflective in their thinking, and be able to question their own thinking through interaction.
2. To develop self-assessment through reflective writing and evaluative discussion. To care for their individual student portfolio and learn how to develop a project portfolio.
3. To understand local industry, how it functions, its organization and management structures.
4. To be aware of the need to consider environmental health and safety factors at all times—site clothing, appropriate materials, safety helmets, safety shoes, protective clothing, all-weather clothing.

Bob's classes have had experience with a topic approach to learning, the last topic having been "space." This project involved investigations into stored energy sources and practical tasks that involved experimenting with elastic, balloons, and springs. They have also studied simple human biology and created imaginary biological systems for creatures from other planets. A project on food required students to "invent" space food: it had to be nourishing, tasty, and of a consistency that would allow it to be eaten from a dispenser that the students themselves had designed and made.

In mathematics, they have studied comparative distances between planets and have made hanging models of the sun and solar system to scale: the sun hung in the entrance to the school; the planet Pluto was half a mile away on the playing field. They have also been engaged in tasks on cubic capacity, layout, and scale measurement. Their topic on houses and homes was designed to build on these experiences and to extend skills, concepts, and capability across the curriculum.

The students have already learned that some form of energy is needed for movement to take place, having experienced energy through the movement of their own bodies and with inflated balloons, batteries, springs, and elastic. They now need to experiment with other simple and readily available energy sources, including gravity, wind, and electricity.

During the year, they will be involved in problem-solving activities that will explore energy, mechanisms, and movement. These activities will include hydraulic systems using syringes, tubes, and valves; electric circuits using switches, bulbs, buzzers, motors, and resistors; levers and linkages; pulleys; and basic gearing using components and kits. Tasks will be implemented through activities that will include scientific and mathematics investigation, applying learned knowledge through "design and make" tasks.

In their planning, the teachers are also covering the concepts of communication and information, in word, symbol, and electronic signal. The intent is to provide students with projects that will allow them to explore visual, verbal, and electronic ways in which instructions, commands, and basic information are delivered. Another concept to be included—control—is generally difficult for students in the age range of sixth to eighth graders. For the lower grades, the teachers are including various experiences with operating mechanisms, switches, systems, and valves; later, the students will learn to program a computer that can provide a sequence of control instructions. As with other concepts, Bob is building on previous experiences and will ensure that the students will learn to operate lifting mechanisms through pulleys and gears, learn about thermostatic control, and begin to understand the control of services to homes.

Planning for High School

As a result of these learning experiences and activities, students in grades six to eight should have acquired a sound content foundation and a well-developed process of inquiry. They should be capable of working cooperatively with others, as well as working to a design brief as an individual. The planning group envisages that the students' individual portfolios will contain mounted sheets of designs covering a full range of design and technology projects. Hence, students should be capable of developing a project portfolio that can act as a guide to themselves and to those involved in the direction and development of ideas and the evaluation of outcomes. A well-structured program of study throughout their time at elementary and middle school will have provided students with a broad knowledge of most types of materials and applications.

In high school, students should be able to consider the services necessary to support a family home—telephone, fax machine, television, electricity, water, waste disposal, sewage, and so on. They might go on to study how a community is organized and constructed. They should be able to map the needs within a largely self-supporting community, including human resources (qualification and expertise) and the range of shops and services needed: gas stations, banks, real estate agents, hospitals, doctors, dentists, and so forth.

A specific service in support of local industry or commerce possibly should be studied and an aspect isolated with the intention of solving a "real" problem through a design and technology task, such as in the following example:

The U.S. Mail Service

What are the specifications needed for a specialized building? What sort of storage, loading, security fencing, parking facilities does it need? What public space is necessary? How many offices? What services?

It would be desirable for this study to be carried out as an education/industry cooperative venture, with students engaged in the real needs of industry. For example, students should be able to make appointments to meet the staffs of local businesses, as well as to meet post office staff to discuss problems with U.S. mail services and to identify areas of profitable study. Students' progress could be monitored by managers and workers. The quality and direction of individual and group portfolios could be discussed with members of the postal service management structure.

A wide range of studies would be possible from this broad opportunity, including individual and group study of mail distribution. Projects could range from postage stamp design, uniform design, corporate identity through logos and letterheads, transportation, sorting, and problems of delivery. Outcomes could involve electronic mail links, and processes developed through computer-aided design.

The planning group set the following broad outcomes for their high school students: given consistent opportunity to work investigatively, students should become independent and self-motivated. At this stage of their schooling, they should be capable of making decisions regarding their personal and group study. They should also be able to set criteria by which the success of a project can be assessed. Most importantly, students should be able to identify real design and technology needs through inquiry and investigation and to sustain a design and technology project from an idea to achieving an acceptable outcome.

This vignette illustrates the in-depth understanding of science, technology, and local resources, and the development of their students' abilities that teachers need in order to design an effective integrated curriculum based on technology concepts and projects. Teachers must have resources available that will help them develop the needed knowledge and skills.

Recommendation

Universities and teacher preparation institutions should develop and support programs for preparing prospective technology education teachers that reflect the vision and goals presented in this book.

Recommendation

Staff developers should work with teachers to construct curriculum from frameworks rather than from prepackaged curricula.

Recommendation

School districts must have in place systems of continuing in-service education to facilitate ongoing revision of technology education, because the subject matter content will demand frequent revision as new technologies are developed and introduced.

Effective Classroom Management and Grouping Techniques

Social interaction is a critical element in the learning process. Students must be given the opportunity to communicate their ideas, to suggest approaches and solutions, and to use data and persuasive argument to convince their classmates about some aspect of their learning. Teachers should build in opportunities for student groups to present their work to their classmates throughout the process, including when they have had a spontaneous breakthrough.

Technology education provides a natural opportunity for students to generate and articulate questions and communicate hypotheses; identify problems and design solutions; and generate ideas for building, testing, and improving prototypes and products. The process requires that students learn to communicate and work in teams effectively. For example, situations in which one or two students dominate the hands-on activities should not be tolerated. Using small groups of two or three students helps to avoid this problem. In successful groups, students assign responsibility, ensure equal access by all participants, listen and consider all students' input, and use direct and honest talk. Allowing children to group with friends can enhance the process. Students tend to form same-sex groups, which eliminates the gender problem associated with boys dominating the construction activities; teachers may use this technique as an affirmative step to encourage girls' access and full participation. Teachers must establish clear expectations for group work and communication. Use of cooperative working groups provides a foundation for effective teamwork. Students at all grade levels must learn to communicate effectively and give feedback to one another.

The importance of managing the learning process without dominating the students is shown in the following vignette, which provides a brief description of the work of Robert McCormick and his colleagues (McCormick, Hennessy, and Murphy, 1993). Their work suggests that teaching intellectual content while also engaging students in design tasks is not easy.

Kites

Studies that examine what students and teachers do on a moment-by-moment basis are expensive and time consuming to conduct, so it is not surprising that such studies are rare. A notable exception is the work of Robert McCormick and his co-workers, who asked whether students actually learn generic problem-solving skills in design and technology classrooms in British secondary schools. This research documents the difficulty of situating conceptual learning in contexts in which students are designing specific products.

In one case study, the students are engaged in building kites. Their own preoccupation is with whether the kite they are building will fly, and whether they have the right kind of paper, glue, scissors, string, and so on. Because the teacher needs to sustain order in the classroom, the pressing concerns of the students (who are focused on actually making the kites) tend to define what the teacher actually does. From the teacher's point of view, however, the point of the lesson is to help the students understand the physics of airfoils, and to develop general problem-solving abilities. McCormick's detailed observations of what ensues show, in a quite poignant way, how the teacher's best efforts are thwarted. For example, when the teacher intervenes to explain some theoretical point or to discuss general problem-solving strategies, the students experience this as an unnecessary interruption to their own productive activity (kite making). The result, according to McCormick, is that students pay superficial attention to systematic problem-solving procedures prescribed by the teachers, while simultaneously adhering to their own product-oriented agendas.

The research of McCormick and colleagues indicates that, even with the requisite content knowledge, teachers may not be able to achieve their instructional goals unless they are also highly skilled in classroom management.

Use of Tools and Equipment

Successful design and technology education as envisaged in the curricular sequence on houses and homes requires that the teachers and the students be familiar with the use of tools and materials in the classroom. Rules must be established for safe use of tools such as saws, soldering or glue guns, and so on (Makiya and Rogers, 1992). Teachers must model the proper use of such tools and guide students to take necessary care in their use. Since many teachers, particularly some female teachers, will not have had experience using tools and building objects, they must take care not to send stereotyped messages about who should use tools—for example, let the boys do the sawing and hammering and the girls do the painting and gluing. Rules should address both safety and access.

Prior to initiating technology activities in the classroom, the teachers should review all the tools, equipment, and materials they will need to ensure that they know how to use all of them in a safe and effective way.

Recommendation

Teachers must be provided with in-service experiences conducted by qualified professionals in technology education to help them learn how to use the various tools they will need and the standard procedures for ensuring safety in the classroom, while at the same time learning key concepts to be shared with their students.

Providing Teacher Education

Throughout this discussion we have implicitly suggested that much of the needed teacher development and education will best proceed through teachers working together toward a common goal. Dennis Sparks and Susan Loucks-Horsley (1989) have identified a number of conditions necessary to support staff development in schools. Among them are (1) schools whose norms support collegiality and experimentation, (2) administrators who work with staff to clarify goals and expectations, and (3) commitment by school authorities to support teachers to change their practice. Leaders who continually shift priorities, deny teachers the time and resources needed to support change, or believe that one-shot in-service is adequate for staff development undermine positive change.

Beyond teachers educating each other, who can provide the staff development? There is no ready answer to this question. The developers of the materials science course at the Pacific Northwest Laboratory described in Chapter Four (see the vignette "Materials Science and Technology"; see also Hayes, 1993; Pacific Northwest Laboratory, 1994) offer institutes to school teams of teachers and administrators who wish to implement the course. This is an example of the necessary staff development provided by a resource deeply grounded in the subject matter content as well as in the technology approach to education. Several of the suppliers of educational equipment and supplies for technology education offer teacher workshops to help educators get started with design technology (for example, LEGO Systems (Connecticut), Links (Maine), Plastruct (California), Unilab (Ohio), and Technology Teaching Systems (Massachusetts). Museums and teacher centers also are good places to contact for teacher training information (for example, the Exploratorium in San Francisco, the Carnegie Science Center in Pittsburgh, and Teachers Workshop in Brattelboro, Vermont). Technology practitioners, including university scientists and engineers, can be valuable resources in staff development.

We noted earlier that institutions of higher education are not particularly hospitable to technology education. Unless institutions of higher education can be persuaded to give greater status to the "practical" and to employ faculty with the relevant knowledge and experience, they may not be very appropriate for education generally, or teacher education specifically. An interesting alternative is emerging at Trenton State College, where technology education is seen as an important part of the college curriculum. All students are required to take a course in society, ethics, and technology, which is team-taught by colleagues in science, philosophy, engineering, psychology, and a range of other subjects, including technology education.

The problem is particularly acute for preservice education, as alternatives for training are generally more available for teachers who are already teaching. New teachers, especially those at the elementary school level, will have had little if any opportunity to take courses in technology education of the type and content necessary to implement in their classrooms the sorts of curricula described in this book. Also at Trenton State College, a unique option is being instituted that will allow preservice elementary school teachers to study technology education as a "major" in technological studies. These options have emerged from processes and strategies very similar to those described by Raizen and Michelsohn (1994) in their book on science education for prospective elementary school teachers. These authors make a number of appropriate recommendations.

Recommendation

"University leaders should facilitate a university-wide emphasis on the improvement of teaching practice in their institution by creating university-wide opportunities for faculty to discuss and improve their practice" (p. 139). The different faculties involved in the education of technology teachers should agree, together with experienced school teachers, on a set of learning principles and activities that will enable the prospective teachers to develop the competencies and behaviors necessary for effective technology teaching.

Recommendation

"Science, engineering, mathematics, education, and other university faculty involved in design and technology-related disciplines must work together with classroom teachers of technology to develop a consensus vision of what prospective teachers in the field need to know and be able to do." After developing the vision, these groups must collaborate on the planning, organization and implementation of the technology and technology education component of preservice teacher education programs.

It will be difficult to prepare technology teachers to teach technology well, no matter the level, "without having them practice with excellent clinical teachers and classrooms. Yet forging meaningful partnerships with schools can be challenging for colleges and universities. Teachers already are overly busy, and only a few see preparing future teachers as an important part of their job. Often, student teachers are accepted because they will lend an extra 'pair of hands' in the classroom. Or worse, the principal assigns student teachers to teachers who are so weak that they need the assistance of a student teacher. Such experiences are hardly likely to produce excellent teachers. . . . Neglect of the final—and critically important— stage of teacher preparation is a major problem" (pp. 143–144).

Recommendation

School districts interested in implementing technology education "should develop at least one professional development school in which design and technology are valued and in which technology teaching is exemplary, to serve as a clinical setting for teacher education programs in technology" (p. 144).

Gender Issues in Technology

Girls need to see the connection between technology education and their future. The labor force projections show that by the year 2000 almost 90 percent of new entrants into the workforce will be women and minorities (American Association of University Women, 1992). Minority and immigrant girls will become almost 30 percent of the new workers in the workforce between now and the year 2000. They will be entering a workplace that is increasingly technological, requiring them to have different experiences and skills than the workers who came before them. Neither of these realities, nor the relevance and importance of a strong base in technology, has been made apparent to school-age girls (American Association of University Women, 1992). Those working to rectify the present inequities must be aware of several issues, including the current status of females in science and technology education; teachers, teaching, and courses; and the role of language and other classroom interactions.

Current Status

Comparisons of performance of male and female students since the mid sixties in mathematics, the physical sciences, and civil engineering have led to much debate and contention. Despite efforts to promote parity of achievement and participation, there is still an unacceptable differential between the sexes. A recent analysis of data from the 1990 National Assessment of Educational Progress found that at age nine, girls and boys tended to have similar proficiencies in the sciences, but that boys had acquired greater proficiencies by age thirteen, with the gap widening even more by age seventeen (Bruschi and Anderson, 1994). At least with respect to the achievement gap at the secondary level, there still is unequal enrollment in high school science classes, particularly in physics. Ensuring equal participation among females and males is a critical issue that must be addressed as technology education is introduced and expanded in U.S. schools.

Technology education is closely connected with two curriculum areas that are primarily viewed as "male domains"—science (particularly physics) and industrial arts education. It is therefore likely to face the same challenges of gender equity that these fields encounter, unless active efforts are taken to understand and address the barriers to girls' participation and success. This section discusses the issues that are apt to contribute to attitude, expectation, and achievement differences between boys and girls in technology education and offers some ideas for reducing the deleterious effects of gender bias in this area.

Attitude and perceptions affect the rate at which girls select and actively participate in technology education. Indeed, "attitudes towards technology and design are established at a very early age" (Granstam, 1988, p. 47). In preschool, boys build things, play with blocks, and create moving objects like race cars and trains out of cartons and other materials. They dominate in the use of computers. Conversely, girls in preschool choose to engage in social play, for example, drama and dress up. These early experiences have their effect. "By the age of ten the difference in attitudes of girls and boys toward technical and science subjects is already substantial, largely due to their earlier exposure and experiences" (Granstam, 1988, p. 47). Technology education in the preschool and early elementary classrooms may actually help to equalize boys' and girls' experiences, as long as teachers create the conditions and expectations for all students to participate.

Presently, schools are not as successful as they should be in interesting girls in science and technology. A number of studies indicate that boys and girls approach and perceive technology in very different ways. The findings of Richard Kimbell (1992), who has studied technology education in England and Wales, support the view that females work through to solutions in a more intuitive and process-related way than their male counterparts. Boys tend to approach problem-solving activities more from a perspective of rules and logic. They view technology as "extensions of their power over the physical universe." Girls tend to see technological devices as "people connectors" and instruments that solve real-life problems (Honey and others, 1991, p. 2). According to researchers at the Center for Children and Technology (Honey and others, 1994), the equity problem in technology education is that "the masculine technological world view . . . is increasingly accepted as the only legitimate model for discussing, developing, and evaluating technology" (Honey and others, 1994, p. 1).

Kimbell (1992) found that females outperformed males when working within a contextual framework. Similar results have been experienced in females' performance on tests in other subjects, notably science and mathematics, when a contextual framework was used (de Lange, 1987). Technology education by its very nature affords the opportunity for teachers to create contextualized learning experiences for girls as well as for boys. Through technology education, students develop their understanding of concepts as they apply them to real projects and problems, thereby contextualizing and helping students to "make meaning" from their experiences. Educators are challenged to use technology in ways that empower boys and girls. One example is a new design program by the Center for Children and Technology called Imagine, a computer graphics program that enables girls to create machines from their own imaginative vantage points (Honey and others, 1994). Use of materials such as these may help educators to take affirmative steps to equalize participation by boys and girls.

Recommendation

Technology education must engage girls equally as much as boys. Teachers should make active efforts to review and select projects, tools, and activities designed to appeal to girls.

Recommendation

School districts and teachers must take active steps to ensure that technology education is equally accessible to all students, particularly girls and minorities, who are often underrepresented in this area.

Teachers, Teaching, and Courses

Gender bias is a concern not only for students in technology education, but also for their teachers. The majority of teachers in elementary schools, who are expected to deliver a broad and balanced curriculum, are women—approximately 85 percent for students seven to eleven years old, and 97 percent for students five to seven years old. Women make up almost 100 percent of preschool and kindergarten teachers.

Only a small proportion of elementary teachers are comfortable with or have qualifications in the areas of physical science or design and technology. Since the typical scientific/technical curriculum reflects male-dominated activities, many women teachers tend initially to be turned off to technology education. Experience with teacher training workshops in design and technology that have been developed especially for the elementary school level has shown that at least 30 percent of elementary teachers are quite technically talented. Once introduced to technology education, these teachers perform well in designing and carrying out activities. If supported with additional training resources, they are able to use design and technology as an approach in their classrooms. Without such training and support, they tend to find the content and the vocabulary that are associated with these curriculum areas alien, and they therefore lack the confidence or incentive to initiate and integrate these curricula into their instructional repertoire. The teachers' discomfort is picked up by the children—reinforcing their perceptions that technology education is not for women and girls. This idea may be inadvertently reinforced by bringing in males (for example, industrial arts teachers or physics teachers) when it is time for technology education.

Conversely, most technology education teachers (formerly industrial arts teachers) at the middle and high school levels are male. They are not accustomed to adapting their materials and instructional practices to include both boys and girls in a meaningful way. They tend to emphasize the technologies linked to males—machines, computers, control, construction, exploration, and warfare—excluding or downplaying those technologies more traditionally associated with women (Layton, 1993). Historically, women have been more involved in so-called life-sustaining and life-enhancing technologies related to foods, textiles, decoration, child rearing, and domesticity. Technology education teachers need guidance and support to integrate their technology activities so that there is a balance between technologies associated with females and those associated with males, while ensuring that stereotyped activities (for example, girls focusing only on design solutions to problems associated with homemaking while boys focus on vehicles) are avoided.

As explained in Chapter One, the study of technology in high schools has often been connected with occupational training—what we called the "technology for employment" approach. Because it is so closely connected with specific male-dom-inated occupations, much of traditional vocational and technical education has often been seen as inappropriate for girls. The assumption has been that, unless a girl wants to become a plumber or an electrician or an air-conditioning technician, she does not need to know about working with metal, about electricity, or about the dynamics of fluid systems.

Technology education for all, as we have emphasized in this book, is very dif-ferent from traditional vocational and technical education. Technology education focuses on problem solving and design; it seeks to develop a generic understand-ing of the nature of materials and systems, while traditional vocational education emphasizes a routine approach to developing psychomotor skills and standard op-erating procedures for work. Courses that concentrate on occupational prepara-tion for the "male" trades contain an inherent gender bias, but if instruction focuses on the nature of materials and systems in their generic form, technology education courses lose much of the gender bias associated with the male trades.

In Victoria, Australia, the amalgamation of the technical schools with the high schools during the mid 1980s meant that the "old-style" vocational courses in metalwork, plumbing, carpentry, and electrical devices were abolished. The new technology education programs that replaced those courses were deliberately designed to be gender fair. To achieve this, it was important that the occupation-ally specific orientation of the old courses be avoided completely. How this was accomplished is illustrated in the following vignette.

Beyond Occupational Specificity and Gender Bias

In the mid 1980s, education authorities in the state of Victoria, Australia, launched a series of reforms aimed at bringing all postcompulsory schooling under a single man-dated system of accredited courses aimed at providing an inclusive education for all students (see the description of the Victorian Technology Studies Curriculum Frame-works in Chapter Four). The new program places more emphasis on project work, problem solving, and collaborative learning than did the subjects that made up the old grade twelve program. The new courses and systems of assessment were intended to redress problems of access and success among all groups in the community. A high priority was placed on improving access for girls to subjects traditionally regarded as boys' subjects, such as mathematics, physical sciences, and technology studies.

From the early 1900s (when technical education was first established in Victoria) to the 1980s, children had been required to choose between an academic or a tech-nical/vocational school at about age twelve. This changed between 1982 and 1987, when the divide between Victoria's 110 secondary technical schools and the 210 high schools was officially abolished, and an inclusive set of "secondary colleges" was created in their place. In some cases, neighboring technical and high schools amalgamated to form a single (sometimes multicampus) college. In other cases, individual schools simply broadened their curriculum offerings to meet the requirements of the inclusive college model.

Before the amalgamation, the high schools had provided six years of general and academic programs, from age twelve to eighteen, while the technical schools had provided five or six years of occupationally specific training. Originally, "techs" had been designed almost exclusively for boys; they led either to apprenticeship positions or to direct employment in the traditional crafts and trades. There were a few domestic arts schools (mainly for the girls). The times were changing during the 1980s, with more girls enrolling in traditionally male classes, but overall, the techs were still for boys.

A key goal for the reformers who masterminded the amalgamation was to create a series of new technology education programs that would not separate boys from girls on the basis of their presumed future destinations in the labor market. They forged a radical reorganization of the curriculum, so that the broad subject area of technology studies was divided into three accredited courses:

Materials and Technology: a study of materials through production, testing, and investigation

Technological Design and Development: a study of design, realization and the evaluation of products

Systems and Technology: a study of automotive, electrical, mechanical, and integrated systems

Each course includes four semesterlong units that are generally taken in grades eleven and twelve. All the units are built around activities that require students to design, make, and evaluate real artifacts or systems. After releasing the accredited study designs, the Victorian Curriculum and Assessment Board (1991) produced a set of curriculum development support materials that helped teachers to transform their courses and practice to meet the new framework guidelines. The support materials helped teachers to develop their own programs and led them to understand that a very wide range of activities were open to them, all of which might be consistent with the framework requirements.

The materials and processes selected for a given unit can reflect the needs and interests of a particular school population. For example, the recognized materials for the materials and technology course are fibers, yarns, and fabrics; food; metals; plastics; wood; and industrial ceramics.

The inclusion of textiles and hospitality-related studies under the heading of technology represented a significant step toward making technology education more accessible to girls. Although it was theoretically possible to continue teaching cooking and metalwork in a gender-stereotyped fashion, in most schools teachers from these different subject-matter areas were brought together, in many cases for the first time.

They were required to work together in joint sessions to design what the school would offer. They were also required to show how the courses they developed would be consistent with the frameworks for each of the technology education courses.

Not only did food and textiles come to be considered as "materials" alongside metal, wood, and plastic, but students learning in the metal and wood shops were required to devote time to matters such as ergonomic analysis, environmental impact evaluation, marketing, and communication. This had the effect of both broadening the outlook of the boys taking the course and attracting girls to traditionally male-dominated areas of study.

Language and Other Classroom Interactions

A balance in the content of courses and classroom activities alone, however, will not ensure equal participation of boys and girls. Teachers need to be aware of how their use of certain vocabulary may inadvertently discourage girls' participation in technology education. Peter Sellwood (1990) found that there was a parallel between the acquisition of positive or negative attitudes toward science and technology and the language and vocabulary employed by teachers when setting tasks and in general classroom discussion.

Some words—for example, lever, structure, pulley, motor, or vehicle—were seen by girls to be masculine. Consequently, girls shied away from any activities that were introduced to them using this type of language. Alternatively, the project found that no gender association existed when an activity was developed to the point where both male and female students were confident in their understanding of the concept introduced. This was the appropriate time to recognize and develop the vocabulary. The vocabulary confirmed the concept and provided a security of knowledge.

In addition, it was found that both male and female students were confused by words in the initiation of a task and that simple language was best. The following example of task setting illustrates this aspect: "Can you make a mechanism that will . . . ?" Girls tended to view the word "mechanism" as being masculine and were put off by the activity, no matter how exciting it might have seemed from the teacher's point of view.

"Can you make a vehicle that will . . . ?" This type of question limited the scope for the male students, but not necessarily for the females. The male students understood the word "vehicle" to mean an automobile or truck, which entails fitting wheels and axles; the females were more likely to understand it to be something that will travel from A to B using the most convenient form of mobility. Such different solutions frequently led to disputes between the sexes. The boys considered any solution not fitted with wheels as cheating, even if it met the objective of the task. In fact, the least confusing way of setting an open-ended task for students was to ask them: "Can you make something that will . . . ?"

Through language and other interactions, classrooms are filled with biased messages about who should participate in what activities, as well as about who should succeed. David and Myra Sadker (1994) conducted extensive studies of the number and types of interactions teachers have with boys and girls. Their findings point to a major problem in classrooms spanning preschool through the university. Teachers interact with males and females in inequitable ways. Boys receive more teacher contact—they are called on, talked to, touched, and praised more than girls. "When teachers evaluate a specific student's performance, the student receiving the comment is most likely to be male" (American Association of University Women, 1992, p. 69). Dale Baker (1986) found similar bias in science and mathematics classes in which teachers provided boys with "more precise" feedback and instruction than they provided for females in terms of both scholarship and conduct.

Interactions between girls and boys also affect the climate for learning in the classroom. Boys are often forceful and aggressive and tend to take over in group work; girls, conversely, are often rewarded for passivity and cooperation, and as mentioned earlier, many learn best in social and contextual settings. Teachers should be sensitive to student interaction and counteract any negative behaviors. Role models can be a powerful influence on girls' participation in areas nontraditional to their gender. Teachers who publicly model their enjoyment of technology and learning send a strong message to their students about what they can do.

In the planning for and implementation of technology education at all levels, it is essential that educators consider the equity issues addressed here, and consider how best to increase girls' interest in technology, design, and inquiry, as well as help teachers develop strategies for promoting gender equity in their technology education classrooms.

Recommendation

Student interactions must be managed to ensure equal participation and opportunity to learn; groups should be balanced and clear rules of participation should be established; and criteria for tasks should be clear to ensure understanding by all. Stereotypes about what boys and girls can do must be discussed and challenged; children need to see the effects of stereotyping on what they learn and on their later options in life.

Recommendation

Teachers should seek to show a variety of men and women engaged in technology and design activities in various ways by bringing visitors to the classroom for demonstrations, through visits to local industry to see design in action, and through appropriate stories featured in the media.

Assessment of Student Achievement

As with any curricular reform in education, change in teaching and learning must be accompanied by change in assessment. Indeed, implementing good technology education can assist in the development of appropriate assessment for other reforms. Three issues in assessment stand out when considering technology education:

1. Classroom assessment by teachers
2. Criteria for assessing student performance
3. Externally mandated assessments

Classroom Assessment by Teachers

Technology education teachers must develop a new view of student assessment. As teachers and students engage in technology education, they will need to rethink how to assess and measure changes in student knowledge and development. Teachers will need to monitor and record student activity and learning on a day-to-day basis. Wynn Harlen (1983) points out that good assessment is about what happens in classrooms each day.

Teachers need to develop new habits around assessment, especially when they gather data about student learning: as teacher and students discuss an investigation the students are working on; when teachers ask open-ended questions that enable students to give their points of view; while teachers listen to what children have to say to each other; as teachers observe how children do their work; and as teachers and students review the finished products diagnostically. A range of methods for gathering this information should be used. To gain access to children's ideas, continuous assessment by teachers has to become more conscious and deliberate. Of primary importance in using this sort of embedded assessment approach is the need for teachers to practice engaging students in active inquiry, to practice observing and questioning students, and to practice reflecting upon and documenting the results of everyday technology work.

The difficulty in doing continuous assessment must not be underestimated. For example, one must collect data without interfering with the teaching/learning dynamic and one must act as a recorder of assessment information at the same time as facilitating activities and monitoring behavior. Most importantly, teachers must define the practices, the criteria, and the standards used to assess quality. Also significant is the need for teachers, students, and parents to have a shared view of these criteria and to agree on a language in which to communicate about them. While assessing student learning in the context of teaching seems natural, it is clearly a difficult challenge well beyond simply administering a test or marking a checklist.

Recommendation

Teachers should use authentic and, where possible, embedded assessments to accompany curriculum.

Recommendation

Curriculum developers must include appropriate assessment tasks in the materials and activities they create and disseminate. Schools and districts considering the use of curriculum materials should downgrade any that lack such built-in assessments.

Criteria for Assessing Student Performance

As previously noted, design and technology is a key element of the secondary school curriculum in England and Wales; since the mid seventies, it has almost become as widespread as the traditional "core subjects" of English, science, and mathematics. Design and technology is not a single subject, however. Through technology courses, students are introduced to the skills, processes, and knowledge of several different subjects, such as art and design; craft, design, and technology; and science and technology.

Between 1985 and 1991, a nationwide research program was launched under the auspices of the department of education's Assessment of Performance Unit (APU) to assess the competencies of students in the area of design and technology. The project focused on the work of students aged fifteen to sixteen, all of whom were enrolled in subjects such as those listed in the previous paragraph. (Students in this age group in England and Wales are mostly enrolled in courses that lead to an intermediate-level qualification known as the General Certificate of Secondary Education, or GCSE). The APU research project led to the development of a range of performance-based assessment instruments (Kimbell and others, 1991). These instruments make it possible to evaluate both the processes students deploy as they carry out design and technology projects and the products they create.

As illustrated in the example in the next vignette, the assessment instruments developed by the APU are criterion-referenced and include holistic as well as analytical evaluations of student performance. They cover the assessment of the attitudes, values, technical ideas, and aesthetic judgments that students bring to their design projects, as well as the knowledge and practical strategies the students use. While these instruments do allow teachers to assess the final products of a student's labor, they also pay substantial attention to the processes of design, to communication with others, and to the ability of a student to evaluate the strengths and weaknesses of his or her own work. As they use these assessment instruments, teachers (and other evaluators) aim to produce a cumulative picture of student project work over time, rather than just one summative assessment at the completion of a project.

The APU developed two assessment processes. One entails holistic scoring (an overall categorization of the way the student worked); the other entails the specific scoring of performance, in terms of nine so-called headline qualities of the student's work. Holistic scoring involves making overall judgments of the processes each student followed and of the products developed. Each student's performance is rated on a five-point scale; in addition, it is described in terms of keyword descriptors and through written comments on how the student approached his or her project. An agreed list of keywords, such as "resourceful," "safe," "methodical," "innovative," "thoughtful," "divergent," "linear," and so on, is used. Holistic scoring needs to be carried out three or four times during the life of a student project.

Specific, or "atomized," scoring allows for the assessment of the "headline qualities" of a student's work. Nine headline qualities were defined by the APU research. The first six relate to the quality of the student's work; the last three relate to the style or approach the student adopts. The first six are "judgmental assessments," which allow evaluators to look at how a student

1. Defines the task and gets started on the project
2. Plans ahead, managing time and resources wisely
3. Understands the task and develops relevant solutions or products
4. Identifies and applies evaluation criteria relevant to the product
5. Identifies appropriate working methods
6. Communicates designs in words or through graphs and models

The last three qualities represent "descriptive profiles" of the student's work. These indicate

7. The principal focus of the work (for example, technical versus aesthetic)
8. The extent to which the student takes "ownership" of the work, rather than following the lead of a teacher
9. The main areas of knowledge and understanding that were used by students in resolving the problems they faced (for example, knowledge of materials, knowledge of energy systems, or knowledge of human factors)

The example presented in the following vignette shows how some of the judgmental assessments just described actually work in practice. Rather than illustrating all nine elements of the assessment system, this example only illustrates the application of (1) starting points, (3) developing solutions, and (6) communications.

Designing and Building a Bite Indicator: An Illustration of a Method for Assessing Design Projects

This is a story about Giles, a keen young fisherman, who had chosen to take "Craft, Design, and Technology" as one of his subjects for the GCSE examinations. At the beginning of his GCSE year, Giles was presented with a list of several hundred possible projects; he chose "the bite indicator" as an obvious project for him.

Starting Point

This is how Giles described his task: "As I am a very keen carp angler, I have noticed the very wide range of 'bite indicators' on the market. However, most of these are too expensive for young anglers. I believe a good, less-expensive bite indicator can be made, so I have resolved to make one for my own project."

Evaluation: Giles gained a high score on item 1 (starting points) because he was able to focus on one task and lay out the details of the task clearly.

Developing Solutions

Giles went through all the correct stages to achieve what his project needed to accomplish, and paid careful attention to how people would use the bite indicator "on location." His first thought was to use an electronic eye as a switching mechanism to turn on the alarm, waking the fisherman when a fish pulled on the line, but this would have made the device too expensive; so instead, he devised a thin wire trigger around which the fishing line had to be wound. This was attached to a pivot point, and when the line was pulled it closed an electrical circuit. Giles built a full-scale model to test his ideas before building the final version.

Evaluation: Giles gained a high score on item 3 (developing solutions) because he was able to solve most of the problems he had set himself. His model did work, both in the bench trials and in the field, but it was not sophisticated enough electronically for reliable long-term operation.

Communication

Giles produced some clear and skillful drawings that described his device, but failed to provide sufficient technical information. In particular, he did not explain how the electronic circuitry he used actually worked.

Evaluation: Giles did not score as highly on communication, because he paid too much attention to pretty drawings and not enough to explaining how his device worked.

Externally Mandated Assessments

A critical issue is the demand for district and state accountability for student learning. Standardized paper-and-pencil tests are generally used for this purpose, since their reliability and generalizability are well established. By their very nature, however, these tests fail to assess several of the most important goals of a field such as technology education, where ability to achieve in the realms of practical action is as important as theoretical understanding, where the process of defining a problem and arriving at solutions is as important as the "right answer," and where trialing and revision is an integral part of carrying a project to completion. For these reasons, the development of alternative assessment in science, in mathematics, and for entry into employment (see the SCANS competencies in Chapter Two) is an active field of research at this time.

In trying to understand various notions of alternative assessment, Shavelson and Baxter (1992) explored techniques of direct observation of students pursuing scientific inquiry. They found that "raters can reliably evaluate students' hands-on performance on complex tasks in real time." They also concluded, however, that "to get an accurate picture of individual student science achievement, the student must perform a substantial number of investigations—perhaps between 10 and 20 . . . [that] continuous assessment throughout the course of instruction is needed to accurately reflect student science achievement . . . [and that] nowhere is the symmetry between teaching and assessment more apparent than with embedded assessments" (pp. 23–25).

Embedded assessment is concerned more with finding out what children do think and what skills they do use than with testing them on what they ought to know or be able to do. Close analysis allows teachers to base judgments on inferences drawn from evidence. The development of this kind of expertise requires practice, coaching, mentoring, and critical reflection. Over time, discrimination increases and teachers are able to become more selective in what they record. To use such methods for large-scale assessments, however, will remain problematic unless the U.S. view of accountability adopts the model used in other countries—accepting teachers' ratings of their students' performance, after establishing common criteria, adequate teacher training, and certain built-in checks.

Recommendation

Districts and states interested in implementing technology education must ensure that their mandated tests are consonant with their goals for technology education. They should give serious consideration to making teacher evaluation of student portfolios a part of their mandated assessments.

Concluding Remarks

This book presents, we believe, compelling arguments for incorporating technology education into the general courses and curriculum in kindergarten through grade twelve. We have argued that the time has come when familiarity and an understanding of technology must be part of the outcomes of a general K–12 education. We have also discussed how to move schools beyond the research and rhetoric to the decision to actually implement technology education. In considering the barriers standing in the way, it is worth noting that most OECD countries—including England and Wales, Scotland, France, Australia, the Netherlands, and Scandinavia—are making much greater progress in introducing technology education than the United States. As for the German-speaking countries, there is a long tradition of technology-based education leading not only to industrial positions but also to admittance (after passing the usual entrance requirements) to both technical and academic universities.

Making technology education a reality in the classrooms of America will require taking advantage of and building on the rich base of knowledge and experience developed here and abroad and on overcoming the obstacles discussed earlier in this chapter. In order to introduce technology education on a widespread scale, with a full sequence of courses from kindergarten to grade twelve, a "systemic" approach will be needed. Essentially, systemic reform means that there is a commitment (at the district, state, and federal levels) to supporting simultaneous change in a number of elements of the educational system. An initial step is to identify the relevant elements of the system. In the case of technology education, these elements must include, at the very least, support for changes in classroom pedagogy, the introduction of new forms of teacher education (preservice and in-service), the creation and adoption of new methods of student assessment, and at the school level, changes in the availability of facilities and in relationships among subject matter departments. The federal government, state and local education agencies, academic departments in colleges and universities, educational policy bodies, educational researchers, and curriculum developers will all have to play key roles in promoting and implementing effective technology education in the nation's schools.

Since the mid 1800s, the processes and products of contemporary technology have had profound effects—for better or for worse—on our lives and on our environment. Dealing with technology has become an inescapable part of everyday life, because the world we live in is largely a made or designed world. The challenge of developing coherent programs of technology education as part of the general education of all young people is one we can no longer afford to ignore.

This young man is setting up a wing in a wind tunnel to determine how effectively his design creates lift and reduces drag.

APPENDIX A

TECHNOLOGY EDUCATION IN OTHER COUNTRIES

This discussion of the evolution of technology education internationally is presented here to put developments in the United States in context. Developments in the United Kingdom are given particular attention because they represent a contrasting approach to that taken in the United States with respect to the balancing of skills, content, and process. In the United States, the efforts to introduce technology education have historically been more attentive to the "content" aspect of technology, while efforts in the United Kingdom have been more attentive to the "process" aspect of technology. Technology education professionals in the United States have been interested and involved in the "structural" aspects of technology, while professional colleagues in the United Kingdom have pursued its "functional" aspects. For further information on technology education in western Europe, the Nordic countries, central and eastern Europe, Latin America, Africa, Australia, and Southeast Asia, the reader is referred to Volume Five of *Innovations in Science and Technology Education,* edited by David Layton (1994a).

Technology Education in the United Kingdom

The United Kingdom, encompassing England, Wales, Scotland, and Northern Ireland, has been most active in developing technology education over the longest period of time. Each of these countries has developed its technology curriculum in its own distinct way. Their efforts extend back over the same period of development as in the United States. Throughout a twenty-year period of development, the main focus on technology education in the United Kingdom has been the process or functional aspect of technology, currently known as Design and Technology (D&T).

As might be expected because of the interest in process, the significant term is "design," with students actually engaged more with the process of designing and building objects than with the study of technology as a subject itself. Learning to work as a designer involves

> three kinds of knowledge and capabilities: procedural knowledge of how to design; capability of communicating complex ideas with clarity, confidence, and skill; and conceptual knowledge and understanding of the use of materials, energy systems, and aesthetics in designing and building technological systems—along with knowledge and awareness of people and their needs. The procedural knowledge of design involves learning how to discern needs and thoroughly investigate them as an architect or engineer would; prepare a design brief or plan for meeting those needs; generate ideas and develop them into a design, build the design, reflect on the quality of the result in meeting the original needs, and then act on the reflection to produce a better design (Wirt, 1994).

D&T is taken by all students, boys and girls, and high- as well as low-ability students, until age sixteen. Students begin D&T in kindergarten, at five years of age, and continue until they leave school, normally at age sixteen. The design and technology program has been developed to appeal to a wide range of students—those interested in arts and humanities as well as those interested in science and technology.

The Development of Design and Technology in Elementary Education

In 1978, Her Majesty's Inspector for schools published the results of a national survey of primary education in England and Wales. Although technology was not considered as a separate subject at that time, the findings provide evidence of initial development of design and technology in the primary system.

The main findings of the survey recognized the way in which science, particularly natural science, had increased in importance, but the survey reported that studies relating specifically to the "made world" were comparatively rare. The report emphasized that mechanisms linked to constructional activities were an aspect of science that was seldom taught, but that could be successfully delivered at the primary level.

In the curriculum area of art and craft, almost every class seen had some materials for drawing and painting, but materials for modeling and three-dimensional construction were available in fewer than two-thirds of the classes. In some cases, older boys and girls were separated for craft activities. On these occasions, girls often undertook needlework while boys did construction work. These findings highlighted the comparative neglect of three-dimensional construction and led to recommendations that opportunities should be provided for boys and girls to undertake some work with wood and other resistant materials and to learn to handle the tools and techniques associated with them.

The survey resulted in a number of national and local initiatives throughout England and Wales through the government's Educational Support Grants, which provided funds for local education authorities to employ advisory teachers and to purchase equipment in support of the growth of science and technology in primary education. In much of the early work, technology was seen as a vehicle for science development. However, as implementation of the National Curriculum proceeded, several professional bodies interested in technology and engineering mounted initiatives and national projects aimed at the development of design and technology as a separate subject. Even so, technology within the National Curriculum at the primary level originated as a subgroup of the Science Working Group and was called "Science and Technology"; within a year, however, it developed into an autonomous "National Curriculum Foundation Subject" at both primary and secondary levels. It was titled "Technology."

The Development of Design and Technology in Secondary Education

Design and technology education originated as a vocational subject immediately after World War II. Boys studied woodwork, metalwork, and technical drawing; girls studied needlework and cookery. Design Education, an integrated approach to the teaching of art, design, craft, textiles, and home economics was introduced into the secondary school system during the late 1960s and early 1970s. This type of faculty organization still remains the norm in many schools in the United Kingdom.

D&T was a natural development from Design Education and was introduced as an examination subject for the General Certificate in Education (GCE) in the mid seventies. Wood, metal, and the introduction of plastics and resins came together as one combined subject, usually within a faculty linked to art and home economics. This triumvirate remained together in a faculty structure until the introduction of the National Curriculum, when D&T was designated to include craft, design and technology, textiles and home economics (including food), and business studies. D&T and Information Technology (IT) were combined as separate components to form the National Curriculum subject of Technology. Identifying technology as a foundation subject was a significant change in the curriculum. Technology had previously only been studied by children beyond age thirteen as an optional subject, representing approximately a third of the school populations, the majority of whom were male.

The National Curriculum for England and Wales made the study of design and technology statutory for students aged five to sixteen, starting in September 1990. The present National Curriculum Orders for England and Wales require technology to be taught to all pupils of compulsory school age in maintained schools. For each subject, there are attainment targets, programs of study, and assessment requirements. The National Curriculum Order for Technology states that it is a new subject that requires pupils to apply knowledge and skills to solve practical problems. The order for Technology contains five attainment targets (ATs) under two distinct sections:

Design and Technology

- AT1: Identifying needs and opportunities
- AT2: Generating a design
- AT3: Planning and making
- AT4: Evaluating

Information Technology

- AT5: Information Technology Capability

Revision of the National Order for Technology

In June 1992, following advice from the National Curriculum Council, the Secretaries of State announced a review of the D&T component (AT1–4) of the National Curriculum Order for Technology. The principal objectives of the review were to

- Clarify what should be taught and ensure that pupils' technical skills, knowledge, and understanding are developed through work with construction materials and related components and systems
- Facilitate assessment by specifying more clearly the skills and knowledge that pupils should acquire at each key stage, so that progression can be ascertained

- Reduce complexity and amount of work required in each key stage
- Improve the manageability of the curriculum and assessment, particularly at the primary level
- Clarify how skills, knowledge, and understanding that have developed through other curriculum orders should be made use of in technology
- Design a framework for short courses at Key Stage 4

The Key Stages are KS1, ages five to seven; KS2, ages eight to ten; KS3, ages eleven to thirteen; and KS4, ages fourteen to sixteen.

The council published its new recommendations in September 1993. The following are significant extracts from the "new" document:

1. The four attainment targets in the original order for D&T should be reduced to two:

Designing and Making. Pupils should be taught to combine their designing and making skills and their knowledge and understanding of products and applications, materials, control, and structures when designing and making. They should also be taught to apply knowledge and skills where appropriate from the programs of study for other subjects, particularly art, mathematics, and science. (AT1: Designing. Investigating, clarifying, and specifying the design task. Modeling, developing, and communicating design ideas.)

Design skills: Activities should allow further scope for pupils to investigate, develop, and refine their design ideas. Pupils should be taught further modeling and communicating skills and be given opportunities to consider examples of models, drawings, and plans done by other people. They should be encouraged to evaluate their work as it develops, bearing in mind the purposes for which it is intended. (AT2: Making. Planning and organizing making. Using a variety of tools, equipment, and processes to make products safely. Testing, modifying, and evaluating.)

Making skills: Pupils should be introduced to additional cutting, shaping, and joining techniques with a wider range of materials, through activities that (1) help them develop their manual dexterity and refine their technical skills, and (2) take account of their developing physical capability. They should be encouraged to consider the quality of their work and to comment on how satisfied they are with it.

2. The attainment targets should be weighted for assessment purposes as follows: 40 percent on AT1, 60 percent on AT2.

3. There should be five supporting sections of the program of study

outlining the knowledge and skills that need to be applied when designing and making. These comprise:

- Construction materials and components
- Food
- Control systems and energy (electrical/mechanical and mechanical/pneumatic)
- Structures
- Business and industrial practices

The council further recommended that the weight of content be reduced by about one-third at each key stage. They also recommended that technology continue to be delivered through the process model developed through the original four attainment targets. Further, IT was to be removed from the Technology Order. The council recognized that D&T offers good opportunities for applying skills in IT and therefore concluded that there is a need to reexamine the position of IT within technology. It recommended that IT should be specified separately from D&T in the National Curriculum, and that pupils' attainment in the two areas should be reported separately.

Technology Education in Germany

Germany has a long history of technical training through which students gain in-depth preparation for jobs in industry. Generally, no technology has been taught at the elementary level, although there is a long tradition of craft instruction. At the secondary level, pupils are divided by ability; those attending "technical high school" receive a thorough training in vocational technology. This training is usually based on such fields as building technology (construction), engineering technology, electrical technology, and so forth. Students attending the academic Gymnasium (pre-university) rarely receive the opportunity to study technology.

The inclusion of technology education as a part of schooling for all students is quite recent and comes in response to the need for general technology education to be part of a broad general education; the need for qualified vocational preparation as part of advanced training or career development; and the need to provide some technical skill for everyone.

These needs are being translated into practice at the elementary school (K–4) level by providing activity-based technology education as part of the other subjects in the curriculum. In grades five and six, the learning experiences become more technical, with arts and crafts instruction emphasizing the handling and experiencing of materials. At the intermediate school level, grades seven to ten, technology education is part of the broad-based technical school curriculum for students pursuing a vocational program. At this level, technological job-oriented education is provided along with the traditional academic subjects. Technology is often taught in conjunction with economics. Most students are provided a four-week practical training experience in industry. At grades eleven and twelve, general technology education includes the science of materials and processes in the context of historical, economical, ecological, and ethical aspects. Technology education generally continues to be excluded from the Gymnasium curriculum.

The objectives of technology education in Germany have been identified to include:

- To understand technology within European cultural and historical dimensions
- To understand where one fits within the technical and economic work environment
- To understand the relationship between technology and the economy
- To understand, identify, and apply technical and economic processes
- To develop technical and economic problem-solving skills
- To develop social responsibility and a responsibility for the learning processes

The content of technology education is strongly linked with science and includes principles of mass, energy, and information transfer. Students are engaged in activities of planning, representing, producing, applying, and judging their technical work. Through these activities they are expected to gain technical competence as well as to enhance their creativity, cooperation, and general expertise. The content and activities are shaped to link the theoretical to the practical and to contribute to gaining transferable scientific and technical concepts and models.

Technology Education in Japan

Japan, unlike the United States, has a strongly centralized system of education, with responsibility for school curricula residing centrally in the Ministry of Education. Curricular review and change are instituted approximately every ten years. Changes in Japanese technology education programs following World War II can be viewed in the context of four eras: (1) the Economic Reconstruction Era, (2) the High Economic Growth Era, (3) the Stabilized Economic Era, and (4) the International Era (Murata, 1990).

During the Economic Reconstruction Era, Japan was subject to a number of external forces for change. For Japan, as for many other countries around the world, the successful launching of the Soviet satellite *Sputnik* signaled a need for educational change generally and the need to improve science and technology education programs specifically. In late 1957, the Japanese government introduced technology education, *gijutsu ka,* as a required subject in all lower secondary schools beginning in 1958. With the introduction of technology education in the lower secondary schools, vocational education was moved to the upper secondary level as an elective course. The major objectives of technology education at the lower secondary school were (1) to help students learn basic skills through creative/productive experiences, to understand modern technology, and to foster fundamental attitudes for practice; (2) through experience of design and realization, to foster skills for representation, creation, and rational attitudes for problem solving; and (3) through experience in manufacturing/operation of machines/devices, to understand the relation between technology and life and to foster attitudes for improving technology and daily life (Murata and Stern, 1993, p. 32).

During the High Economic Growth Era, student enrollments continued to increase, and industrial sector employers wanted workers to have greater flexibility and trainability. In response, the Ministry of Education decreed that fundamental subjects were to include "Fundamentals of Industry," "Mathematics in Technology," and "Practice." The goal of these subjects was to improve the students' fundamental knowledge and skills, as well as to accommodate new teaching materials and methods (Tamaura, Arai, and Murata, 1985).

In the late 1980s, during the Stabilized Economy Era, the Ministry of Education initiated several additional changes. Of particular note was the inclusion in lower secondary education of a new computer literacy course in the technology education programs. The primary objective of the new course was to help students understand the roles and functions of computers and develop capability for the use of computers and information. This has become the most popular of the technology courses, with 76 percent of all students wanting to take it (Murata and Stern, 1993, p. 33). During this same period, the Ministry of Education revised technical courses in the upper secondary school level to help students develop basic skills and flexibility. A significant revision in the upper secondary technical curriculum was the introduction of new integrated problem-solving courses, such as "mechatronics," "applied mechatronics," and independent-assignment project study. ("Mechatronics" is a combination of the words "mechanics" and "electronics.")

The primary object of the new mechatronics course is to promote the understanding of fundamental knowledge and skills related to mechanics and electronics. As shown in Exhibit A.1, content areas include basic machines and devices, sensors, analog-to-digital conversion, logic circuits actuators, and mechanics and power transmission devices.

EXHIBIT A.1. NATIONAL COURSE OF STUDY.

Objectives	*Contents*
Mechatronics. To understand fundamental knowledge and develop skills related to mechatronics and to foster the ability to apply them in a practical setting.	1. Integration of electronics and mechanics in machines and devices 2. Principles and characteristics of sensors 3. Sensors and computers; analog-digital conversion, logic circuits, and signals 4. Types and characteristics of actuators 5. Actuator control 6. Mechanics and power transmission devices

Source: Murata and Stern, 1993, p. 34.

In general, there has been a movement in Japan toward a broader view of technology education. There is some concern, however, that the broader and less "subject-specific" approach could result in a relatively shallow education experience. The primary objective of independent project study for students is to deepen and integrate their knowledge and skills through problem solving and industrial projects. The major content areas reflected in these problem-solving projects include design, manufacture, research, experimentation, and the study of workplace practice. (Murata, 1990).

Technology Education in the Netherlands

Secondary education in the Netherlands traditionally has consisted of several different types of schools, notably, junior vocational education, junior and senior secondary general education, and pre-university education. Technology education has not been taught at the primary school level, but has generally been provided within the curriculum at the junior vocational level and at some combined secondary schools. It is legally possible for all schools in secondary education to place technology in their curriculum.

The National Institute for Curriculum Development constructed a technology curriculum for implementation in secondary schools in 1991. It is hoped that technology education will be accepted by all of the schools when school reforms are fully implemented between 1996 and 2000. Technology education as envisioned in this reform has three subgoals:

1. Teaching pupils to produce technical products
2. Teaching pupils to handle several products of technology
3. Teaching pupils to form opinions on the application of technology and on the resulting effects on society

Dutch schools are currently involved in a large-scale innovation in education for students from twelve to fifteen years of age. This innovation, called the "Basisvorming Act," became effective in August 1993. Instead of entering different types of lower secondary schools after grade six, all pupils in the-twelve-to-fifteen age group will study the same set of fifteen subjects, with "technology" included as one of the compulsory subjects; after age fifteen, students are to choose one of four different tracks of upper secondary education. In the general required three-year curriculum, the technology courses are aimed at familiarizing students with aspects of technology that are significant to the understanding of culture, with the way in which students function in society, and with concepts and skills significant to the pupil's further technical development. The students are to acquire knowledge and understanding of the three main components of technology (materials, energy, and information), and of the close relationships between technology and the natural sciences and between technology and society. The students also are expected to learn how to produce technology, by becoming actively involved with applications of technology. Pupils are to learn how to use a number of technological products and are given the opportunity to explore their abilities and interests with regard to technology. The Dutch elaboration of the curriculum for technology has indications of offering equal opportunities for boys and girls and of appealing to both sexes. The core objectives of the curriculum are defined within three domains:

1. Technology and society
   - Technology in everyday life
   - Industry
   - Professions
   - The environment
2. Using products of technology
   - Mechanical principles
   - Technical systems
   - Control techniques
   - Use of technical products

3. Producing functional workpieces
   - Preparatory activities
   - Design; drawing and reading technical drawings
   - Processing materials
   - Inspection of workpieces

The new curriculum in the Netherlands positions problem solving as a key working method in technology, used to develop, refine, or maintain technological products. To become skilled in problem solving, students should have insight into theoretical principles, as well as practical knowledge and skills and an understanding of the problem-solving process. To accomplish this, students must have adequate resources at their disposal so they can translate their ideas into real objects (National Institute for Curriculum Development, 1993).

There are several problems, however. The activities in the technology lessons focus on practicing technical skills through practical work and the production of workpieces and assignments. For this reason, teachers wishing to emphasize the relationship between technology and society do not find it easy to bring this into practice. On the one hand, it is hard to show the connection between this relationship and the (concrete) practice of skills; on the other hand, good classroom materials are still lacking. Many teachers also feel the need for developing a clearer concept of this relationship. A second problem is that the introduction of the technology curriculum requires additional class time, at least two to three hours per week; hence, school hours have been increased by two hours a week, while at the same time the hours for science have been decreased from seven to five, and time for geography has been decreased as well. A third problem is the preparation of teachers. It is expected that science teachers will staff these courses, with some assistants. Training is being offered to teachers in the new technology curriculum; teachers are able to reduce their teaching load by half for two years to attend the training. The aim is to have at least one teacher in each school trained; however, some schools have two or three teachers who attended the training, others have none. Unfortunately, the same barriers exist in the Netherlands as exist in the United States between teachers of science, specifically physics, and technology teachers: schools that have been observed by researchers in the course of implementation studies show no evidence of discussions among teachers of technology and physics on coordinating or building on each others' courses.

Discussion

As these summaries show, the form and focus of technology education differ considerably within and across countries. There is also considerable diversity of technology education within each of the countries. For example, in the United States and Germany, where the responsibility for schooling resides at the state level, schools differ significantly from state to state. In the United Kingdom and Japan, where National Curriculum initiatives are being implemented, programs are more similar from school to school.

Other than centralization, it has not been possible within the purposes of this book to consider such important influences on the diversity of technology education programs as the method and extent of funding support, the place of technology education in the educational delivery system of a country, and the means by which students are directed into or elect the subject. It should be noted, however, that the United States is significantly behind other major industrialized countries in the development of technology education as a part of the school curriculum.

The status of technology education in the United States and internationally is better understood if viewed from the context within which it continues to develop. As indicated by Layton (1993), technology is so new as a school subject it lacks both a history and a tradition as a component of general education for all students; it has no core of commonly accepted beliefs, values, standards, or practices; and it has no role model in higher education. Layton makes a point of particular significance for this document:

> A general characteristic of school technology and one which makes it different from many other school subjects is its engagement with practical action in the made world. No subject challenges the historic role of schools as institutions which decontextualize knowledge quite so strongly as does technology. It represents a major revaluation of the kinds of knowledge which a society deems important. Academic knowledge has hitherto been king and, in most subjects, learning has been an end in itself. What technology signals is the recognition that practical knowledge, that is, knowledge which empowers its possessors in the realms of practical action, is now being accorded equal status [pp. 14–15].

In many countries, including the United States, education that is theoretical and lacks application generally is seen as more important, even more liberalizing than education that is practical and applied. The roots to this view are deep indeed, reaching back some two thousand years to classical Greece. There have been periods of time in the United States, however, when practical knowledge was held in higher esteem. This situation appears about to change, however, as U.S. industrialists and educators observe practices in other countries and come to value the important role that technology education might play in bringing theoretical and practical knowledge back together in more fruitful and powerful relationships.

A THEMATIC APPROACH ACROSS GRADES

The following description provides a detailed example of how subjects in the elementary and middle grades can be integrated around a central theme, and how instruction can be built coherently from level to level. It is drawn from Project UPDATE (Upgrading Practice through Design and Technology/Engineering), an effort funded by the National Science Foundation. This extended example concludes with the capabilities that can be expected of high school students who have engaged in such a curriculum.

Kindergarten Through Grade Three

During kindergarten and early elementary classes, the teacher's role is one of setting up learning situations. The teacher guides pupils in their learning through setting challenging tasks and posing challenging open-ended questions.

An appealing toy might be made the focus for the learning situations developed by the teacher. This is the stage when young students can be given activities based on their favorite soft toys, such as teddy bears, using materials to make things for the bears, such as a house, a bed, a chair, clothes, food, and—depending on the season—a sleigh, a boat, or some other vehicle. Different subjects merge as the pupils address tasks of interest to them woven around "Teddy":

Language, Stories, and Drama

- Telling each other about their teddy bears
- Making up adventures for their bears (done verbally)
- Listening to and talking about stories
- Practicing early lettering and naming skills
- Beginning to read (stories about bears)
- Having a picnic in the woods and role-playing Teddy's adventures

Art

- Painting a picture of Teddy; painting Teddy's garden
- Decorating Teddy's home with patterns; making a hanging mobile for Teddy's house
- Making clay teddy bears; making pretend food

Music and Movement

- Learning and singing songs about bears
- Making teddy bear movements: little bear, big bear, teddy bear dances
- Making up teddy bear musical sounds

Science, Design, Technology, and Mathematics

- Designing and making a house for Teddy
- Designing and making a bed for Teddy
- Designing clothes for Teddy to wear, in the rain, at play, to a party
- Planning food for a picnic
- Making a vehicle for Teddy to ride in: for example, a sleigh or a cart
- Studying materials: for example, using a magnifier to study textures
- Making comparisons: for example, testing to see what material is waterproof
- Studying plants: deciding which to grow in Teddy's garden
- Measuring and arithmetic operations

The following questions can be asked of pupils concerning the design of a home for their toys:

- Can you make a house for your Teddy?
- What is it going to look like?
- How many windows will it have?

- How does Teddy get in and out?
- Will it have a door?

Children can be involved in designing the house, discussing appropriate materials, learning where to bend and where to cut, estimating sizes, measuring Teddy against the home. The teacher can stimulate design considerations and measurement by asking:

- Is Teddy the right size to fit inside?
- Does the house need to be bigger?

Aesthetic considerations can be introduced:

- What color would Teddy paint the house?
- Does Teddy want a garden?
- Can you design a garden for Teddy?

Other activities can be drawing a map showing where Teddy lives, or discussing Teddy's recreational activities: the picnic, winter sports, water sports. All of these activities will require a consideration of the things that are needed and the type of materials necessary to make them: Will they need to be hard, strong, soft, warm, and so forth?

Through such a curriculum for kindergarten through third grade, the following knowledge and concepts can be developed:

Science

- Properties of materials: soft, hard, bendable, strong, floppy, floater, sinker
- Energy: movement (moving ourselves, moving things, making things move by dropping, pushing, rolling, sliding, rocking, revolving); using the sun's heat to warm things, the light to help plants grow; cooking food using heat in an oven

Technology

- Structures: housing structures, moving structures, floating structures; structures that protect us from the sun's heat, from hurting ourselves, from getting wet
- Control: making things go where you want them to go, guiding direction by pathways, tunnels, slopes; switching things on, plugging things in, turning heat up or down
- Communication (nonverbal): making drawings of things, showing how things work

Mathematics

- Measurement: linear, time, size, comparative area, developing an understanding of measurement by units
- Size: comparative, rather than measured—which is longer, shorter, taller, fatter?
- Understanding the concept of containing something: How many teddy bears can fit in the box? How much water will a plastic bottle hold? Will it hold as much as a similar bottle that is wider but not as tall?
- Shape: Recognizing and being able to name basic shapes—squares, rectangles, circles, triangles

The following materials, tools, and equipment will be useful for carrying out the proposed curriculum:

- *Materials:* boxes, tubes, plastic containers, soft wood, dowels, clay, plasticine, dough, string, sticky tape, fabric scraps, food, drawing materials, painting materials, cotton spools, threads, natural materials
- *Tools:* scissors, pencils, paint brushes, pens, junior hacksaw, lightweight hammers, mallets, small pliers, measuring calipers, sewing needles, knitting needles, cooking utensils
- *Equipment:* small bench or table with vice, bench hooks, cutting boards, water tray, sand tray, weaving loom, small oven, protective clothing, goggles, plastic gloves. Educational construction kits are helpful, but not necessary.
- *Learning resources:* photographs, slides, viewers, magnifiers, reference books, natural objects (shells, fossils, stones, driftwood), made objects (pieces of machinery, knitted things, woven things, sewn things, padded things, moving toys, soft toys)

Grades Four Through Eight

The goal of the sequence is for students to come to understand that all physical structures are made from materials, that different types of material have different properties, and that understanding the properties of materials and the ways in which they can be processed and used is the means by which human living conditions are advanced. Such knowledge has provided the means to create a wide range of shelters and other types of buildings; to develop transport systems, the manufacturing industry, clothing, food, and recreational facilities; and to change the environment to meet human needs.

Pupils need to be provided with a range of problem-solving activities requiring them to plan, organize, and evaluate their ideas. Learning skills should have advanced to a point where they are introduced to the value of working in teams: listening to others' points of view; making joint decisions; and planning, organizing, and carrying out a task. They will need to recognize the importance of setting criteria by which the success of the task and their efforts can be judged.

The foundation of science, technology and allied mathematical concepts will be laid, and students will be prepared for more advanced learning tasks in the next stage of their education. The following examples of activities and concepts to be learned illustrate how the theme of building houses and homes can be used throughout the curriculum.

Humanities

Research and study human homes in different cultures and at different times in history.

- What effect does culture have on the design of homes?
- What major changes can you find in homes through the ages, in materials, style, construction techniques, furnishings, grouping of families, location of community services and social functions, and so forth?

Study the materials used in construction and furnishing and discuss with your group:

- Why were they chosen?
- What are their properties?
- How does climate affect the design? Choice of materials?

Science

- *Properties of materials:* Understand that materials can be malleable, flexible, or brittle; they can have various degrees of hardness; they can be porous, non-porous, waterproof, conductors, nonconductors, buoyant or nonbuoyant, or insulating; they can be constructed into structures that will provide shelter and into frameworks to support things. Understand where materials come from, their general uses and value, that earth's resources are not unlimited; understand the toxic nature of some materials, the health and safety concerns of working with some materials, and so on.
- *Energy:* Understand the various sources of energy relevant to the home and

industry—heat, gravity, running water, food, and so on; that energy can be utilized to make things work; the various forms of stored energy—batteries, springs, elastic.

• *Testing:* Understand the need to plan a fair test, to make a hypothesis and test theories, and to conduct trial and error tests; understand that failure is necessary in the pursuit of success; understand the need to test materials for water resistance, porosity, insulation qualities, and structural strength, and to test soil and conduct a survey of the plants in the area—do some plants grow best in different types of soil?

• *Plan, hypothesize, and predict:* What makes cement harden? Conduct experiments on materials that solidify when mixed; test for strength; interpret results and findings.

Technology

• *Site layout:* Draw a map for the site showing the position of domestic housing, shops, recreation facilities; also show on your map/layout the necessary domestic systems—electricity, water, gas, sewage, TV cabling, roads.

• *Look at the materials used to build houses:* Do they vary from house to house? Can you think of a reason why this may be so? Describe the materials in terms of their use.

• *Consider the function of different rooms:* What is a good layout for a kitchen? For a bedroom? For a bathroom? Where should windows and doors be placed? Design and make a vehicle to deliver building materials around the site; it must be driven by electricity and be capable of forward and reverse movement; an alarm must be activated when reversing.

• *Lifting and lowering:* Design and make a pulley system to carry building materials up and down.

• *Structures:* Understand more complex standing structures, cantilever structures, pillars, beams, struts, balance and equilibrium in structures.

• *Control:* Understand control through guiding, steering, switching, regulating, lighting, heating, and flow.

• *Communication:* Understand that there are many forms of communicating information and commands: symbols, flags, sound, vision, touch, smell, electronics.

• *Reasoning through doing:* Come to solutions through working with basic materials and constructing with educational construction kits; come to understand patterns through making toys, clothing, houses, constructions.

• *Problem solving:* Recognize that there is more than one solution to simple problems.

Language

- *Develop a technical, observational, and imaginative vocabulary:* modeling, span, structure, cantilever, taut, corrugated, malleable, pliable, flexible, rotate, gear, cam, pump, circuit, valve, switch, suspension, construction.
- *Verbal expression:* Describe how things work, how they are joined/fixed, and so forth; learn oral reasoning, to verbalize ideas, to discuss with peer group.
- *Writing:* Learn to write descriptively and observationally regarding the nature and location of a site; write a sales description for the new homes; learn technical writing for describing the site vehicle (material transporter); write directions for how to get to the site from the nearest turnpike; draw up simple job descriptions when working in teams; write imaginatively about a community celebration.

Mathematics

- *Use shape and space:* Recognize and use patterns, relationships, and sequences.
- *Measurement:* Make comparisons—bigger than, smaller than; linear, area, cubic measurement. Know units of measurement— fractions and decimals; area of building site, individual housing units, shops, recreation facilities.
- *Construct geometric shapes:* cones, cubes, pyramids, triangular tubes.
- *Proportion, scale, use of graphs and charts:* Make bar graphs showing site use; make room areas and furniture to scale and experiment with placement; handle data in practical tasks.
- Understand that containing something is not only how many, but also how much in solids, liquids, powders, electricity, and information. Understand the difference between volume and capacity.
- *Introduction to simple algebraic equations:* Estimate and calculate probabilities.

Music and Art

- Listen to the building-site sounds; compose a building song, or music and songs about homes.
- *Observation and drawing/picturing:* See houses as shapes against the sky, pattern of shapes, color patterns using repeated geometrical shapes; record situations and ideas through drawings.
- *Decoration:* Observe the shapes and colors of furnishings; choose art for walls, flowers for garden.

Attitudes

- *Learn how to work with others:* Learn to understand others' points of view, to cooperate with others, to be open to criticism, to appreciate others' efforts, to persevere to get something finished, to care for your own and other students' work.
- Learn to care for living things and the environment.

Practical Skills

- *Building and assembly:* Make a variety of structures with a range of materials—textiles, hard materials, fiber and thread; make models that have articulated joints and moving parts, that can be steered; make things to measured size, to scale.
- *Fitting, fixing, building, constructing, joining, bending, molding, tying, stitching, weaving, modeling, forming, mixing, and so on:* Understand that some things have to fit together to make a whole; understand simple modules within construction kits.
- *Cutting, bending, and forming:* Use a range of tools safely; cut, form, bend, and shape materials to size; work a range of different materials, connecting through sticking, fixing, and slotting.
- *Testing:* Test for strength and appropriateness for task. Use the computer for word processing, to develop graphic skills, for modeling and design.

The following materials, tools, and equipment will be useful for carrying out the proposed curriculum:

- *Materials:* cardboard, paper, cardboard boxes, tubes, plastic containers, soft wood, various sections (square, triangular, rectangular), dowel, flexible wire, rigid metal rod (1/32-inch, 1/16-inch), rigid plastic sheet, flexible plastic sheet, plastic rod, plastic tube, cotton fabric, tape, string, clay, plaster of paris, food, thread, wool, synthetic textiles, and so on.
- *Tools:* scissors, pencils, paintbrushes, pens, mallet, junior hammer, junior hacksaw, pliers, wood saw, craft knives, wood-shaping tools, hand drill, drill bits, card drill, safety rulers, measuring calipers, sewing needles, knitting needles, food utensils, and so forth.
- *Equipment:* educational kits (LEGO, technical LEGO), electricity kits, oven, small loom, benches, vises, cutting boards, bench hooks, water tray, syringes, valves, cotton reels, pulleys, plastic gears, wheels of various sizes, batteries, electricity wires, bulb holders, electric motors, connectors, switches, balances, microscopes,

computers, interfaces, graphic programs, control programs, design programs, a wide range of manufactured kits, and so on.

* *Resources for learning:* photographs, photographic slides, magnifiers, natural objects, made objects (for study), items made from different types of materials, printed and woven textiles, reference books, puppet theaters, small items of machinery cranks, gear wheels, and so on.

APPENDIX C

TECHNOLOGY AT MERLYN HIGH

The following (fictitious) excerpts from a high school handbook and student transcripts illustrate one of many alternatives for a linked set of science/technology programs for grades nine through twelve. (This material is adapted from *The High Stakes of High School Science,* National Center for Improving Science Education, 1991.)

Excerpts from the Merlyn High Handbook for Students and Parents

Students entering Merlyn High School are able to individualize their technology and science program to suit their backgrounds, interests, and career aspirations. Students design their program in cooperation with the school's guidance counselors; they must obtain their parents' or guardians' consent. At the end of each school year, students review their program with the guidance counselor and modify it as their interests and career aspirations change.

All students must take four years of technology and/or science. The first two years consist of a technology/science core, followed in the third and fourth years by courses selected from three alternative options. The options are designed to prepare students for postsecondary study in the liberal arts or in technical fields or for entry into the workplace. Students are able to move from one option to another; even while working to complete one option, they sometimes chose electives from another. All of the options have some technology components.

Technology/Science Core

Course Offerings

Core Technology/Science 1
  1A Contemporary Ecological Concerns
      Managing Low-Radiation Nuclear Waste
      Supplying Our Water Needs
      The Benefits and Risks of Modern American Agriculture
      The Disappearing Seafood
      Greenhouse Emission Gases: How Much Is Too Much?
  1B Case Studies in the History and Philosophy of Science and Technology
      The Story of Time and Its Measurement
      Unfamiliar Women of Science: Lise Meitner, Roselyn Frankel, Annie
        Cannon, Carolyn Herschel
      The Lives and Times of Black Scientists: Charles Drew, Booker T.
        Washington, George Washington Carver
      The Science, Technology, and Politics of the Cotton Gin
      How the Earth Under Our Feet Shifted: The Development of Plate Tectonics Theory
Core Technology/Science 2
  2A Themes Across the Disciplines
      The Use of Models in Technology and the Sciences
      Form and Function in Nature and in Human Design Types and Sources
        of Energy and Energy Transformations
      Evolution in Physical, Biological, and Designed Systems
  2B Contemporary Ethical Dilemmas
      Safe Drugs, Late Drugs
      Diagnosis of Genetic Defects
      High-Tech in Hospitals: Organ Transplants, Life Support Systems, and
        Neonatal Care for High-Risk Infants
      Frost-Resistant Strawberries
      The Endangered Species Act: Success or Failure?

The Core

The content of the modules in the Core Program at Merlyn High is organized in different ways so as to achieve the purposes of general education in technology and science. While some modules stress science more heavily than technology and others focus on technology with science concepts brought in as needed, all core modules are interdisciplinary in approach and include a variety of hands-on activities. The content of the modules may change from year to year, depending on the interests of the teacher and current developments. This is particularly true for modules CTS1A and CTS2B. Curriculum may be supplied from many sources other than traditional texts. Solid waste management, for instance, taught last year in CTS1A, used a module designed by the New York State Department of Education's Science, Technology, and Society Program. The CTS1A water supply module uses units from the American Chemical Society's *ChemCom* Program (1988).

By examining historical events, Core Technology/Science 1B allows students to gain insights into the links between science and technology, how society has affected the development of science and technology, and how science and technology in turn have affected society. This course often is team taught by a technology teacher and a social studies teacher; when this is the case, it serves as a core requirement for both technology/science and social studies.

Core Technology/Science 2A takes a thematic approach to technology and the science disciplines, examining similarities and differences in constructs across the different fields. Concepts and themes for Merlyn High's CS2A are drawn from *Science for All Americans* (American Association for the Advancement of Science, 1989) and the National Research Council's (1994) draft of *National Science Education Standards*.

Core Technology/Science 2B deals with ethical dilemmas arising from social and individual choices made possible by scientific and technological advances. It provides students from diverse cultural and religious backgrounds the opportunity to develop the scientific and technological understanding needed for a thoughtful consideration of the issues surrounding the choice to utilize technological artifacts that prolong or appear to enrich life.

Preparation for Postsecondary Education

Course Requirements

> *Freshman Year:* Core Technology/Science 1A and 1B
> *Sophomore Year:* Core Technology/Science 2A and 2B
> *Junior and Senior Years:* Courses selected from

- Introductory Biology, half year
- Introductory Concepts of Technology/Biology, half year

- Introductory Chemistry, half year
- Introductory Concepts of Technology/Chemistry, half year
- Introductory Physics, half year
- Introductory Concepts of Technology/Physics, half year
- Introductory Earth/Space Science, half year
- Advanced Concepts of Technology/Chemistry, one year
- Advanced Concepts of Technology/Biology, one year
- Advanced Concepts of Technology/Physics, one year
- Advanced Placement Biology, one year
- Advanced Placement Chemistry, one year
- Advanced Placement Physics, one year

Preparation for Postsecondary Education: Options One and Two

Students in this program may select from conventional introductory science courses and technology courses. A major difference is that these courses are all just a half year long rather than the conventional one year for equivalent junior or senior high school courses. This is possible because all students are required to take the Core Technology/Science courses in their first and second years; these courses build a strong foundation of subject-matter knowledge. Merlyn High continues to provide for students planning on college the traditional advanced placement courses in the natural sciences. Students may also take advanced technology courses that equal in rigor the advanced placement courses.

The principles of technology courses are team taught by science and technology teachers and linked to the relevant science courses. Science teachers take primary responsibility for the introductory technology series, focusing on science but using examples from technology. Technology teachers take primary responsibility for the advanced technology series, focusing on design problems and execution but co-teaching fundamental scientific concepts with the science teachers. Any course in the introductory technology series can be substituted for the conventional science courses. Thus, a student interested in an approach to chemistry that is more applied than academic may elect to take introductory principles of technology/chemistry in place of introductory chemistry.

Workplace Preparation

Course Requirements

Freshman Year: Core Technology/Science 1A and B

Sophomore Year: Core Technology/Science 2A and B

Junior and Senior Years: Courses selected from introductory college preparatory courses as well as two years of internship and seminar in technology education

Workplace Preparation: Option Three

Students in this program take a mixture of introductory science and introductory concepts of technology courses. They also are required to participate for two years in the internship and seminar series jointly sponsored by the Technocity Board of Education and the Technocity Chamber of Commerce. Students are assigned to internships according to their interests and competencies; their progress is monitored periodically by a committee composed of teachers from the program and cooperating business and industry representatives. Related seminars are organized by the teachers and industrial representatives to reinforce the students' work experience and concepts stressed in their school courses. The connected school and work experiences enable students to see the relevance of education to their ability to perform on the job. Close cooperation between the school and the employers provides students with work experience while at the same time encouraging full attention to their school responsibilities. Students have been so well received in local businesses that this aspect of the Merlyn High School Program is quickly evolving into a cooperative work-study program. Option Three has proved particularly attractive for students who otherwise might drop out before completing high school.

Transcript Stories

The following success stories illustrate how students with different interests organized their Merlyn High Program.

Merlyn High School Student Transcript
Student: Latisha Jefferson

Technology / Science

Freshman Year:	Core Technology/Science 1A and B
Sophomore Year:	Core Technology/Science 2A and B
Junior Year:	Introductory Chemistry, Introductory Biology

Senior Year: Introductory Concepts of Technology/
                        Biology, Introductory Physics

Latisha entered Merlyn High with a strong technology and science background. Both the elementary and middle schools she attended had implemented technology and science programs that followed national recommendations. Latisha planned to enter college following graduation from high school. Consequently, she planned her program (in consultation with her mother and the guidance counselor) to meet college entrance requirements as well as general education goals.

The core technology and science courses at Merlyn High gave Latisha the opportunity to engage compelling topics in a safe but intellectually and culturally rich environment. In the introductory technology course she took in her last year, she and her fellow students from diverse backgrounds were exposed to some of the difficult intellectual and ethical issues raised by the use of biotechnology. The difficulties the students faced in reaching consensus on the issues they confronted led Latisha to think about switching her prospective college major from economics to sociology or anthropology.

Latisha's third- and fourth-year science program engaged her in the study of the natural sciences structured in the conventional way and also through the lens of technology. Because Latisha planned to major in one of the social sciences in college, she did not take any advanced courses in her senior year. Even so, the cumulative effects of a strong elementary- and middle-level technology and science program and the intellectually rigorous content in her freshman and sophomore core courses enabled her to complete each of the half-year science courses in the college preparatory program. She will enter college with a well-structured base of knowledge equivalent to what she would have achieved in three full-year traditional science courses, enriched by a much deeper understanding of historical and present-day developments in science and technology.

Merlyn High School Student Transcript
Student: Martin Garcia

Technology/Science

Freshman Year: Core Technology/Science 1A and B
Sophomore Year: Core Technology/Science 2A and B
Junior Year: Introductory Concepts of Technology/
                        Physics, Internship and Seminar in T/E

Senior Year: Advanced Placement Physics, Internship
                        and Seminar in T/E

Martin entered Merlyn High knowing that he wanted to take as little science as possible. He did not think he needed any more academic science to get a
good job after high school; he had found science boring in middle school; and
he was convinced he could not do it. He was therefore distressed to learn from his
guidance counselor that, even if he did not plan to go on to college, he was required to take science/technology for four full years at Merlyn. He was only
partially reassured by the guidance counselor's description of the core technol-
ogy/science program; it certainly did not resemble any science course Martin had
ever taken before. After hearing about the alternative option available for students
interested in the workforce, Martin agreed to consider taking Introductory Principles of Technology/Physics in his junior year, the prerequisite for the study of
hydraulic, pneumatic, electrical, mechanical, and optical systems of household
appliances and workplace equipment.

Martin did credibly well in his core program. Some of the topics in CTS1A
and CTS2A led him to expand his interest in fixing and redesigning a variety of
appliances and equipment—a hobby he had pursued since his early teens, but that
had previously been completely dissociated from his school work. He still did
not believe, however, that he could do science; he did not think of the core course
as real science, since it was so different from what he had experienced in middle
school. Martin went ahead with the Introductory Principles of Technology/Physics
course in his junior year. Because the science content studied in this course was
presented in the context of devices and situations familiar to Martin, he learned
the material with surprising ease. In fact, he not only learned the content but also
came to enjoy it. Although he knew it was going to be hard, he decided to take AP
Physics in his senior year. He discovered that, while he struggled with much of the
mathematical work in the course, his experiences with how physics is used in the
worlds of home and work, gained from his technology course, made it easier for
him to understand many of the complex topics in the course. To his surprise, some
of the students who had taken the introductory physics course actually asked him
to help them with understanding how the abstract concepts they were learning
apply to everyday phenomena.

When Martin entered Merlyn he was working at Darcey & Sons Plumbing, Heating, and Air Conditioning. Through Mike Darcey's cooperation, this part-time job
was converted to an internship for Martin. The Darcey brothers became involved in
the T/E Seminar committee, and now not only Darcey & Sons but also the All-
Purpose Auto Clinic (owned and run by John Darcey) provide not only internships
but also equipment for the Advanced Concepts of Technology/Physics course.

Martin still plans to accept the full-time job offered him by Darcey & Sons after graduation, but he is negotiating flexible hours so he can continue his education at Tech Community College. His long-term plans include going to school on a full-time basis, once he has saved enough money, and obtaining an engineering degree at Leeland Polytech, so he can set up his own business.

Merlyn High School Student Transcript
Student: Jeanne Carvas

Technology / Science

Freshman Year:	Core Technology/Science 1A and B
Sophomore Year:	Core Technology/Science 2A and B
Junior Year:	Introductory Concepts of Technology/Physics, Introductory Concepts of Technology/Chemistry, Internship and Seminar in T/E
Senior Year:	Advanced Placement Physics, Introductory Earth/Space Science, Internship and Seminar in T/E

Jeanne Carvas entered Merlyn High planning to be an aerospace engineer. The program she planned in preparation for entry into postsecondary education was highly skewed toward physical science and engineering. She developed this interest through her part-time job at the local Aeroflight General Plant, which not only helped her save money for college but also gave her insights into career potentials for women in aerospace engineering.

The guidance counselor was quite concerned about the overemphasis in Jeanne's program on the physical sciences, but was assured by her parents that she was very committed to her goal. He knew that the life science topics in CST1A and CST2B would provide some balance in Jeanne's science knowledge and skills. Jeanne did well despite her heavy load in the last two years of high school; she especially enjoyed the T/E seminar series during senior year, which allowed her to advance to more challenging assignments at Aeroflight General. She was accepted at several top-level engineering schools on the basis of her school and work records and she looks forward to her college experience. She plans to accept Aeroflight General's offer to work full time during the coming summer.

RESOURCE LIST

Cave, J. *Technology in School: A Handbook of Practical Approaches and Ideas.* London: Routledge, 1986. Essentially an ideas resource book, this text is designed for teachers who want to introduce a larger element of technology into their teaching at all levels. The book is packed with relevant and realistic suggestions and illustrations for activities in school. It will also be of interest to science and primary teachers.

Darrow, K., and Pam, R. *Appropriate Technology Sourcebook.* Stanford, Calif.: Volunteers in Asia, 1978. A guide to practical plans and books for village and small community technology. Critical reviews of selected publications on a wide range of practical applications are provided on the basis of low price, clarity of presentation, easily understandable nontechnical language, and unique subject matter.

Deming, W. E. *Out of Crisis.* Cambridge, Mass.: Center for Advanced Engineering Study, Massachusetts Institute of Technology, 1982. This book teaches the transformation that is required for survival, a transformation that can only be accomplished by people. A company cannot buy its way into quality—it must be led into quality by top management and by a serious implementation of fourteen points for long-term improvement.

Engineering Concepts Curriculum Project. *The Man-Made World.* New York: McGraw-Hill, 1971. This book was a product of the Engineering Concepts Curriculum Project, which started in 1965 as an effort to interest more students in entering careers in science and technology. The text organizes the content of technology into three major categories: systems, materials, and energy. Although somewhat dated, the book remains a useful reference for teachers who want to introduce engineering concepts into the classroom.

Gardner, H. *To Open Minds.* New York: Basic Books, 1989. Gardner weaves lessons garnered from three vantage points—his own traditional education as an American child, his years of research on creativity at Harvard, and what he saw in modern Chinese classrooms—into a program for creativity that draws on the best of both traditional and progressive modes.

"General Certificate Student Examination (GCSE) Technology." Leckhampton, Cheltenham, England: Stanley Thornes, 1991. A modular series of four books on *Pneumatics, Electronics, Mechanisms,* and *Structures with Materials.* Each book covers one of the core topics of technology on the General Certificate Student Examination given to students in England and Wales. Each book applies an accessible problem-solving approach to the "harder" edge of technology, is rich in illustrations and examples, and contains many activities for individual and group work.

Hickman, L. A. *John Dewey's Pragmatic Technology.* Bloomington: Indiana University Press, 1990. This book provides insights into the concept of instrumentalism, the pragmatic critique of technology that Dewey developed and refined during his sixty years of public life. Dewey's lifelong preoccupation with the problems, methods, aims, and prospects of technology can provide unique insights for those who would be serious teachers or students of technology.

Inose, H., and Pierce, J. R. *Information Technology and Civilization.* New York: Freeman, 1984. Commissioned by the Club of Rome, the authors explore the opportunities and problems arising from changes in information technology. They show how technological imperatives and humans needs drive this revolution.

Jacobs, J. A., and Kilduff, T. F. *Engineering Materials Technology.* Englewood Cliffs, N.J.: Prentice Hall, 1985. The authors introduce the nature, properties, and applications of engineering materials that technology teachers should find helpful as they give additional attention to this important resource of technology.

Kreighbaum, E., and Barthels, K. M. *Biomechanics: A Qualitative Approach for Studying Humans Movement.* Minneapolis, Minn.: Burgess, 1981. A comprehensive introduction to biomechanics, following the guidelines and standards for undergraduate kinesiology, this text provides an important reference for teachers who wish to consider the relationship of humans to the tools, machines, and environments that are products of technology.

Lubar, S., and Kingery, D. W. *History from Things: Essays on Material Culture.* Washington, D.C.: Smithsonian Institution, 1993. This collection of eighteen essays explores the many ways objects can reconstruct and help to reinterpret the past. The essays are helpful to teachers in that they describe how to "read" artifacts, how to "listen to" landscapes and locations, and how to apply methods and theories to historical inquiry.

Markert, L. R. *Contemporary Technology: Innovations, Issues, and Perspectives.* South Holland, Ill.: Goodheart-Willcox, 1989. This is a reference book related to technology and society that is intended to introduce the reader to the pervasive nature of technological innovations and to increase awareness of both the promises and the uncertainties associated with the use of technology as a creative human enterprise.

McCrory, D. *Technology Education: Industrial Arts in Transition, A Review and Synthesis of the Research.* Columbus: Ohio State University, 1987. (ED 290 935) This publication covers the following aspects of technology education: (1) history, philosophy, and objectives; (2) human resources related studies; (3) status studies; (4) curriculum; (5) learning process variables; (6) instructional media, materials, and methods; (7) student personnel and guidance; (8) facilities; (9) evaluation; (10) teacher education; (11) administration and supervision; (12) professional concerns; and (13) recommendations for further research.

McLounghlin, M. *Electronics for You.* London: Hutchinson, 1989. This reference includes more than seventy interesting projects and applications, more than a thousand questions, and more than six hundred line illustrations that will help teachers see practical uses of electronics not normally found in the United States. The component details and construction plans provided increase the usefulness of the text.

Needham, J. *Science in Traditional China.* Cambridge, Mass.: Harvard University Press, 1981. Written by the world's authority on Chinese science, the book explores the philosophy, social structure, arts, crafts, and military strategies that form our understanding of Chinese science. Considerable attention is given to Taoist alchemy, which led not only to the invention of gunpowder and firearms, but also, through the search for macrobiotic life-elixirs, to the rise of modern medical chemistry.

Pierce, J. R. *An Introduction to Information Theory: Symbols, Signals and Noise.* New York: Dover, 1980. In this revision of his 1961 work, Pierce provides an overview of the field of information theory, its origins and development. He continues with an impressive, nontechnical account of how information theory relates to physics, cybernetics, psychology, and art.

Rutherford, F. J., and Ahlgren, A. *Science for All Americans.* New York: Oxford University Press, 1990. This book is about scientific literacy and consists of a set of recommendations on what understandings and ways of thinking are essential for all citizens in a world shaped by science and technology. These recommendations will be essential to the education of today's children for tomorrow's world.

Secretary's Commission on Achieving Necessary Skills. *SCANS: Learning a Living: A Blueprint for High Performance.* U.S. Department of Labor, 1992. This is the first in a series of documents that provide an overall look at the types of competencies that will be required of those who will work in the coming century. The language, concepts, and competencies mirror those of technology education. This document is an important source of support for those defending the central role that technology education should play in schooling for all.

Shimizu, Y., and others. *Models and Prototypes.* Tokyo: Graphics-sha Publishing, 1991. This richly illustrated book, written in both English and Japanese, provides detailed treatments of such aspects of modeling as concept sketching, paper model making, concept development through study models, and clay modeling. An excellent source for those serious about the use of modeling in design and technology.

Temple, R. *The Genius of China: 3000 Years of Science, Discovery, and Invention.* New York: Simon & Schuster, 1986. This is a captivating introduction to the astounding and unparalleled achievements of ancient China. The book presents a wide range of developments and contributions in engineering, medicine, technology, mathematics, science, warfare, transportation, and music that helped inspire the European agricultural and industrial revolutions.

Tickle, L. (ed.). *Design and Technology in Primary School Classrooms.* Washington, D.C.: Falmer Press, 1990. Presents a comprehensive account of the development and nature of D&T in the primary classroom from modest beginnings in the 1980s to detailed information within the U.K. National Curriculum. Includes original classroom research data and extensive illustrations, resource information and summaries of what D&T in the National Curriculum involves.

Tufte, E. R. *Envisioning Information.* Cheshire, Conn.: Graphics Press, 1990. This richly illustrated work presents a remarkable range of examples for use in visual thinking. The author helps the reader look for the best means of displaying information. This is a

"must" for those interested in adding substance to information, one of the key resources of technology.

Whaley, C. E. *Future Studies: Person and Global Possibilities*. New York: Trillium Press, 1984. This
short book introduces a range of usable tools and approaches to the study of the future. It serves as a straightforward aid to those who wish to integrate future studies
with their teaching about technology.

Related Resources for Use by Students

Burke, J. *Connections*. Boston: Little, Brown, 1978. This publication provides a unique examination of the ideas, inventions, and coincidences that have culminated in the major
technological achievements of the day. Accompanied by a series of ten hour-long
videos, the book makes a valuable resource for teachers interested in broadening students' insights into the development and impact of technology.

Caborn, C., and others. *Design and Technology*. Walton-on-Thames, Surrey, England: Nelson,
1989. Adopting a fully integrated approach, this text highlights the links between design and technology. It includes up-to-date material on electronics, microelectronics,
mechanisms, structures and energy, product modeling, and graphic techniques, and relates school-based practice with the real world.

Cave, J. (ed.). *Starting Design and Technology*. London: Cassell, 1992. This is a series of books
that provide substantial resource materials for introductory design and technology
courses across the range of student abilities. Teachers can select areas for study and
create their own teaching plans, using different combinations of the books, which address such topics as electronics, energy and control, materials, structures, mechanisms,
graphics, modeling, and more.

Breckon, A. *Craft, Design and Technology (CDT)*. London: Collins Educational, 1986. This book
series provides a practical approach to introducing the hands-on approach of CDT.
The titles of these books include *Foundation Course, Technology, Design and Communication*,
and *Design and Realization*.

Davies, D. *Information Technology at Work*. London: Heinemann Educational Books, 1986. This
reference is activity based and gives students the opportunity to learn and understand
through practical work. A variety of tasks centered on job-related or everyday experience will give students the opportunity to consolidate learning and to work at their
own pace.

De Old, A. R., and Judge, J. *Space Travel: A Technological Frontier*. Worcester, Mass.: Davis, 1989.
This well-illustrated book provides a valuable resource for those interested in teaching
about space travel. It includes information on the development of the space shuttle
program and underscores how transportation is dependent on other systems of technology.

De Vore, P., Horton, F., and Lawson, A. *Creativity, Design and Technology*. Worcester, Mass.:
Davis, 1989. This is a hands-on guide to fostering creative thinking in students, a practical resource that offers teachers useful information on the creative process through a
step-by-step analysis of the creative-technical process on which are built strategies and
activities for applying creative solutions to present and future situations.

Garratt, J. *Design and Technology*. New York: Cambridge University Press, 1991. This colorful
and stimulating book is designed for use by high school students. It covers the requirements of the National Curriculum for Design and Technology's equivalent to upper

high school level. It includes topics ranging from aesthetics and ergonomics to mechanisms, structures, pneumatics, and system control.

Hacker, M., and Barden, R. *Living with Technology.* Albany, N.Y.: Delmar, 1992. This text is designed to help middle school and junior high school students become technologically literate. It considers the impact of technology on humans, provides an overview of generic technological resources, and focuses on problem-solving methods as applied to technological systems.

Hacker, M., and Barden, R. *Technology in Your World.* Albany, N.Y.: Delmar, 1991. This general text on technology education for middle school and junior high school students discusses the technological process central to communication, manufacturing, construction, and biotechnical and transportation systems. It makes considerable use of the systems approach and integrates aspects of the U.K. approach to design and problem solving.

Hanks, K., Belliston, L., and Edwards, D. *Design Yourself.* Los Altos, Calif.: Kaufman, 1978. This book views design as making the optimum use of mental and physical tools for the creation of a better life and the solution of problems. It is a worthwhile reference for teachers learning about design and its use in the classroom.

Hutchinson, J., and Karsnitz, J. *Design and Problem Solving in Technology.* Albany, N.Y.: Delmar, 1994. This book is intended to help all students gain an understanding of technology. The design process has been used as the framework for the book, which links with and extends the content or structure of technology. The end purpose of the book is to make all students better and more knowledgeable technological problem solvers.

Hutchinson, P., and Sellwood, P. *Design and Problem Solving.* Cincinnati, Ohio: Thomson Learning Tools, 1995. This text is intended to help students learn about the design process and how to use it, improve their problem-solving skills with practice, and construct their own personal thinking skills for facing familiar and unfamiliar problems. Further, the book relates design-based technology with other subjects across the curriculum.

Kasicki, O. *Resources and Projects Book: Key Stage 3 Technology.* Walton-on-Thames, Surrey, England: Nelson, 1991. This book consists of two main sections: resources, which provides students with essential technology skills; and projects, which helps to develop problem-solving skills in a relevant context. It uses a colorful, cartoon approach and includes many tips on skills to help students improve their techniques.

Kimbell, R., and others. *Craft, Design and Technology.* London: Hutchinson Educational, 1987. This text provides a foundation for design and technology and includes lessons on identifying problems and needs, investigating tasks, generating and developing ideas, modeling, communication, producing provisional solutions, and evaluating. The book is supported by a series of videos produced by Thames Television.

Myerson, J. *Technology: A Systems Approach.* Leckhampton, Cheltenham, England: Stanley Thornes, 1990. This publication covers the main principles of technology as a framework for design and project work, without relying on excessive amounts of factual knowledge. It presents a variety of activities for students from short-term tasks to extended projects.

Poor, G. W. *The Illusion of Life: Lifelike Robotics.* San Diego, Calif.: Educational Learning Systems, 1991. This is a book about machines that give the illusion of life. It illustrates a wide range of robots that can be mistaken for humans and animals. The book also discusses in some detail how these robots, as well as fantasy figures from movies and exhibitions, are made.

Porter, T. and Greenstreet, B. *Manual of Graphic Techniques 1*. London: Butterworth Architecture, 1980. This is the first comprehensive guide to the use of graphic presentation tools and techniques for both the beginner and the professional. Hundreds of drawings and photos, including twelve color plates, provide step-by-step instructions for more than 120 techniques in surface, line and tone, color media and methods, orthographic and perspective drawing, and more.

Robertson, B. *How to Draw Charts and Diagrams*. Cincinnati, Ohio: North Light Books, 1988. This text provides a useful step-by-step guide on how to evaluate data, select the chart or diagram style that best communicates the data, and then use a variety of mediums to complete a final presentation. The book includes hundreds of examples of both good and poor examples of data treatment.

School Council. *Modular Courses in Technology*. Edinburgh, Scotland: Oliver & Boyd, 1983. This is a series of books to be used for existing courses in science, applied science, technology, technical studies, design, and technology, or for modular courses. The titles include *Energy Resources, Electronics, Mechanisms, Structures, Problem Solving, Pneumatics,* and *Instrumentation*. A teacher's guide and a student workbook are available for each book.

Staffordshire Technology Education Program. *STEP 5–16 Design and Technology*. New York: Cambridge University Press, 1992. This is a comprehensive series of books and resource materials for introducing D&T (ranging from biotechnology to control technology) into the classroom. The series includes data files of cards on technical aspects of D&T that are particularly helpful to inexperienced teachers and students.

Thode, B., and Thode, T. *Technology*. Albany, N.Y.: Delmar, 1994. This is a middle-level textbook that introduces students to a collection of technology experiences and activities.

Tickle, L. (ed.). *Design and Technology in Primary School Classrooms*. Washington, D.C.: Falmer Press, 1990. Presents a comprehensive account of the development and nature of D&T in the primary classroom from modest beginnings in the 1980s to detailed information within the U.K. National Curriculum. Includes original classroom research data and extensive illustrations, resource information and summaries of what D&T in the National Curriculum involves.

Todd, R., McCrory, D., and Todd, K. *Understanding and Using Technology*. Worcester, Mass.: Davis, 1985. This text for junior high school students provides a progressive treatment of the concepts and content of technology. Illustrations, text, and activities help students integrate the systems and problem-solving approaches and move to more sophisticated insights into the nature of technology and its resources, systems, changes, and impacts.

Todd, R., Todd, K., and McCrory, D. *Introduction to Design and Technology*. Cincinnati, Ohio: SouthWestern, 1995. This text extends the earlier book by the three authors and integrates the design and technology approach with a sound content framework of technology. The book also provides a detailed look at the resources, systems, and impacts of technology as the basis for sound technological decision making.

Tufnell, R. *Design and Communication*. London: Hutchinson, 1986. An exciting textbook that introduces middle and junior high school students to the ways in which ideas may be communicated through good design. It includes basic information on techniques for successful drawing in many different styles. In addition, the design process is analyzed through the work of specific designers and through project suggestions.

Williams, D. *Design Graphics*. Oxford: Blackwell, 1987. This is a major new book for students of design and technology. It combines techniques in graphic communication with practical studies and explores the role of graphics as an integral part of the design process. The book concentrates on generating and recording ideas, developing design concepts, communicating technical detail, and presenting design solutions.

Magazines

Adastra—To the Stars, National Space Society, 922 Pennsylvania Avenue, SE, Washington, DC 20003–2140

American Heritage of Invention and Technology, Forbes Building, 60 Fifth Avenue, New York, NY 10011

Arts and Activities, 591 Camino de la Reina, Suite 200, San Diego, CA 92108 (619/297–8032)

Bulletin of Science, Technology & Society, STS Press, Materials Research Laboratory, University Park, PA 16802 (814/865–1137)

Compressed Air, 253 East Washington Avenue, Washington, NJ 07882–2495

Data, Smallpiece House, 27 Newbold Terrace East, Leamington Spa, Warwickshire, England CV32 4ES

Design Perspectives, 1142 East Walker Road, Great Falls, VA 22066 (703/759–0100, 703/759–7679)

Discover, P.O. Box 420105, Palm Coast, FL 32142–0105 (800/829–9132)

Electronic Learning, 555 Broadway, New York, NY 10012 (800/544–2917)

Futurist, World Future Society Headquarters, 4916 Saint Elmo Avenue, Bethesda, MD 20814–5089

Journal of Technology Studies, Technology Building, Bowling Green State University, Bowling Green, OH 43403–0305 (419/372–2438, 419/372–6066)

Multimedia, Multimedia World, Subscription Department, 501 Second Street, #110, San Francisco, CA 94107

Photonics, Laurin Publishing Company, Berkshire Common, P.O. Box 4949, Pittsfield, MA 01202 (413/499–0514, 413/442–3180)

Popular Science, P.O. Box 5096, Harlan, IA 51593–2596 (800/289–9399)

Science News, P.O. Box 1925, Marion, OH 43305 (800/247–2160)

Sensors, Sensors Subscriptions, 174 Concord Street, Petersborough, NC 03458

Smithsonian, P.O. Box 55593, Boulder, CO 80322–5593 (800/766–2149)

Spinoff, U.S. Government Printing Office, Superintendent of Documents, Mail Stop SSOP, Washington, DC 20402–9328

T.H.E. Journal (Technological Horizons in Education), 150 El Camino Real, Suite 112, Tustin, CA 92680–3670

Technology Review, P.O. Box 978, Farmingdale, NY 11737–9878

Technology Teacher, International Technology Education Association, 1914 Association Drive, Reston, VA 22091 (703/860–2100)

TIES Magazine, Trenton State College, 3 Armstrong Hall, Trenton, NJ 08650–4700 (609/771–3344, 609/771–3330, ties@trenton.edu)

Associations

American Association for the Advancement of Science, Project 2061, 1331 H Street, NW, Washington, DC 20005 (202/326–6666, 202/842–5196)

American Chemical Society, 1155 16th Street, NW, Washington, DC 20036–4800 (202/872–4388, 202/872–8068, saw97@acs.org)

American Institute of Aeronautics and Astronautics, 370 L'Enfant Promenade, SW, Washington, DC 20024 (202/646–7444, 202/646–7508)

American Society of Mechanical Engineers (ASME), 345 East Forty-Seventh Street, New York, NY 10017–2330 (212/705–7448, 212/705–7143)

American Solar Energy Society, 2400 Central Avenue, G-1, Boulder, CO 80301 (303/443–3130, 303/443–3212, econet:ases)

ASM International, Student Outreach Program, Materials Park, OH 44073 (216/338–5151, 216/338–4634)

Design and Technology Association (DATA), Smallpiece House, 27 Newbold Terrace East, Leamington Spa, Warwickshire, England CV32 4ES (926/315984, 926/450679)

Epsilon Phi Tau (EPT), Technology Building, Bowling Green State University, Bowling Green, OH 43403–0305 (419/372–2438, 419/372–6066

IDATER, Department of Design and Technology, Loughborough University of Technology, Loughborough, Leicestershire, England LE11 3TU (0509/222644, 0509/610813)

Industrial Designs Society of America (IDSA), 1142 East Wallur Road, Great Falls, VA 22066 (703/759–0100, 703/759–7579)

Institute of Electrical and Electronics Engineers (IEEE), United States Activities, 1828 L Street, NW, Suite 1202, Washington, DC 20036–5104 (202/785–0017, 202/785–0835, a.hartfiel@ieee.org)

International Technology Education Association (ITEA), Kendall Starkweather, Executive Director, 1914 Association Drive, Reston, VA 22091–1539 (703/860–2100, 703/860–0353)

National Association for Science, Technology and Society (NASTS), 133 Willard Building, Pennsylvania State University, University Park, PA 16802 (814/865–3044)

Society for the History of Technology, Department of Social Science, Michigan Technological University, 1400 Townsend Drive, Houghton, MI 49931–1295 (906/487–2113)

Society of Automotive Engineers (SAE), 400 Commonwealth Drive, Warrendale, PA 15096–0001 (412/776–4841, 412/776–5760)

Society of Manufacturing Engineers (SME), One SME Drive, Dearborn, MI 48121 (313/271–1500, ext. 506; 313/271–2861)

Technical Education Research Centers, 2067 Massachusetts Avenue, Cambridge, MA 02140 (617/547–0430)

APPENDIX E

UNIVERSITY AND SCHOOL SITES

Universities Sponsoring Teacher Education Collaboratives

Ball State University, Dr. Ray Shackelford, Department of Industry and Technology, College of Applied Sciences and Technology, 2000 University Avenue, Muncie, IA 47306 (317)285–5641, (317)285–2162

Bowling Green State University, Dr. Ernest Savage, Visual Communications and Technology Education Department, College of Technology, Bowling Green, OH 43403–0300 (419)372–2437, (419)372–6066

Brigham Young University, Dr. Garth Hill, Technology Education Department, 230 Snell Building, Provo, UT 84602 (801)378–2021, (801)378–7519

California State University at Los Angeles, Dr. Ethan Lipton, School of Engineering and Technology, 5151 State University Drive, Los Angeles, CA 90032 (213)343–4550, (213)343–4555

California University of Pennsylvania, Dr. Stanley Komacek, Department of Industry and Technology, College of Science and Technology, 250 University Avenue, California, PA 15419–1394 (412)938–4086, (412)938–4572

Central Connecticut State University, Dr. Tad Foster, Technical and Vocational-Technical Education Department, School of Technology, 1615 Stanley Street, New Britain, CT 06050 (203)827–1850, (203)832–1868

Central Missouri State University, Dr. William Downs, Department of Graphics, College of Applied Sciences and Technology, Warrensburg, MO 64093 (816)543–4727, (816)543–8031

City College of New York, Dr. Howard Sasson, Technology and Occupational Education Department, School of Education, Convent Avenue and 138th Street, New York, NY 10031 (212)650–7139, (212)650–7534

Colorado State University, Dr. Gene Glockner, 200 West Lake Street, Fort Collins, CO 80523 (303)491–7353, (303)491–7801

Fairmont State College, Dr. Gary Bolyard, Division of Technology, Locust Avenue, Fairmont, WV 26554 (304)367–4156, (304)366–4870

Georgia Southern University, Dr. Alexander Creighton, Department of Vocational and Adult Education, College of Education, Statesboro, GA 30460 (912)681–5301, (912)681–5093

Illinois State University, Mr. Michael Daugherty, Department of Industrial Technology 5100, College of Applied Science and Technology, Normal, IL 61761 (309)438–3661, (309)438–5037

Indiana State University, Dr. Lowell Anderson, School of Technology, Department of Industrial Technology Education, 6th and Cherry Streets, Terre Haute, IN 47809 (812)237–2642, (812)237–4479

James Madison University, Dr. Arvid Van Dyke, Human Resource Development, College of Integrated Science and Psychology, Harrisonburg, VA 22807 (703)568–2876, (703)568–2761

Kent State University, Dr. Lowell Zurbuch, School of Technology, College of Fine and Professional Arts, 123 Van Deusen Hall, Terrace Drive, Kent, OH 44242 (216)672–2892, (216)672–2894

Millersville University, Dr. Perry Gemmill, Department of Industry and Technology, Division of Education, Osborn Hall, Frederick Street, Millersville, PA 17551 (717)872–3316

Montclair State University, Dr. Vincent Walencik, Department of Technology, School of Professional Studies, Valley Road and Normal Avenue, Upper Montclair, NJ 07043 (201)655–4161, (201)655–7206

Murray State University, Dr. Bert Siebold, College of Industry and Technology, Murray, KY 42071 (502)762–3393, (502)762–6919

North Carolina State University, Dr. Dick Peterson, Department of Occupational Education, Yarbrough Drive, Raleigh, NC 27695–7801 (919)515–2234, (919)515–7634

Ohio State University, Dr. Karen Zuga, Technology Education, College of Education, 190 West 19th Avenue, Columbus, OH 43210–1184 (614)292–7471, (614)292–2662

Old Dominion University, Dr. John Ritz, Occupational and Technical Studies Department, College of Education, 4600 Hampton Boulevard, Norfolk, VA 23529 (804)683–4305, (804)683–5227

Oregon State University, Dr. Sam Stern, Professional Technical Education, School of Education, Education Hall 230, Corvallis, OR 97331–1631 (503)737–6392, (503)737–2040

Pittsburgh State University, Dr. John Iley, Department of Technology Studies, School of Technology and Applied Science, Pittsburgh, KS 66762 (316)235–4371, (316)231–4231

State University of New York College at Oswego, Dr. Vincent D'Ambrosio, Department of Technology, School of Education, Oswego, NY 13126–3599 (315)341–3011, (315)341–3363

Trenton State College, Dr. John Karsnitz, Department of Technological Studies, School of Technology, CN 4700, Trenton, NJ 08650–4700 (609)771–2543, (609)771–3353

University of Missouri, Dr. Michael Dyrenfurth, Technology and Industry Education, 105 London Hall, College of Education, 6th and Stewart Streets, Colombia, MO 65211 (314)882–2782, (314)882–9935

University of Nebraska at Lincoln, Dr. George Rogers, Program of Industrial Education, 513 Nebraska Hall, Lincoln, NE 68588–0359 (402)472–5926, (402)472–5907

University of North Dakota, Dr. Myron Bender, Department of Industrial Technology, College of Business and Public Administration, Grand Forks, ND 58202 (701)777–2249, (701)777–3650

University of South Florida, Dr. Kenneth Smith, Industrial and Technical Education Program, College of Education, 4202 Fowler Avenue, Building FAO 100U, Room 226, Tampa, FL 33620 (813)974–3456, (813)974–5423

University of Wisconsin-Stout, Dr. Kenneth Welty, Communications, Education and Training Department, School of Industry and Technology, 1102 Union Street, Menomonie, WI 54751 (715)232–1137, (715)232–1274

Utah State University, Dr. Maurice Thomas, Industrial Technology and Education Department, College of Engineering, Logan, UT 84322–6000 (801)750–1795, (801)750–2567

Virginia Polytechnic Institute, Dr. Jim LaPorte, Technology Education Program, College of Education, 144 Smyth Hall, Blacksburg, VA 24061 (703)231–6480, (703)231–4188

Western Washington University, Dr. Robert Raudebaugh, Department of Engineering Technology, 516 High Street, Bellingham, WA 98225–9086 (206)676–3380, (206)647–4847

Sites: Elementary Schools

Name: Paramus Elementary Schools

Address: East 99 Century Road, Paramus, NJ 07652

Phone: (201)261–7800, ext. 3063

Fax: (201)261–3833

Chief education officer: Janice Dime

Director of curriculum: Paul Maramaldi

Contact: Ellen Van Howling, Supervisor of Creative Arts, K–12

Department name: Industrial Arts and Technology

Type of school: Suburban

Number of students: 1,400

Number of students in technology education: 288

Number of teachers in technology education: 12

Paramus Elementary is in the process of implementing technology education in kindergarten through grade four using technology learning activities (TLAs) through the science curriculum. The K–12 science supervisor and others are formulating a goal for two successive years to add TLAs using science content. At the end of two years, every K–4 teacher will have used TLAs with their students. They will use the TLA format and design loop as a process. They are working with Montclair State University to place their K–3 student teachers who are receiving a course in technology education as preparation.

Name: Cook-Wissahickon Elementary School

Address: Righter and Salaignac Streets, Philadelphia, PA 19128

Phone: (215)487–4463

Fax: (215)487–4808

Principal: Anne Marie Bucci

Contact: William Metz

Department name: Science/Math/Technology

Program Name: Connections for 2000

Type of school: Urban

Number of students: 540

Number of teachers: 25

Number of students in technology education: 200

Number of teachers in technology education: 5

The Cook-Wissahickon Elementary School has blended its design and technology program in grades three to five with thematic units as well as with their language skills program. This obvious integration of curricula strands affords numerous opportunities for students to be challenged in the upper level skills of problem solving and critical thinking as they work through a variety of hands-on assignments. Student evaluation is continuous throughout each unit. Authentic assessment of projects and documentation in the form of journals, design briefs, and appropriate data collection techniques are coupled with observation of student laboratory skills, student self-assessment, and cooperative group work.

Name: Hopkinson Elementary School

Address: "L" and Lucerne Streets, Philadelphia, PA 19124

Phone: (215)537–2526

Fax: (215)537–2901

Contact: Joseph Huttlin, technology education specialist

Hopkinson Elementary is a K–8 school that has used a middle school technology education program as a focal point to support elementary teachers' efforts to integrate design and technology into their classrooms.

Name: Dranesville Elementary School

Address: 1515 Powells Tavern Place, Herndon, VA 22070

Phone: (703)709–7789

Fax: (703)709–9448

Principal: Beverly Morrison

Contact: Diane Harazin, technology specialist

Type of school: Suburban

Number of students: 920

Number of students in technology education: 920

Dranesville Elementary School's mission statement and yearly objectives emphasize technology, stating the goal of strengthening the mathematics, science, and technology programs at all grade levels. The goal is carried out by integrating technology into all curricula. Technology education is therefore not a separate curriculum area, but a vehicle for applying the concepts acquired in math, science, social studies, language arts, and other subjects. The application of technology is used to solve current problems and needs. Technology education at Dranesville includes more than just teaching with technology such as computers. It involves teaching about the past, present, and future of technology. This program uses the students' "know-how" and "ability-to-do" capabilities and a carefully planned interdisciplinary learning situation.

Sites: Middle Schools

Name: Middle School of Plainville

Address: 150 Northwest Drive, Plainville, CT 06062

Phone: (203)793–3250

Fax: (203)793–3265

Chief education officer: James J. Ritchie

Principal: Paul Cavaliere Jr.

Contact: Joseph Spagna, teacher

Department name: Technology Education

Type of school: Suburban

Number of students: 650

Number of teachers: 50

Number of students in technology education: 650

Number of teachers in technology education: 2

This program provides a wide range of design and technology-oriented experiences for students. Examples of activities include the design and development of a powered ice boat, the conversion of a gas go-cart to solar power, and the erecting of an underwater geodesic dome. The design problem activities integrate the content and skills of science, mathematics, and technology, as well as other school subjects across the curriculum.

Name: Brooker Middle School

Address: 2250 Myrtle Street, Sarasota, FL 34234

Phone/Fax: (813)359–5824

Fax: (813)359–5898

Chief education officer: Charles Fowler

Principal: Andrew Jones

Contact: Ms. Arnall Cox, teacher

Department name: Exploratory/Vocational-Technical

Program name: Technology Education

Type of school: Urban

Number of students: 1,200

Number of teachers: 60

Number of students in technology education: 180 per semester

Number of teachers in technology education: 1

In this program, sixth graders are given an orientation to technology; in the seventh grade, they are introduced to integrated technology studies; and in the eighth grade, integrated technology studies are supplemented with an exploration of manufacturing. Sixth graders are introduced to team assignments that include problem-solving activities, which prepare them for the modular learning approach in the seventh grade. This approach centers on use of a modular technology lab with twenty stations; students are given the opportunity to explore possible careers while being introduced to the newest technologies in the various areas.

Name: Greenwood Middle School

Address: 523 South Madison Avenue, Greenwood, IN 46142

Phone: (317)889–4163

Fax: (317)889–4163

Chief education officer: Joe DiPietro

Contact: Rex Harris or Mike McQueen, industrial technology teachers

Type of school: Suburban

Number of students: 900

Number of teachers: 50

Number of students in technology education: 775

Number of teachers in technology education: 2

Greenwood Middle School is located ten minutes south of Indianapolis, off I-65. The technology facility is a modular unit with twenty-five work stations. These work stations are used in conjunction with bar-coded textbooks in the classroom phases. These sixth- through eighth-grade courses are called "Exploring Technology." Rex Harris and Mike McQueen are described as "facilitators of learning." Student are held responsible for their own learning. Through the use of hands-on experiences, students are motivated to learn. This facility has been visited by hundreds of educators across the nation. It was recently filmed by the Korean *60 Minutes* television program for a special on learning in the twenty-first century. Many visitors proclaim that this concept makes more sense than anything they have seen in education.

Name: Powell County Middle School

Address: 770 West College Avenue, Stanton, KY 40380

Phone: (606)663–3307

Chief education officer: Jimmy Potts

Principal: Darryl Abner

Contact: Ronnie Cooper, technology education teacher

Department name: Vocational and Technical Education

Program name: Technology Education

Type of school: Rural

Number of students: 600

Number of teachers: 35

Number of students in technology education: 450

Number of teachers in technology education: 1

At Powell County Middle School, technology education for seventh and eighth graders has been designed to allow students to view and have hands-on experience in many different areas of technology. The lab is equipped with lasers, computer numerical control (CNC) mills, computers, robots, satellites, audio and video equipment, and numerous other high-tech equipment. Classes are self-directed and self-paced for learners at all levels, to ensure that students obtain technological literacy and learn how technology affects society and the environment. One of the highlights of the year is centered around a collaborative effort between the technology and math departments. The students design and build their own bridges, and then test the bridges' weight capacity. This always proves to be a very memorable and educational project. Teachers are constantly teaching and reinforcing with hands-on experience that technology does indeed affect all aspects of life. They view technology education as the key to a brighter future for students, the community, and the nation.

Name: Bloomfield Hills Middle School

Address: 4200 West Quarton Road, Bloomfield, MI 48302

Phone: (810)932–6100

Fax: (810)932–6026

Chief education officer: Gary Doyle

Principal: Gary Grosnickle

Contact: Gary Grosnickle

Department name: Integrated Math/Science/Technology Program

Type of school: Suburban

Number of students: 468

Number of teachers: 32

Number of students in technology education: 52

Number of teachers in technology education: 3

The integrated mathematics, science, and technology program is designed to be used by seventh-grade students to replace the traditionally separate courses of mathematics, science, and technology. The program integrates knowledge, skills, and attitudes normally taught in the separate courses, in ways that are consistent with current understandings of how children learn.

Name: Winona Middle School

Address: 166 West Broadway, Winona, MN 55987–3320

Phone: (507)454–9402

Fax: (507)454–9586

Chief education officer: Ron McIntire

Principal: Scott Hannon

Department head: Jerry Lowery

Contact: Dan Picha, instructor

Department name: Technology Education

Program name: Manufacturing/Engineering

Number of students: 1,100

Number of teachers: 70

Number of students in technology education: 1,100

Number of teachers in technology education: 2.5

Manufacturing deals with the study of manufacturing firms from the top administration to shipping and receiving. Manufacturing floor plans are developed. A mass production unit is included using a working gumball machine as a prototype. A computer robotics unit is used to enhance excitement toward learning. In engineering, students study terms dealing with careers in engineering while teams of students build and test a bridge.

Name: Will James Middle School

Address: 1200 30th West, Billings, MT 59102

Phone: (406)655–3124

Fax: (406)655–3129

Principal: Harold Olson

Contact: Curt Prchal, technology teacher

Department name: Technology and Computer Applications

Type of school: Suburban

Number of students: 550

Number of teachers: 35

Number of students in technology education: 380

Number of teachers in technology education: 2

Will James Middle School operates a comprehensive, self-directed technology learning lab that focuses on promoting technological literacy, lifelong learning, and workplace skills. The program offers modular-based learning stations woven together with a unique laboratory management and delivery system. The program has been developed to integrate critical thinking skills through the learning processes of brainstorming, creativity, cooperative learning, risk taking, decision making, and problem solving.

> *Name:* Paramus Middle Schools
>
> *Address:* East 99 Century Road, Paramus, NJ, 07652
>
> *Phone:* (201)261–7800 ext. 3063
>
> *Fax:* (201)261–3833
>
> *Chief education officer:* Janice Dime
>
> *Director of curriculum:* Paul Maramaldi
>
> *Contact:* Ellen Van Howling, Supervisor of Creative Arts, K–12
>
> *Department name:* Industrial Arts and Technology
>
> *Type of school:* Suburban
>
> *Number of students:* 1,100
>
> *Number of students in technology education:* 1,100
>
> *Number of teachers in technology education:* 5

Technology education is required as a cycle for all students at both Paramus Middle Schools in the sixth and seventh grades; in the eighth grade, it is offered as an elective. Both Middle Schools were listed as demonstration sites by Technology Education Association of New Jersey (TEANJ). The program was established in 1989.

> *Name:* Soule Road Middle School
>
> *Address:* 8340 Soule Road, Liverpool, NY 13090
>
> *Phone:* (315)453–1283
>
> *Fax:* (315)453–1286
>
> *Chief education officer:* John Cataldo
>
> *Principal:* Joseph Pecori
>
> *Department head:* Thomas La Clair
>
> *Contact:* Steve Poydock
>
> *Department name:* Technology Education
>
> *Program name:* Introduction to Technology
>
> *Type of school:* Suburban

Number of students: 538

Number of teachers: 33

Number of students in technology education: 538

Number of teachers in technology education: 3

Soule Road Middle School's technology education program is a unique situation in which three classes are presented simultaneously in one large technology laboratory. The curriculum parallels New York State's mandated Introduction to Technology syllabus. Visitors can quickly observe students actively experiencing how to understand, use, and control technology and its impacts on society. Youngsters apply principles of math, science, and technology during hands-on experiments in areas such as robotics, control technology, materials testing and fabrication, engineering structures and problem solving, desktop publishing, computer-aided drafting, computer-aided manufacturing, and technology's impacts on society.

Name: Bay Trail Middle School

Address: 1760 Scribner Road, Penfield, NY 14526

Phone: (716)248–0983

Fax: (716)248–0735

Chief education officer: Richard Mace

Principal: Doreen DeCamp

Department head: Ried Doe

Contacts: Joseph Rieger and Thomas Douglas, teachers

Department name: Technology Education

Program name: Introduction to Technology, Seventh and Eighth

Type of school: Suburban

Number of students: 1,150

Number of teachers: 115

Number of students in technology education: 800

Number of teachers in technology education: 4

The technology education program at Bay Trail Middle School revolves around three distinct laboratories. All seventh- and eighth-grade students explore numerous activites in each of three facilities: a communications lab, a technology lab, and a production lab. The emphasis of the program is to develop students who, when they leave the middle school setting, will have been exposed to a variety of technical areas. The department uses common pre-engineering projects to unify all three labs. This enables the students to see how each lab is dependent upon the others to produce a final product. In addition to the pre-engineering projects, students also complete activities in the field of black and white photography, digital imaging, computer applications, aerospace, plastic fabrication, manufacturing projects, structures, robotics, database management, lego dacta, and much more.

Name: Queensbury Middle School

Address: 75 Aviation Road, Queensbury, NY 12804

Phone: (518)793–2258

Fax: (518)793–4476

Chief education officer: David Gee

Principal: Arthur Gottlieb

Contact: Douglas Purdy, technology teacher

Department name: Technology

Type of school: Suburban

Number of students: 1,052

Number of teachers: 69

Number of students in technology education: 525

Number of teachers in technology education: 3

The technology program at Queensbury Middle School includes information technology such as computer-aided design (CAD), and a computer bulletin board system (BBS). Physical technology involves the application of concepts of physics and mathematics by using various components, including LEGO blocks. For example, using the properties of solids, liquids, and gases, the student designs a diving device that is suspended underwater. Math is used to find pressures and volumes used in the activity. Cloning of plants by tissue culturing is the main focus of the biotechnology area. Another biotechnology activity involves using rapid-cycling laboratory plants to investigate the effects of various chemicals on the environment. The student is evaluated on individual learning progress. Documented formalized problem solving is part of the assessment process.

Name: Dake Junior High School

Address: 350 Cooper Road, Rochester, NY 14617

Phone: (716)336–2997

Fax: (716)336–2929

Chief education officer: Joseph Sproule

Principal: Deborah Springpeace

Department head: Dudley Carlson

Contact: Dudley Carlson, coordinator, occupational education

Department name: Occupational Education Department

Program name: Technology Education

Type of school: Suburban

Number of students: 604

Number of teachers: 55

Number of teachers in technology education: 7 (grades 7–12)

The program at Dake Junior High School focuses on an integrated study of transportation, fabrication, and photography as used in today's society. These are followed by the study of materials found in the construction, aerospace, and electronics industries, and by an array of practically oriented computer activities.

Name: Felix V. Festa Junior High School

Address: Parrott Road, West Nyack, NY 10994

Phone: (914)639–6410

Fax: (914)634–5073

Chief education officer: William Heebink

Principal: Gerard Gretzinger

Contact: Alan Horowitz, Chairman of Technology

Department name: Technology Education

Type of school: Suburban

Number of students: 1,400

Number of teachers: 105

Number of students in technology education: 1,400

Number of teachers in technology education: 8

Technology education at Felix Festa V. Junior High School is an exciting hands-on program that includes a broad variety of topics in fields such as production, transportation, construction, and communications. CAD, robotics, alternative energy sources, aerospace, satellite communication, magnetic levitation, hydroponics, and laser technology are some of the subjects included in the seventh- and eighth-grade curricula. Technology education provides students with experiences that encourage them to question what they do not understand, to promote exploration and problem solving, to foster limitless growth through lifelong learning, and most of all, to motivate and inspire youngsters to achieve their maximum potential.

Name: Discovery Junior High School

Address: 1717 South 40th Avenue, Fargo, ND 58104

Phone: (701)241–6090

Fax: (701)241–6095

Principal: Warren Gullickson

Contact: Garry Roth, department chair, technology education

Department name: Technology Education

Type of school: Suburban

Number of students: 1,050

Number of teachers: 68

Number of students in technology education: 720

Number of teachers in technology education: 3

Three technology-oriented classrooms focus on manufacturing, construction, electronics, transportation technology, and computer communications. The three rooms run on a seven-day module schedule. All classes are elective and a semester in length.

Name: Sells Middle School

Address: 150 West Bridge Street, Dublin, OH 43017

Phone: (614)764–5919

Fax: (614)764–5923

Contact: Kevin Burns (E-mail: kburns@magnus.acs.ohiostate.edu)

Sixth- and seventh-grade programs consist of technology education with a focus on problem solving. Some of the problem-solving activities include microelectronics, vehicle design, and crash testing. At the eighth-grade level, technology teachers have been involved in working with the academic teams on integrating all the subject areas.

Name: Garden Spot Middle School

Address: Box 609, 669 E. Main Street, New Holland, PA 17557

Phone: (717)354–4031

Fax: (717)354–1534

Chief education officer: William Rohrer

Principal: Joyce Wilkinson

Contact: Bruce Ventura

Department name: Technology Education

Type of school: Suburban

Number of students: 550

Number of teachers: 35

Number of students in technology education: 550

Number of teachers in technology education: 2

Technology education at Garden Spot Middle School uses an interdisciplinary, thematic approach to drive a problem-solving problem. Science, social studies, English, and other disciplines are teamed with technology education around themes such as energy conversion, transportation, space colonization, biomes and biospheres, or projects such as creating models of DNA molecules or Punnett squares. Traditional hand- and machine-tool skills are emphasized through individual project work. The technological systems model is used to identify various inputs, processes, and outputs of systems. Problem solving is overtly taught by employing several heuristics. Design briefs pose realistic problems for the students to solve. Computers are employed in testing designs, researching information, desktop publishing, and preparing reports.

Name: Margaret Bell Miller Middle School

Address: 126 E. Lincoln Street, Waynesburg, PA 15370

Phone: (412)852–2722

Fax: (412)627–9591

Chief education officer: Linda McCraken

Principal: Donna Sybert

Contact: Dave Shulz

Department name: Technology Education

Program name: Technology Education Five to Eight

Type of school: Rural/Suburban

Number of students: 800

Number of teachers: 60

Number of students in technology education: 800

Number of teachers in technology education: 2

At Margaret Bell Miller Middle School, technology education is defined as the discipline for the study of the application of knowledge, creativity, and resources to solve problems and extend human potential. It is a comprehensive, activity-based program that is concerned with understanding the evolution, application, and significance of technology; its organization, personnel, systems, processes, resources, and products; and the associated social, cultural, and environmental impacts. The school's philosophy is that technology education should be exploratory in nature, meaning that it should give students experiences in as many technological areas as possible to aid them in future educational and vocational choices.

Name: Marshall Middle School

Address: 5145 Wexford Run Road, Wexford, PA 15090

Phone: (412)934–6060

Fax: (412)935–2474

Chief education officer: Larry Buzzomo

Principal: John Schwoebel

Contact: Tim Vermillion, teacher

Department name: Technology Education

Type of school: Suburban

Number of students: 758

Number of teachers: 40

Number of students in technology education: 758

Number of teachers in technology education: 3

Marshall Middle School's technology education program is an award-winning program recognized by the local, state, and federal governments. Sixth-, seventh- and eighth-grade students are taught how to use technology. Students perform activities designed to provide hands-on experiences in communications (CAD, telecommunications, hypermedia), manufacturing (product development), transportation (technology timeline), and construction (bridge building). All of these activities include discussion of the environment. Students do all this in the form of a company called "The Toy Company." This thematic approach has provided students with the "big picture" of technology.

Name: Albright Middle School—Alief Independent School District

Address: 6315 Winkleman, Houston, TX 77083

Phone: (713)983–8411

Fax: (713)568–7759

Principal: Dennis Paul

Contact: Julie Moore, teacher/facilitator

Department name: Technology Education

Type of school: Suburban

Number of students: 1,087

Number of teachers: 64

Number of students in technology education: 384

Number of teachers in technology education: 1–2

Albright Middle School is helping students make informed occupational choices by providing them with an opportunity to explore different technologies in a modular technology education center. Using the Synergistic System, paired students rotate through twenty-one different work stations to study various technologies using computers, videos, hands-on activities, and other educational materials. The center allows students to become responsible for their own learning while developing problem-solving and critical-thinking skills.

Name: Chisholm Trail Middle School

Address: 500 Oak Ridge Drive, Round Rock, TX 78681

Phone: (512)255–7866

Fax: (512)388–1471

Principal: Darla Regner

Contact: Chuck Bridge, industrial technology teacher

Department name: Industrial Technology Department

Type of school: Suburban

Number of students: 1,100

Number of teachers: 98

Number of students in technology education: 170

Number of teachers in technology education: 2

The program at Chisholm Trail Middle School might be considered "middle-tech," as opposed to high-tech or low-tech. The school is fourteen years old, and it utilizes computers (for desktop publishing, graphics, word processing, databases, spreadsheets, telecommunication, and simulation), robots, video and still photography, electronics learning units, digitizers and scanners, and other such tools, along with traditional equipment usually incorporated into a production/manufacturing/construction course. The curriculum was developed around three technology areas of communication (audio, visual, and electronic), production (manufacturing and construction), and transportation (energy/power, space, land, water, air, and stationary). Development of curricula in the area of biotechnology is just beginning. Activities use student experiences in problem solving, brainstorming, systems models, cooperative learning, role-play/simulation, parliamentary procedure, and entrepreneurship. Community and administrative support are great, which is essential to such a program. The teachers and administrators are always looking for new and creative means for educating young people in the wonders of a technological world.

Name: Franklin Middle School

Address: 3300 Lees Corner Road, Chantilly, VA 22021

Phone: (703)904–5100

Fax: (703)904–5197

Principal: Mrs. Johnnie Hamilton

Department head: Bob Sciabica

Contact: Charles Harris

Department name: Technology Education

Type of school: Suburban

Number of students: 1,400

Number of teachers: 70

Number of students in technology education: 750

Number of teachers in technology education: 2

The technology education program at Franklin Middle School is a comprehensive program that includes studies in basic technical drawing, CAD, aerospace engineering, pneumatics, hydraulics, structures, CNC electronics, animations, and robotics. Students work in small cooperative groups as they use problem-solving techniques, computers, and traditional tools and machines to construct solutions to design-brief problems.

Name: Saint Clare Walker Middle School

Address: Route 33 East, P.O. Box 9, Locust Hill, Va 23092

Phone: (804)758–0317

Chief education officer: W. Ernest Worley

Principal: Joseph Fears

Department head: Michael Willis

Contact: Kevin Rose, project coordinator

Department name: Technology Education

Type of school: Rural

Number of students: 350

Number of teachers: 24

Number of students in technology education: 350

Number of teachers in technology education: 1

The MARS Technology Lab consists of fourteen areas of technology in a modular form. Each module consists of three levels of activities. The first level introduces history, present-day innovations, and enabling activities of the area; the conclusion is an open-ended activity to test the student team's knowledge and skill in that module area. In the second level, teams do more in-depth research and apply that research to a problem-solving activity. The third level requires understanding of the two previous levels in the module area. Student teams are expected to collaborate with each other to do special projects that involve two or more module areas. The two student teams are given nine days to do a level, with a labwide seminar on the tenth day. The goal of the lab is to show the student how to become an independent researcher. The intention is that students will become leaders in technology, not followers waiting for somebody to "teach" them.

Name: Buckhannon Upshur Middle School

Address: P.O. Box 250, Buckhannon, WV 26201–0250

Phone: (304)472–1520

Fax: (304)472–6864

Principal: Steve L. Paine

Department head: Thomas Withers

Contact: Rick Dye, teacher

Department name: Technology Education

Type of school: Rural

Number of students: 1,100

Number of teachers: 81

Number of students in technology education: 468

Number of teachers in technology education: 2

Buckhannon Upshur Middle School meets the need for seventh- and eighth-grade students to explore technology. The school uses two approachs, the world in which students live and the world in which they will work. Both are an accumulation of four different technology systems: communication, transportation, manufacturing, and construction. In the seventh grade, the students work in groups. They explore the systems-input process and output as a group by using books and readings, hands-on activities, and problem solving. In the eighth-grade program, students explore systems through the modular approach. The students work in pairs, cooperatively exploring nine systems of technology with the use of TV, VCR and a computerized self-paced curriculum in a synergystic modular lab. Research and problem-solving skills are strengthened as well as math and science skills.

Name: Frankfort Middle School

Address: Route 3, Box 170, Ridgely, WV 26753

Phone: (304)726–4339

Chief education officer: Charles Kalbaugh

Principal: Clarence Golden

Department head: Terry Cannon

Contact: John Watson

Department name: Technology Education

Type of school: Rural

Number of students: 560

Number of teachers: 40

Number of students in technology education: 560

Number of teachers in technology education: 1

The program at Frankfort Middle School is a "synergistic" technology education lab. Students are paired up and placed in work stations, where they receive video-based instruction. In specific areas of technology, the students rotate to a new station every seven days. While at each station, the students complete various problem-solving activities using many different pieces of high-tech equipment.

Name: Winfield Middle School

Address: 3280 Winfield Road, Winfield, WV 26201

Phone: (304)586–3072

Fax: (304)586–0553

Chief education officer: Samuel Sentelle

Principal: Eugene G. Andersen

Contact: Dale Slack

Department name: Technology Education

Type of school: Rural

Number of students: 550

Number of teachers: 36

Number of students in technology education: 525

Number of teachers in technology education: 1

Winfield Middle School will soon be taking a new curricular approach to education. Currently, the industrial arts classroom is being renovated to accomodate a twelve-station technology education modular classroom with a separate production area. Each module will have two students working in the areas of communication, transportation, manufacturing, construction, and biotechnology. Topics such as robotics, desktop publishing, and flight technology will be covered. With this new approach, students will use self-directive lesson plans, acquire cooperative learning techniques, develop problem-solving skills, and participate in many hands-on activities.

Sites: Middle and High Schools

Name: Grundy Center Middle School and High School

Address: 1006 M Avenue, Grundy Center, IA 50638

Phone: (319)824–5449

Fax: (319)824–6415

Chief education officer: Robert Crouse

Principal: Harold Dole

Contact: Bruce Huber, technology teacher

Department name: Industrial Technology

Program name: IMAST (Integrated Math/Science/Technology)

Type of school: Rural

Number of students: 342

Number of teachers: 22

Number of students in technology education: 108

Number of teachers in technology education: 1

The IMAST program consists of activities for seventh graders that integrate concepts and processes from the disciplines of mathematics, science, and technology education. The IMAST program emphasizes the connections among the traditional disciplines as well as to other disciplines. The curriculum teaches in a global context, is related to daily life, develops problem-solving strategies, and includes cooperative learning experiences as well as experiential learning activities. A curriculum design team is in the process of expanding this idea at the high school level to include such curriculum areas as language arts, science, and technology. Interdisciplinary learning enables students to make connections and attach relevance to the work they are doing, thereby increasing their level of interest.

Name: Lyon County High School

Address: 209 Fairview Avenue, Eddyville, KY 42038

Phone: (502)388–2296

Principal: Carroll Wadlington

Contact: Doug Cotton, technology education teacher

Department name: Vocational-Technology Education

Type of school: Rural

Number of students: 450

Number of teachers: 31

Number of students in technology education: 200

Number of teachers in technology education: 1

In the seventh and eighth grade, students are taught an exploratory class in technology. The students are exposed to the principles of design, hands-on problem solving, engineering structures, and aerospace technology. In grades nine to twelve, students are offered drafting, computer graphics, a survey of technology, and woods. A wide range of projects and creativity can develop from students who have a choice.

Name: Randolph Middle/High Schools

Address: Millbrook Avenue, Randolph, NJ 07869

Phone: (201)361–2400

Fax: (201)361–1661

Chief education officer: Robert Gordon

Principal: Cecil Beavers

Contact: Joyce Maehrlein, district supervisor

Department name: Business/Technology Education

Type of school: Suburban

Number of students: 2,200

Number of teachers: 181

Number of students in technology education: 975

Number of teachers in technology education: 7

Technology education at the Randolph Middle and High Schools is an interdisciplinary approach to looking at the technological world. In this approach, the teacher acts as facilitator as students explore and develop solutions to technological problems. Methodology includes critical thinking, problem solving, and portfolio development. A new offering for 1995–96 will be a collaboration between the science and technology departments called physics/technology. It will be team taught by a physics and technology teacher, and the methods used will be problem solving through engineering projects that reinforce the application of physics principles. Courses are taught in technology and design, power and energy technology, robotics and control technology, transportation technology, electronics, and inventions and innovations.

Name: Boyertown School System

Address: South Madison Street, Boyertown, PA 19512

Phone: (610)369–7471

Fax: (610)369–7483

Contact: Arvid Seifarth, technology education supervisor

This school system has used technology education as a focal point for bringing together the interest and efforts of school faculty in the redesign of what and how students will learn.

Name: Bryan Independent School District

Address: 101 North Texas Avenue, Bryan, TX 77803

Phone: (409)361–5214

Fax: (409)361–9649

Chief education officer: Sarah Ashburn

Principal: Jerry Ellis

Department head: Nina Wright

Contact: Ward McCain, director of careers and technology

Type of school: urban

Number of students: 2,796

Number of teachers: 205

Number of students in technology education: 1,732

Number of teachers in technology education: 57

One of the most innovative programs at Bryan Independent School District is Tech Lab 2000. This facility provides a computer activity–based course with emphasis on communications, energy, and production technology. Students use and develop critical thinking skills, problem solving, and decision making. Students also experience how the computer serves the needs of people and society. The curriculum places emphasis on construction, programming, operation, applications, and socioeconomic impacts of computers in industry. This course also fills graduation requirements for computer science.

Name: Lopez Middle/Senior High School

Address: Route 1, Box 1190, Lopez Island, WA 98261

Phone: (360)468–2219

Fax: (360)468–2212

Chief education officer: Daniel Levine

Contact: Steve Adams, technology education teacher

Department name: Science-Technology

Type of school: Rural

Number of students: 150

Number of teachers: 8

Number of students in technology education: 100

Number of teachers in technology education: 1

Lopez school has an integrated science and technology curriculum. These courses use design-based activities in an engineering environment. The core content includes the history and future of science and technology; computer skills; systems of technology; and electronics controls. Students learn through a series of exciting projects that include building solar-powered vehicles, electrothons, computer-controlled robots, and various wind tunnel activities. Students are evaluated through portfolios, projects, presentations, and showing creative solutions to problems.

Name: Wauzeka Public Schools

Address: P.O. Box 347, Wauzeka, WI 53826–0347

Phone: (608)875–5792

Fax: (608)875–5100

Chief education officer: Jerome Fiene

Principal: Rodney Gardner

Contact: Pete McConnell, technology educator

Department name: Technology Education

Type of school: Rural

Number of students: 389

Number of teachers: 35

Number of students in technology education: 175

Number of teachers in technology education: 1

The Wauzeka Public Schools' 7–12 Technology Education Program was modeled after the Wisconsin Small School Technology Education Model. Exploration is a seventh- and eighth-grade eighteen-week course for boys and girls. The four clusters are taught to freshmen in the introduction to technology course for nine weeks per cluster. Level One courses include separate classes in power and energy, communications, home mechanics, and manufacturing process. Level Two courses include CAD, electricity, construction, and woods technology. (All courses are taught by semester, except construction, which is a full-year course.) Also taught are applied math, principles of technology (along with power and energy), and eighth-grade engineering and design. The transition into this program has been tiring for the teachers as they have continued to expand with applied academics and engineering. The emphasis is maintained by problem solving, decision making, and team involvement. The school's population of both male and female students continues to grow. Students raise money to purchase computers, and the school also has an active VICA Club that competes at the state and national levels.

Sites: High Schools

Name: Berlin High School

Address: 139 Patterson Way, Berlin, CT 06037

Phone: (203)828–6577

Fax: (203)829–0526

Chief education officer: Ted Rokicki

Principal: Thomas Galvin

Department head: Robert Poglitsch

Contact: Robert Recor, technology educator

Department name: Technology Education

Type of school: Suburban

Program name: Computers in Technology

Number of students: 750

Number of teachers: 80

Number of students in technology education: 378

Number of teachers in technology education: 4

This course is set up to give students the opportunity to explore both the vocational and avocational uses of the computer. Students explore applications such as graphic design, CAD, desktop publishing, robotic control, two- and three-dimensional computer graphics and animation, word processing, database creation, simulations, video capture and manipulation, CNC and computer operating systems such as MSDOS, Mac OS, and Windows. Students are also introduced to telecommunications and the use of modems for accessing remote services such as Prodigy and America Online. In addition, students access the technology education department's student-run BBS, the Berlin Wall. Activities include sending and receiving E-mail, uploading and downloading text graphics files, and completing on-line assignments with students from other schools. Other activities on the Berlin Wall include accessing on-line CD-ROMs, on-line simulations and games, and on-line chatting.

> *Name:* Somers High School
> *Address:* Ninth District Road, Somers, CT 06071
> *Phone:* (203)749–0719
> *Fax:* (203)749–9264
> *Chief education officer:* Paul Gagliarducci
> *Principal:* Daniel Lynch
> *Contact:* Roy Slater
> *Department name:* Somers Technology Education Program (STEP)
> *Type of school:* Rural
> *Number of students:* 425
> *Number of teachers:* 31
> *Number of students in technology education:* 185
> *Number of teachers in technology education:* 2

Somers High School's technology education program provides experiences within three domains of instruction: communication, production, and power/energy/ transportation. Students are exposed to technology concepts through a hands-on/minds-on systems approach, traditional human and machine tool processes, and the latest technological methods. Students are empowered to become self-learners and to embrace change as a positive progression of life. The various programs offered to students have enhanced their math and science concepts through challenging applied activities. A course in the scientific principles of technology is also offered. Courses are designed to instill critical thinking, problem solving, research and design, quality principles, interpersonal skills, and career awareness through a variety of learning experiences.

> *Name:* Ben Davis High School
> *Address:* 1200 North Girls School Road, Indianapolis, IN 46214
> *Phone:* (317)244–7691
> *Fax:* (317)243–5506
> *Chief education officer:* Edward Bowes
> *Principal:* James Mifflin

Department head: John Clark

Contact: Tony Suba, instructor

Department name: Industrial Technology Education

Type of school: Suburban

Number of students: 2,352

Number of teachers: 182

Number of students in technology education: 628

Number of teachers in technology education: 7

If students are interested in hands-on activities, they should check out the industrial technology department at Ben Davis High School. These activities occur in courses relating to manufacturing, communication, construction, and transportation. Work involves real applications that business and industry use in everyday life. The Ben Davis High School industrial technology education department has designed an educational program to lead into the twenty-first century. The staff recognized a need to look at the future and implement a technology program for high school students to use and value. The department designed a curriculum to blend the best of its courses with the activities of modern technology. Thirty-two semesterlong courses are offered. This provides a flexible way to enroll in many industrial technology education classes in three years at Ben Davis High School.

Name: Emporia High School

Address: 3302 W. Eighteenth, Emporia, KS 66801–5998

Phone: (316)341–2365

Fax: (316)341–2376

Chief education officer: Richard Gregory

Principal: Jerry Baumgardener

Contact: John Wyrick

Department name: Technology Education

Type of school: Urban

Number of students: 1,300

Number of teachers: 80

Number of students in technology education: 600

Number of teachers in technology education: 4

Emporia High School has an articulated grade seven to nine program with articulation agreements with a technical school for postsecondary training. Key features are module delivery and explorations in technology in grades seven and eight; investigations of technology, introduction to careers; systems courses; classes in production, construction, transportation, and communication; tech-prep courses; principles of technology; applied math; engineering preparation; hobby/consumer courses; auto maintenance; and woodworking in grades nine through twelve.

Name: Marshall County High School

Address: 416 High School Road, Benton, KY 42025

Phone: (502)527–1453

Fax: (502)527–0578

Chief education officer: Kenneth Shawowen

Principal: Gene Brooks

Contact: Bobby Woods

Department name: Technology Education

Type of school: Rural

Number of students: 1,450

Number of teachers: 90

Number of students in technology education: 175

Number of teachers in technology education: 2

The technology education program at Marshall County High School is a modern holistic program that integrates academics into a comprehensive study of technology and its applications. An introduction to technology is provided through sixteen self-directed study modules in a high-tech environment using current hardware and software. The technology in the twenty-first century lab served as one of three pilot sites for the state of Kentucky. A more in-depth study in technology is provided by a course in technology systems, which gives students the opportunity to explore current and emerging technologies in the areas of communication, transportation, production, and bio-related technology. Speciality courses in CAD, multimedia, and computer graphics provide intense, concentrated studies in specialized areas. The program has an articulated tech-prep agreement with a local university and a state vocational school. It received ITEA's program excellence award in 1994.

Name: Warren East High School

Address: 6867 Louisville Road, Bowling Green, KY 42101

Phone: (502)781–1277

Fax: (502)843–2610

Chief education officer: Leonard McCoy

Principal: Aaron Milliken

Contact: Edwin Moss, department head/teacher

Department name: Technology Education

Program name: Technology Education

Type of school: Rural

Number of students: 942

Number of teachers: 81

Number of students in technology education: 280

Number of teachers in technology education: 2

The technology education department of Warren East High School provides students in grades nine through twelve with a full program in technology education. Currently, five courses in technology education are offered, including an introduction to technology course, and systems courses in communication technology and production technology, with plans to create a course for biotechnology as soon as time and funding permit. The systems courses offer students concentration in a particular area such as production technology, with time to work with CNC mills, a CNC lathe, programmable controls, electricity and electronics, robotics, applied physics, laser/fiber optics, material processing, and engineering structures. In the multifunction lab, mechanical drafting/CAD and architectural CAD courses are taught while students from other departments work on projects and applications.

Name: South Floyd High School

Address: P.O. Box 310, Hi Hat, KY 41636

Phone: (606)452–9600 ext. 100

Fax: (606)452–2551

Principal: Alan Osborne

Contact: Paul Fletcher, technology education instructor

Department head: Gwinetta Mitchell

Department name: Vocational Technical Education

Program name: Technology Education

Type of school: Rural

Number of students: 500

Number of teachers: 29

Number of students in technology education: 130

Number of teachers in technology education: 1

The technology education program at South Floyd High School is a semester-long course offered primarily to incoming freshman and in some cases to older students who have not had the benefit of the class. The course is designed to provide a brief overview of fifteen different areas of technology (for example, desktop publishing, computer graphics, CAD, robotics, CNC, and so forth). During their time in this course, students engage in hands-on activities that are designed to introduce them to the technological area. If students have developed an interest in specific areas of technology upon completion of the course, they are given the opportunity to continue in the program by enrolling in classes that focus on specific technological areas (such as advanced computer topics, publishing, radio and TV production, general drafting CAD).

Name: Apollo High School

Address: 2280 Temerack Road, Owensboro, KY 42301

Phone: (502)685–3121

Fax: (502)685–1730

Principal: Robert Combs

Contact: Stan Scott, department head

Department name: Technology Education

Type of school: Suburban

Number of students: 1,450

Number of teachers: 90

Number of students in technology education: 300

Number of teachers in technology education: 3

Apollo High School's technology education department provides students with course offerings that include hands-on experiences using more than forty Novell-networked computers equipped with such programs as Autodesk AutoCAD Release 13, for teaching computer-aided drafting. In the technology lab, students experience sixteen different technology modules, including aerospace, CAD, desktop publishing, computer numeric lathe, problem solving, and lasers. The students' attitudes toward the new programs have been great. They seem to enjoy working with technology, and to understand why it will be important to their future. The classes offered by the technology education department help develop real-world, up-to-date, market-hungry job skills.

Name: Russellville High School

Address: 1101 West Ninth Street, Russellville, KY 42270

Phone: (502)726–8432

Fax: (502)726–6303

Chief education officer: Gary Rye

Principal: Mickey Mequiar

Contact: Timothy Bollenbecker, technology teacher

Department name: Technology Education

Type of school: Suburban

Number of students: 430

Number of teachers: 28

Number of students in technology education: 85

Number of teachers in technology education: 1

Russellville High School has had a modular technology education program since 1990. It was funded by the local board, after an unsuccessful attempt to secure a grant. It was one of the first modular labs in the state. Student assessment is performance based using rubrics. The teacher-written curriculum is integrated with math and science content, and associated careers are identified throughout the modules. Students are encouraged to participate in the Technology Student Association and have competed in the past seven state and national conferences. The high school is heavily involved in Tech-Prep, School-to-Work, and the Southern Regional Education Board Initiatives.

Name: Pulaski County High School

Address: 511 East University Drive, Somerset, KY 42501

Phone: (606)678–0443

Chief education officer: Bert Minton

Principal: Mike Hicks

Contact: Mike Crowhurst, School Technology Coordinator

Department name: Technology Education

Program name: Technology Education I and II

Type of school: Rural

Number of students: 1,150

Number of teachers: 57

Number of students in technology education: 120

Number of teachers in technology education: 1

Originally started in 1992 by a $62,000 grant from the Pulaski County Board of Education, the technology education laboratory at Pulaski County High School consists of eleven technology modules. Examples of subjects covered include computer graphics, desktop publishing, computer-aided drafting, computer animation, robotics, BASIC programming, and electronics. The technology education laboratory is also the home of the school's Student Technology Leadership Program (STLP). The STLP Program serves the entire school by assisting in instructional technology training, and by performing technology-based service projects for the school and the district. Students in this department have also worked closely with school yearbook and newspaper publications. The program also serves as a cornerstone for the school's Tech Prep initiatives. The program has recently received a grant from the Partnership for Reform Initiatives in Science and Math (PRISM), a statewide initiative funded by the National Science Foundation. With this grant, students in the technology education department are developing a new module to study the technology of sound.

Name: Seaholm High School

Address: 2436 West Lincoln, Birmingham, MI 48009

Phone: (313)433–8440

Fax: (313)642–6059

Chief education officer: John Hoefler

Principal: Helene Mills

Contact: Mike Pierno, head, Department of Technology

Department name: Industrial Technology

Type of school: Suburban

Number of students: 1,150

Number of teachers: 90–95

Number of students in technology education: 350–425

Number of teachers in technology education: 3.5

Seaholm High School's industrial technology department gives students an early look at present and future technology and works to help students learn to use this cutting-edge technology. The emphasis in every class is to put the students in a hands-on environment in which there is more than one possible solution, and to let them use their problem-solving skills to overcome the challenges presented. Classes include automation/robotics, systems engineering technology, engineering drawing/CAD, energy technology, and visual communication technology.

Name: Paramus High School

Address: East 99 Century Road, Paramus, NJ 07652

Phone: (201)261–7800 ext. 3063

Fax: (201)261–3833

Chief education officer: Janice Dime

Principal: Richard Zanella

Contact: Ellen van Howling, Supervisor of Creative Arts K–12

Department name: Industrial Arts/Technology

Type of school: Suburban

Number of students: 1,000

Number of teachers: 125

Number of students in technology education: 300

Number of teachers in technology education: 3

The program at Paramus High School consists of elective courses only. These include courses in invention and design, electronics/robotics technology, TV and video, architectural drawing and design (AutoCAD), engineering drawing and design (AutoCAD), and graphics communications I and II.

Name: Carthage High School

Address: Martin Street Road, Carthage, NY 13619

Phone: (315)493–1690

Fax: (315)493–6252

Chief education officer: Kenn C. Rishel

Principal: Stewart Amell

Department head: Marvin Tyler, coordinator of industrial technology

Department name: Technology Department

Type of school: Rural

Number of students: 950

Number of teachers: 75

Number of students in technology education: 300

Number of teachers in technology education: 4

The technology program at Carthage High School is a broad-based curriculum that includes the full range of systems, foundations, and elective courses required by New York State for an occupational sequence in technology education. Beyond the core curriculum, the faculty has come to be recognized as another resource area for all students. Because of the focus on performance-based projects, students employ multiple technologies in completing assignments. The program offers a full technical drawing sequence and opportunities for students to gain experience in the operation of CCS-TV, the local access educational television station.

Name: Hilton Central High School

Address: 400 East Avenue, Hilton, NY 14468

Phone: (716)392–6849/4940

Fax: (716)392–3965

Chief education officer: C. Bogden

Principal: M. J. Brook

Department head: Deb Godlove

Contact: Ronald Hindmarch, technology teacher

Department name: Technology

Type of school: Suburban

Number of students: 1,300

Number of teachers: 89

Number of students in technology education: 800

Number of teachers in technology education: 4.2

Hilton Central High School's technology program is well rounded and includes eighteen course titles. Emphasis is given to establishing links with the local industries and technology in the Monroe County area. These links include partnership with companies, shadowing experiences, guest speakers, articulation with local colleges, and acquiring donation of equipment and supplies. A technology sequence includes courses in introduction to occupations, materials processing, basic electronics, technical drawing, communication systems, and production systems; a total of five units is required.

Name: Lincoln Orens High School

Address: Trafalgara Boulevard, Island Park, NY 11558

Phone: (516)431–7194

Fax: (516)431–7550

Chief education officer: Erich Stegmeier

Principal: Sy Rosen

Contact: Neil Swernofsky, teacher

Department name: Technology Education

Type of school: Suburban

Number of students: 200

Number of teachers: 26

Number of students in technology education: 200

Number of teachers in technology education: 1

The program uses carefully designed, hands-on problem solving activities. The curriculum drives the activities, which are centered on the teaching of technological concepts, processes, and impacts. Portfolio assessment is used along with more traditional assessment to evaluate the student and the program.

Name: Arlington High School North Campus

Address: 263 Route 55, LaGrangeville, NY 12540

Phone: (914)486–4860

Fax: (914)486–4879

Chief education officer: Edward Lynn

Principal: Linda Horisk

Department head: Glen Botto

Department name: Technology

Type of school: Rural, urban, suburban

Number of students: 2,100

Number of teachers: 200

Number of students in technology education: 500

Number of teachers in technology education: 7

The technology program course offerings at Arlington High School provide a wide selection for students. These include three separate courses in engineering, a course in communications, and courses in design and drawing, materials processing, and electricity/electronics. In addition, a technology sequence is offered in production, communications, and transportation systems. Finally, a range of lectures and technology electives are available to interested students.

Name: Irondequoit High School

Address: 260 Cooper Road, Rochester, NY 14617

Phone: (716)336–2997

Fax: (716)336–2929

Chief education officer: Joseph Sproule

Principal: Stewart Agor

Department head: Dudley Carlson

Contact: Dudley Carlson, coordinator, occupational education

Department name: Occupational Education

Program name: Technology Education

Type of school: Suburban

Number of students: 1,149

Number of teachers: 115

Number of teachers in technology education: 7 (grades 7–12)

Technology education at Irondequoit High School is an integrated discipline designed to develop technological literacy through activity-based study as part of all students' fundamental education. The high school program consists of an array of courses. These include auto/transportation, communication/graphics, carpentry/construction, electricity/electronics, drafting, and other electives.

Name: Sauquoit Valley Central High School

Address: 2601 Oneida Street, Sauquoit, NY 13456

Phone: (315)839–6316

Fax: (315)839–5352

Chief education officer: Robert Hanna

Principal: Ken Ford

Department head: Craig Kopper

Contact: Edward Zak, technology instructor

Department name: Technology Education

Type of school: Rural

Number of students: 394

Number of teachers: 36

Number of students in technology education: 280

Number of teachers in technology education: 4

Sauquoit Valley Central High School, a vanguard school in technology education, offers students some of the most advanced software and equipment available. A highly trained technology education staff offers a full list of course offerings, and promotes a five-unit sequence for students. Courses are offered in sequences for pre-engineering, electronics, transportation, materials processing, and graphic communications.

Name: Clinton High School

Address: 1201 West Elizabeth Street, Clinton, NC 28328

Phone: (910)592–2067

Fax: (910)592–6185

Chief education officer: Charles Gainey

Principal: Carl Herman

Contact: Kathleen Barrows, department head/teacher

Department name: Technology Education

Program name: Technology Education

Type of school: Rural

Number of students: 730

Number of teachers: 45

Number of students in technology education: 268

Number of teachers in technology education: 2

Clinton High School has a four-year technology program available to all students. Courses include fundamentals of technology, manufacturing technology, structural technology, advanced structural technology, communication technology, advanced communications, and technology studies. A synergistic approach to teaching is used. Students rotate through sixteen modular activities that emphasize concepts and principles of technology. They use critical thinking skills and creative problem solving principles and processes to research, design, develop, and assess an identified technological problem. The technology studies course provides an opportunity for students to pursue a serious and creative topic of their choice using the knowledge, skills, and insights previously gained in technology education courses. Students investigate technological concepts or apply the tools of technology to better understand other fields of study.

Name: Worthington Kilbourne High School

Address: 1499 Hard Road, Columbus, OH 43235

Phone: (614)431–6220

Fax: (614)431–6238

Principal: Ron Porta

Contact: Roger Beck

The technology education program at Worthington Kilbourne offers coursework in manufacturing, construction, communication, and electronics. The facility truly complements the program. The communications program in particular is integrated with other subjects in the school.

Name: Nordonia High School

Address: 8006 South Bedford Road, Macedonia, OH 44056

Phone: (216)468–4690

Fax: (216)468–4690

Chief education officer: Mike Szabo

Principal: Roger Sidoti

Contact: Mike Szabo, technology education teacher

Department name: Fine and Professional Arts

Number of students in technology education: 225

Number of teachers in technology education: 1

The Nordonia High School education technology program uses a modular format of instruction. The school has implemented the program with grants and private donations totaling over $50,000 to date. They are trying to implement the next step of technology, which they believe will be engineering concepts. They are always willing to share or swap ideas.

Name: Peters Township High School

Address: 631 East McMurray Road, McMurray, PA 15317

Phone: (412)941–6251

Fax: (412)941–6565

Chief education officer: Dennis Urso

Principal: Thomas Hajzus

Department head: Bruce Lubak

Contact: Thomas Hajzus

Department name: Technology Education

Type of school: Suburban

Number of students: 962

Number of teachers: 65

Number of students in technology education: 118

Number of teachers in technology education: 2

The program at Peters Township High School is in the second year of a three-year phase-in to technology education. All previously titled industrial arts courses have been replaced, as has the overall program philosophy. In concert, the applied academics focus is 50 percent complete and the articulation agreements with schools of higher education are beginning to function. By 1997, Peters Township High School believes it will have "the" model program.

Name: Forest Hills High School

Address: 489 Locust Street, Sidman, PA 15955

Phone: (814)487–7613

Fax: (814)487–5937

Chief education officer: Paul Robinson

Principal: Don Bailey

Department head: Robert Myers

Contact: Terry Crissey, technology teacher

Department name: Technology

Type of school: Rural

Number of teachers in technology education: 2

The new technology area at Forest Hills High School is arranged in three sections. First, the manufacturing lab is extremely versatile, and the equipment is movable to meet the requirements of any activity. Second, a CAD lab with sixteen computers is used for computer programming and word processing. The third area is the most adaptable. This room is equipped and used to teach principles of technology, computer applications, and transporatation technology. Computer application is supported by robotics and CAM.

Name: Rapid City Central High School

Address: 433 North Eighth Street, Rapid City, SD 57701

Phone: (605)394–4041

Fax: (605)394–4023

Chief education officer: Maurice Haugland

Principal: Gordon Kendall

Contact: Wayne D. Lang, department chair

Department name: Technology Education

Type of school: Urban

Number of students: 2,200

Number of teachers: 130

Number of students in technology education: 380

Number of teachers in technology education: 4

Rapid City Central's technology education department features an introduction to engineering course that emphasizes technological problem solving through individual and team design activities. The class activities highlight the relationship between physics, geometry/trigonometry, and technology. An entry-level applied technology course is structured around ten "core technologies." Students study selected core technologies, determined by which system cluster they choose. Traditional electronics, drafting, woodworking, and welding courses are in place until facility updates permit conversion to an applied technology format.

Name: Eastern Hills High School

Address: 5701 Shelton, Fort Worth, TX 76112

Phone: (817)496–7625

Fax: (817)497–7621

Chief education officer: Thomas Tocco

Principal: John Largent

Department head: Duane Rogers

Contact: David Greer, Program Director

Department name: Career and Technology Education

Program name: Technology Education

Type of school: Urban

Number of students: 1,250

Number of teachers: 71

Number of students in technology education: 300

Number of teachers in technology education: 3

All twelve high schools and seventeen middle schools in the Fort Worth Independent School District (FWISD) have new high-technology laboratories. The implementation of these laboratories across the district has brought national recognition to the technology education program. The program was featured on ABC news and has had a positive impact on other districts in the metroplex and around the world. The nearly two thousand visitors to the program include individuals and groups from local and regional school districts from many states across the nation, and visitors from countries such as Australia, England, Brazil, and Canada. The program has been called the "New Basic" in education, because of its ability to provide an "application of reading, writing, and arithmetic" in a meaningful way.

Name: W. T. Woodson High School

Address: 9525 Main Street, Fairfax, VA 22031

Phone: (703)323–1911

Fax: (703)239–9351

Chief education officer: Anthony Casipit

Principal: Gary Miller

Department head: Marvin Brown

Contact: Anthony Casipit, engineering/electronics instructor

Department name: Professional Technical Studies

Program name: Engineering and Electronics

Type of school: Suburban

Number of students: 1,600

Number of teachers: 150

Number of students in technology education: 300

Number of teachers in technology education: 2

The engineering and electronics programs are designed to integrate math, science, technology, computer skills, and technical communication into real-time problem solving. Concurrent engineering and group dynamic principles are incorporated. Major activities include sumo robots, robotics, laser optics, balsa bridges, mousetrap-driven egg elevators, machine automation, cybernetics, holography, and so on.

Name: Heritage High School

Address: Lynchburg City Schools, 10th and Court Streets, Lynchburg, VA 24505–1599

Phone: (804)522–0723 ext. 139

Fax: (804)846–0723

Chief education officer: James McCormick

Principal: Roger Roberts

Department head: Richard Glover

Contact: Gregory Sullivan, supervisor for instruction

Department name: Career-Technical Programs

Program name: Technology Education

Type of school: Urban

Number of students: 1,089

Number of teachers: 90

Number of students in technology education: 215

Number of teachers in technology education: 3

The technology education curriculum at the middle school offers twenty exploratory modules in a variety of topics including bridge engineering, screen printing, flight technology, problem solving, desktop publishing, systems and controls, materials processing, rocket technology, electronics technology, computer programming, robotics technology, sensor technology, manufacturing systems, CAD, research technology, car design technology, power and energy, communications technology, and fiber optics. The high school program currently being developed will include one eighteen-week course devoted to technology foundations, based on the technological actions of designing, developing, producing, using, and assessing technology. In a second eighteen-week course devoted to the technology challenge, students will study group dynamics, discuss brainstorming techniques, learn responsibilities in group endeavors, sharpen presentation skills, and use the problem solving process.

Name: Brookpoint High School

Address: Stafford, VA 22554

Phone: (703)720–1750

Fax: (703)720–2123

Chief education officer: Russell Watson

Principal: Kerri Tillery

Department head: David Eschelman

Contact: Peter Vernimb, assistant principal for technology

Department name: Technology Education/Instructional Technology

Program name: Technology Foundations/Technology Transfer/Technology Broadcasting

Type of school: Suburban

Number of students: 1,300

Number of teachers: 95

Number of students in technology education: 375

Number of teachers in technology education: 3

The technology education program at BPHS uses state-of-the-art equipment to present the first course of Virginia's design and technology curriculum. Students rotate through a number of learning centers in construction/production, robotics, hydroponics, communications, electricity/electronics, holography, and other systems of technology. Students work out of a networked facility with access to library media center technologies as well as to the Internet and to weather data systems. Introduction to engineering students apply systems of technology to problem-solving activities. Broadcast students work to prepare video productions of events at school and in the community using state-of-the-art equipment. Technology transfer students apply foundational knowledge to real-life problems in the community and the environment.

Name: Ocean Lakes High School

Address: 885 Schumann Drive, Virginia Beach, VA 23454

Phone: (804)721–4110

Fax: (804)721–4309

Principal: Jerry DeViney

Contact: Scott Brown, technology education department chair

Department name: Technology Education

Type of school: Suburban

Number of students: 1,450

Number of teachers: 72

Number of students in technology education: 257

Number of teachers in technology education: 3

Located in the front of the school, the technology education department is a design highlight of the building. A foundations/resource lab is surrounded by labs for materials/production, drafting/engineering, communications, and electronics/control. Offerings in the eighteen-course program of studies include materials science, principles of technology, and technology foundations. A state-of-the-art facility and a dedicated, forward-thinking staff made the first year of this school a hotbed of technology education.

Name: Winooski Junior–Senior High School

Address: 80 Normand Street, Winooski, VT 05404

Phone: (802)655–3531

Fax: (802)655–6538

Chief education officer: George Cross

Contact: Ted Burton, technology education teacher

Department name: Technology Education

Type of school: Suburban

Number of students: 400

Number of teachers: 25

Number of students in technology education: 265

Number of teachers in technology education: 1

The technology education program at Winooski consists of five levels of technology education from grade six through grade twelve. The Level I and Level II courses are required for the sixth, seventh, and eighth grades consecutively. The Level III courses are elective technology systems courses available to all students in grades nine through twelve. The Level IV courses are design and engineering I and II courses required of all students enrolled in high school chemistry and physics. A unique feature of these courses is the integration and block scheduling of the engineering and chemistry or physics courses for a three-hour period. All activities for the engineering courses center around case studies relevant to today's society. There are also Level IV courses in design and manufacturing and design and construction, which are semi-independent in nature. A Level V advanced drafting and CAD course is available to students with permission only. As the technology education program evolves, design briefs at the middle school level and case studies at the high school level will be the basis for all activities and instruction.

Name: Athens High School

Address: Athens, WI 54411

Phone: (715)257–7511

Fax: (715)257–7651

Chief education officer: Robert Clinton

Principal: Lance Alwin

Department head: Patrick T. Kelley, technology education coordinator

Department name: Technology Integration Education

Type of school: Rural

Number of students: 514 (K–12)

Number of teachers: 37

Number of students in technology education: 411

Number of teachers in technology education: 20

The Alpha Center at Athens High School consists of three distinct components: (1) an integrated/applied curricular lab, (2) a model classroom, and (3) an integrated elementary satellite. The major premise of the Alpha Center is that the technology-oriented program is based on student's experiences and revolves around applied activities. At its most basic level, the Alpha Center Project provides integrated and applied learning opportunities for all students. The curriculum is designed to teach all disciplines in an integrated technology center. Students see connections between subjects that are traditionally taught in isolation. In addition, by developing the center around business- and industry-developed competencies (such as SCANS), students see the connection of the subjects to the world outside of school.

Name: North High School

Address: 2700 Mercury Avenue, Eau Claire, WI 54073

Phone: (715)839–6227

Fax: (715)839–2947

Chief education officer: Lee Hansen

Principal: J. T. Downen

Department head: Dennis Skurulsky

Department name: Technology Education

Type of school: urban

Number of students: 1,641

Number of teachers: 92

Number of students in technology education: 1,364

Number of teachers in technology education: 6.5

North High is very excited and proud of the type of curriculum that it offers to its students. The technology education department feels that it offers courses that prepare students for the twenty-first century. It was selected to be a pilot program in engineering for the state of Wisconsin. Instructors from the school have written curriculum in the areas of engineering and computer applications for the state. Students have a selection of thirty-five courses that they can choose from, including principles of technolgy, applied algebra, introduction to technology, TV production, cooperative education, and youth apprenticeship.

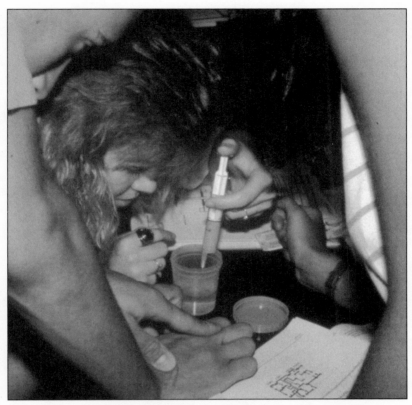

This member of a design team is making alginate beads to use in testing the impeller system for the bioreactor the team is developing.

REFERENCES

American Association for the Advancement of Science. *Science for All Americans.* Washington, D.C.: American Association for the Advancement of Science, 1989.

American Association for the Advancement of Science. *Benchmarks for Science Literacy.* Washington, D.C.: American Association for the Advancement of Science, 1993.

American Association of University Women, Educational Foundation. *How Schools Shortchange Girls.* Washington, D.C.: American Association of University Women, 1992.

American Chemical Society. *ChemCom: Chemistry in the Community.* Dubuque, Ia.: Kendall/Hunt, 1988.

Baker, D. "Sex Differences in Classroom Interactions in Secondary Science." *Journal of Classroom Interaction,* 1986, *22,* 212–218.

Boyce, L. N., and others. *Consumer Guide to Science Curriculum.* Williamsburg, Va.: College of William and Mary, 1993.

Bruschi, B., and Anderson, B. T. "Gender and Ethnic Differences in Science Achievement of Nine-, Thirteen-, and Seventeen-Year-Old Students." Paper presented at annual meeting of Eastern Educational Research Association, Feb. 10, 1994.

Bybee, R. W., and others. *Science and Technology Education for the Elementary Years: Frameworks for Curriculum and Instruction.* Andover, Mass.: The NETWORK, Inc., National Center for Improving Science Education, 1989.

Bybee, R. W., and others. *Science and Technology Education for the Middle Years: Frameworks for Curriculum and Instruction.* Andover, Mass.: The NETWORK, Inc., National Center for Improving Science Education, 1990.

Chen, D. and Stroup, W. "General System Theory: Toward a Conceptual Framework for Science and Technology for All." *Journal of Science Education and Technology,* 1993, *2*(3), 447–459.

Clinchy, E. "Higher Education: The Albatross Around the Neck of Our Public Schools." *Phi Delta Kappan,* 1994, *75,* 745–751.

de Klerk–Wolters, F., Raat, J. H., and de Vries, M. J. "Assessing Students' Attitudes Towards Technology." In D. Layton (ed.), *Innovations in Science and Technology Education,* Vol. 5. Paris: United Nations Educational, Scientific and Cultural Organization (UNESCO), 1994.

de Lange, J. *Mathematics, Insight and Meaning: Teaching, Learning and Testing of Mathematics for the Life and Social Sciences.* Utrecht, Netherlands: OW & OC, 1987.

de Vries, M. J. "The Role of Technology Education as an Integrative Discipline in Integrating Advanced Technology into Technology Education." In M. Hacker, A. Gordon, and M. J. de Vries (eds.), *Integrating Advanced Technology into Technology Education,* NATO ASI Series VF78. Berlin: Springer-Verlag, 1991.

de Vries, M. J. "Technology Education in Western Europe." In D. Layton (ed.), *Innovations in Science and Technology Education,* Vol. 5. Paris: United Nations Educational, Scientific and Cultural Organization (UNESCO), 1994.

Department for Education and the Welsh Office. *Technology for Ages Five to Sixteen (1992): Proposals of the Secretary of State for Education and the Secretary of State for Wales.* London: Department for Education and the Central Office of Information, 1992.

Driver, R., and others. "Constructing Scientific Knowledge in the Classroom." *Education Researcher,* Oct. 1994.

Duckworth, E. *The Having of Wonderful Ideas and Other Essays on Teaching and Learning.* New York: Teachers College Press, 1987.

Dunn, S. and Larson, R. *Design Technology: Children's Engineering.* Washington, D.C.: Falmer Press, 1990.

Engineering Concepts Curriculum Project. *The Man-Made World.* Brooklyn, N.Y.: Polytechnic Institute of Brooklyn, 1970.

Federal Coordinating Council for Science, Engineering, and Technology (FCCSET). *By the Year 2000, First in the World: A Report of the FCCSET Committee on Education and Human Resources to Congress* (Doc. No. EA022727). Springfield, Va.: CBIS System, 1992.

Fullan, M., and Hargreaves, A. *What's Worth Fighting For? Working Together for Your School.* Andover, Mass.: The Regional Laboratory for Educational Improvement of the Northeast Islands and Toronto: Ontario Public School Teachers' Association, 1991.

Gardner, H. *The Unschooled Mind: How Children Think and How Schools Should Teach.* Basic Books: New York, 1991.

Gott, R. *Electricity at Age 15.* London: Department of Education and Science, 1984.

Granstam, I. "Girls and Women in Science and Technology Education." In D. Layton (ed.), *Innovations in Science and Technology Education,* Vol 2. Paris: United Nations Educational, Scientific and Cultural Organization (UNESCO), 1988.

Hales, J., and Snyder, J. (eds.). *Jackson's Mills Industrial Arts Curriculum Theory.* Fairmont, W.Va.: Fairmont State College, 1982.

Hall, G., and Hord, S. *Change in Schools: Facilitating the Process.* SUNY Series in Educational Leadership. Albany: State University of New York Press, 1987.

Harlen, W. *Guides to Assessment in Education: Science.* London: Macmillan, 1983.

Harlen, W. (ed.). *Primary Science: Taking the Plunge.* London: Heinemann Educational Books, 1985.

Hayes, I. D. "Twisting the Dragon's Tail." *Washington Science Teachers' Journal,* Nov. 1993.

Hill, A. M. "Technology in the Elementary School." *MSTE News,* 1994, *4*(1), 1–4. (Mathematics, Science, and Technology Education Group, Queens University, Kingston, Ontario.)

Holbrook, J. B. "Teaching Science the STS Way." In R. E. Yager (ed.), *ICASE Yearbook 1992: The Status of Science-Technology-Society Reform Efforts Around the World.* Washington, D.C.: National Science Teachers Association, 1992.

Honey, M., and others. *Girls and Design: Exploring the Question of Technological Imagination.* Technical Report No. 17. New York: Center for Technology in Education, 1991.

Honey, M., and others. "Designing for Equity: A New Approach for Girls and Engineering." Final Report to the National Science Foundation. New York: Center for Children and Technology, Education Development Center, 1994.

Howe, H., and Vickers, M. "Standards and Diversity Down Under." *Education Week,* July 14, 1993, p. 36.

Hutchinson, J., and Hutchinson, P. "Process-Based Technology Education." *Technology Teacher,* 1991, *50*(8), 3–6.

Hynes, H. P. "Gender and the Teaching and Learning of Technology." In D. Layton (ed.), *Innovations in Science and Technology Education,* Vol. 5. Paris: United Nations Educational, Scientific and Cultural Organization (UNESCO), 1994.

Johnsey, R. *Problem Solving in School Science.* London: Simon & Schuster, 1986.

Johnson, S., and Fuhrman, S. "Lessons from Victoria." *Phi Delta Kappan,* June 1994, *75*, 770–774.

Kimbell, R. *Progression in Learning and the Assessment of Children's Attainments.* London: Goldsmiths' College, 1992.

Kimbell, R., and others. *The Assessment of Performance in Design and Technology.* London: School Examinations and Assessment Council, 1991.

Layton, D. "Science Education and Praxis: The Relation of School Science to Practical Action." *Studies in Science Education,* 1991, *19*, 43–79.

Layton, D. *Technology's Challenge to Science Education: Cathedral, Quarry, or Company Store.* Buckingham, England: Open University Press, 1993.

Layton, D. "A School Subject in the Making? The Search for Fundamentals." In D. Layton (ed.), *Innovations in Science and Technology Education,* Vol. 5. Paris: United Nations Educational, Scientific and Cultural Organization (UNESCO), 1994a.

Layton, D. (ed.). *Innovations in Science and Technology Education,* Vol. 5. Paris: United Nations Education, Scientific and Cultural Organization (UNESCO), 1994b.

Layton, D., Jenkins, E., Macgill, S., and Davey, A. *Inarticulate Science? Perspectives on the Public Understanding of Science and Some Implications for Science Education.* Driffield, East Yorkshire, England: Studies in Education, 1993.

Loucks-Horsley, S., and others. *Developing and Supporting Teachers for Elementary School Science Education.* Andover, Mass.: The NETWORK, Inc., National Center for Improving Science Education, 1989.

McCormick, R., Hennessy, S., and Murphy, P. "Problem-Solving Processes in Technology Education." Paper presented at the 55th Annual Conference of the International Technology Education Association (ITEA), Charlotte, North Carolina, Apr. 18–21, 1993.

Makiya, H., and Rogers, M. *Design and Technology in the Primary School: Case Studies for Teachers.* New York: Routledge, 1992.

Massachusetts Department of Education. *Massachusetts Mathematics, Science and Technology Framework.* (Draft). Malden: Massachusetts Department of Education, 1994.

Moore, J. A. "Science as a Way of Knowing: Evolutionary Biology." *American Zoologist,* 1984, *24,* 421–534.

Murata, S. *New Trends of Vocational Technical Education in Secondary Education in Japan.* Paris: Development Committee, Organization for Economic Cooperation and Development, 1990.

Murata, S., and Stern, S. "Technology Education in Japan." *Journal of Technology Education,* 1993, *5*(1), 29–37.

National Center for Improving Science Education. *The High Stakes of High School Science.* Andover, Mass.: The NETWORK, Inc., 1991.

National Commission on Excellence in Education. *A Nation at Risk: The Imperative for Educational Reform.* Washington, D.C.: U.S. Department of Education, 1983.

National Institute for Curriculum Development. "Technology: A New Subject in Dutch Schools." *Special Techniek Koerier,* Aug. 1993.

National Research Council. *National Science Education Standards.* (Draft). Washington, D.C.: National Academy Press, 1994.

National Science Board Commission on Precollege Education in Mathematics, Science and Technology. *Educating America for the 21st Century.* Washington, D.C.: National Science Foundation, 1983.

National Science Foundation. *Local Systemic Change Through Teacher Enhancement: Grades K–8.* Program Solicitation and Guideline No. 94–73. Arlington, Va.: National Science Foundation, 1994.

Nelson, D. *Transformations: Process and Theory.* Santa Monica, Calif.: Center for City Building Educational Programs, 1984.

New York State Education Department. *Curriculum, Instruction, and Assessment: Framework for Mathematics, Science, and Technology.* Albany: New York State Education Department, with cooperation from the University of the State of New York, 1994.

Olson, D. W. *Industrial Arts and Technology.* Englewood Cliffs, N.J.: Prentice Hall, 1963.

Pacific Northwest Laboratory. *Materials Science and Technology Teachers Handbook, 1994.* Richland, Wash.: Science Education Center, Pacific Northwest Laboratory, 1994.

Parnell, D. *The Neglected Majority: American Association of Community and Junior Colleges.* Washington, D.C.: Community College Press, 1985.

Phillips, K. "A Progression of Technology in Industrial Arts Education." In *Technology Education: A Perspective on Implementation.* Reston, Va.: International Technology Education Association, 1985.

Raizen, S. A. *Reforming Education for Work: A Cognitive Science Perspective.* Berkeley: National Center for Research in Vocational Education, University of California, 1989.

Raizen, S. A. *Linkages in Vocational-Technical Education and Training: Challenges-Responses-Actors.* Paper prepared for "Learning and Work: The Research Base," a seminar organized by the U.S. Department of Education and the Organization for Economic Cooperation and Development, 1991.

Raizen, S. A., and Colvin, R. L. "Commentary: Apprenticeships, a Cognitive-Science View." *Education Week,* Dec, 26, 1991.

Raizen, S. A., and Michelsohn, A. M. (eds.). *The Future of Science in Elementary Schools: Educating Prospective Teachers.* San Francisco: Jossey-Bass, 1994.

Resnick, L. B. "Learning in School and Out." *Educational Researcher,* 1987, *16*(9), 13–20.

Roberts, P. "The Place of Design in Technology Education." In D. Layton (ed.), *Innovations in Science and Technology Education,* Vol. 5. Paris: United Nations Educational, Scientific and Cultural Organization (UNESCO), 1994.

Rogoff, B., and Lave, J. (eds). *Everyday Cognition: Its Development in Social Context.* Cambridge, Mass.: Harvard University Press, 1984.

Rosenholtz, S. J. *Teachers' Workplace: The Social Organization of Schools.* White Plains, N.Y.: Longman, 1989.

Sadker, D., and Sadker, M. *Failing at Fairness: How America's Schools Cheat Girls.* New York: Scribner, 1994.

Science Curriculum Framework and Criteria Committee. *Science Framework for California Public Schools: Kindergarten Through Grade Twelve.* Sacramento: California State Department of Education, 1990.

Scottish Consultative Council on the Curriculum. *A Framework for Technology Education in Scottish Schools.* Broughty Ferry, Dundee, Scotland: Scottish Consultative Council on the Curriculum, 1994.

Scottish Office Education Department. *Curriculum and Assessment in Scotland National Guidelines, Environmental Studies, 5–14.* Edinburgh, Scotland: Scottish Office Education Department, 1993.

Sellwood, P. M. "Progression and Development for the Practical Curriculum." In *National Project: Practical Problem Solving, 5–13, Standing Conference on Schools, Science and Technology, Department of Trade and Industry.* London: Department of Trade and Industry, 1989a.

Sellwood, P. M. "The Role of Problem Solving in Developing Thinking Skills." *Technology Teacher,* 1989b, *49*(3).

Sellwood, P. M. "A Practical Problem-Solving Approach to Education." In *National Project: Practical Problem Solving, 5–13, Standing Conference on Schools, Science and Technology, Department of Trade and Industry.* London: Department of Trade and Industry, 1990.

Sellwood, P. M. "The Investigative Learning Process." *Design and Technology Teaching,* 1991, *24*(1), 4–12.

Shavelson, R., and Baxter, G. "What We've Learned About Assessing Hands-On Science." *Educational Leadership,* 1992, *49*(8), 20–25.

Sparks, D., and Loucks-Horsley, S. "Five Models of Staff Development for Teachers." *Journal of Staff Development,* 1989, *10*(4), 40–57.

Spilka, G. J., and Nutter, L. *Design as a Catalyst for Learning.* Final Report for the National Endowment for the Arts: Design Arts, D.C. (Draft). Philadelphia: OMG, Inc., 1995.

Staudenmaier, J. M. *Technology's Storytellers: Reweaving the Human Fabric.* Cambridge, Mass.: Society for History of Technology/MIT Press, 1985.

Tamaura, S., Arai, I., and Murata, S. *Kinrotaiken gakushu no nerai to jiseen* [Objectives and practice of work experience activities]. Tokyo: Gyosei, 1985.

Todd, R. "Theory and Model Building in Industrial Arts and Technology." *Epsilon Pi Tau,* Spring 1975, pp. 29–32.

Todd, R. "The Natures and Challenges of Technological Literacy." In M. Dyrenfurth and M. Kozak (eds), *Technological Literacy.* 1991 Yearbook of the Council of Technology Teacher Education. Peoria, Ill.: Macmillan/McGraw-Hill, 1989.

Todd, R., McCrory, D., and Todd, K. *Understanding and Using Technology.* Worcester, Mass.: Davis, 1985.

U.S. Department of Education. *Mathematics, Science and Technology Education Programs That Work: A Collection of Exemplary Education Programs and Practices in the National Diffusion Network.* Washington, D.C.: U.S. Department of Education, Office of Educational Research and Improvement, 1994.

U.S. Department of Labor. *Learning a Living: A Blueprint for High Performance.* Washington,

D.C.: U.S. Department of Labor, Secretary's Commission on Achieving Necessary Skills, 1992.

Victorian Curriculum and Assessment Board. *The Technology Studies Framework: P–10. Materials and Technology: Study Design.* Victoria, Australia: Ministry of Education, 1991.

Whittaker, G. "Materials Science and Technology: What Do the Students Say?" *Journal of Technology Education,* 1994, *5*(2), 52–67.

Wirt, J. *Testing and Assessment in Vocational Education.* OTA-BP-SET-123. Washington, D.C.: U.S. Government Printing Office, 1994.

Yager, R. E., and Roy, R. "STS: Most Pervasive and Most Radical of Reform Approaches to Science Education." In R. E. Yager (ed.), *What Research Says to the Science Teacher,* Vol. 7: *The Science, Technology, Society Movement.* Washington, D.C.: National Science Teachers Association, 1993.

Zoller, U., Donn, S., Wild, R., and Beckett, P. "Teachers' Beliefs and Views on Selected Science-Technology-Society Topics: A Probe into STS Literacy Versus Indoctrination." *Teacher Education,* 1991, *75*, 541–561.

INDEX

239

DATE DUE

NOV 3	2004		
ILL 6/13/05			
GAYLORD			PRINTED IN U.S.A.